HAMMOND INNES' EAST ANGLIA

50   50

48   48

46   46

44   44

42   42

40   40

38

Books by Hammond Innes

HAMMOND INNES'
East Anglia

PHOTOGRAPHS BY NEVILLE FOX-DAVIES

☒ HODDER AND STOUGHTON
London Sydney Auckland Toronto

HAMMOND INNES' EAST ANGLIA

British Library Cataloguing in Publication Data
Innes, Hammond
Hammond Innes' East Anglia.
1. East Anglia (England) – Description and travel.
Rn: Ralph Hammond-Innes
1. Title
914.26′04858   DA670.E14

ISBN 0-340-32450-3

First printed 1986

Designed by Mavis Henley

Printed in Italy for
Hodder and Stoughton Limited
Mill Road, Dunton Green, Sevenoaks, Kent
by New Interlitho S.p.A., Milan

Origination by Adroit Photo Litho.

Photoset by Rowland Phototypesetting Limited
Bury St Edmunds, Suffolk

Hodder and Stoughton Editorial Office
47 Bedford Square, London WC1B 3DP.

For Dorothy,
who is so very much a
part of this book

CONTENTS

LINCOLNSHIRE

*Historically the
East Anglian boundaries
are those of Norfolk
and Suffolk.*

*However, for the
purposes of this book
I have included
the whole of
the East Anglian bulge
from the Blackwater
north, and including
Cambridge and the Fens.*

*The water complex
of the area is so
unique that I felt
this was justified.*

HAMMOND INNES

Sutton Bridge

WISBECH

Welland

Nene

Thorney ●

Peterborough ●

March ●

Bedford Levels

Chatteris ●

Old Bed

Haddenha

Huntingdon ● Earith

Ouse

CAMBRIDGE ●

CAMBRIDG

BEDFORDSHIRE

Bishop's Stortford

HERTFORDSHIRE

1. Footsteps in a strange land

My approach to East Anglia has been that of a stranger, taking first one step and then another until finally I cannot imagine having a base anywhere else. Those estuaries up which the longship invaders came, both to devastate and to settle, those wide skies, that sparkling light, the air so dry and clear, the great churches and those exquisite villages of timber and plaster – there's nowhere else in England quite like this.

When I say my approach to East Anglia has been that of a stranger, this is not quite true, for the first part of what is really my surname stems from Essex, where the Hammonds apparently built a large number of churches, schools and public houses, one of the Romford descendants commenting drily that the public houses paid best.

Such a mixed constructional connection, whilst making me wonder as I pass through Essex who built what, does not alter the fact that I came to East Anglia a step at a time and that this may perhaps help me to explain to others how the fascination for it has grown upon me.

The first step of all was made when I worked on a City newspaper. I was earning nine pounds a week, had a bedsitter in Bloomsbury, an Austin 7 Sports and a girlfriend who was an actress. Early morning and late evening I wrote books, at weekends I got out of London, when I could afford to.

The Friday I first put wheel into East Anglia was one of those still cold spring evenings when the mist creeps up off the saltings and everything is ghostly strange. I was headed for Clacton because Dorothy had most conveniently arranged it so that she had a fill-in week at this seaside resort between theatre engagements in the big cities.

I suppose I left London by the Mile End Road and the A12 and headed north-east through Chelmsford, Witham, Kelvedon, Marks Tey and Colchester, but all I remember is the last part of the journey, from Colchester to Clacton, with the narrow road winding above Wivenhoe Park through Keelars Tye, High Elms and Tenpenny Heath, a flat land full of fruit trees in full blossom, night closing in and a mist with it. I think I can recall a signpost that said Clacton 9 miles, but I can't be sure, for by then I was playing Box and Cox with the chauffeur of one of those old-fashioned straight up-and-down Rolls Royces.

It was an odd arrangement, the mist drifting over in low-lying veils about a yard deep and beautifully layered – like ectoplasm. One minute my low-slung little roadster was below it, streaking past the Rolls whose chauffeur could scarcely see a yard ahead of him, the next the mist was

Near East Bergholt.

down on the deck and it was I who was reduced to a crawl, the Rolls hurtling by to the music of its horn, the chauffeur's head above the ectoplasm with a clear view of the hedgetops and the fruit blossom on either side.

Where would I end up – an old rectory, a haunted hall? All those Dunsanian stories, the ghosts, the terrible cold, the lonely empty houses and the mists coming up off the marshes – all that I had read and therefore expected of Essex, the Rolls a phantom and myself doomed to go hurtling into oblivion down a non-existent road to end in the deep

Withermarsh Green.

mud of an estuary.

It was an extraordinary journey, and of course with a blissfully happy ending, for Dorothy was there at the end of it, and she was certainly no ghost.

The next time I ventured into East Anglia, it was the same car, the same girl. We were married then and making an exploratory Sunday search for a dream of mine, a totally impractical dream for anyone working on a London paper. I wanted to live on a boat, either on the Thames or on an estuary.

Somewhere between the Roach and the Crouch I followed my nose on a wild track that led into nowhere, nothing ahead of us but endless salt flats, an infinity of sky, and in the distance disembodied sails scurrying across the land. Finally I stopped, for there was water on the track. It wasn't deep and it wasn't continuous, but even while we stood there, watching the sails we knew we could not reach, it spread to the wheels of the car, lapped at our shoes, the tide making and time to go back.

Six months later, much further north, in Norfolk, I at last made the first tentative step towards my dream. All winter I had been studying a little teach-yourself-to-sail book and in early May we hired a small sailing boat and tried putting theory into practice. I think we both knew it was our last chance. Four months later the country was at war.

This little interruption to our lives went on and on, and it was not until it was over and we were together again that we took the final step that brought us permanently into East Anglia. I was then writing full time, our little thatched cottage in Wiltshire far too small. I needed a working base in an attractive setting that was not too far from London – and one that a writer after five years of war service could afford. I had just revised a book on old coaching inns, some of the best of them in Suffolk where the temperance trust house movement had been strongly supported, so to Suffolk we went, to stay at one of the oldest of them, the Bull at Long Melford.

It was May and the chestnuts on the huge green that faced the entrance gates and towers of that lovely warm brick Tudor mansion had all their candles standing white against the bright new green of their leaves. My agent and his wife joined us. Our needs were very different, but we house hunted together and one night we drove from Lavenham through Brent and Monks Eleigh to a little medieval timbered village, and there, by the watersplash, were some wrought iron gates and a house that was so exactly what we wanted that we turned down everything else we looked at. And then, in the autumn, the unbelievable happened – that very house came on the market.

It had a well and an old 'toffets tool' of a pumping engine, a very temperamental electric light plant and its own drainage system. But we could just afford it, and its tumbled roofs and beautifully planned garden . . . this has remained home to us ever since. So many changes in the world at large, but our house, the village, the whole East Anglian scene, I don't know what it is, those wide skies perhaps, but it has proved a marvellous working base. And because it has been my working base, I have never set out consciously to explore, so that this book is the story of a land that has come upon me almost unawares, growing on me gradually until now I think of it as home and cannot imagine myself living anywhere else.

The Stour near Flatford Mill.

2. Reaching out from an old Wool Village

They said of East Anglia that it was flat, that it was out on a limb where nobody ever went, cut off from the rest of the country with an appalling train service – nobody, they said, would dream of living in East Anglia. A cold, bleak world, where the east wind blew and only arctic migrants flourished. Well, that's true, the arctic migrants come pouring into Norfolk over saltmarsh, fen and broad, up the estuaries into Suffolk, great skeins of geese flying in formation, the beat of their wings sighing through the crisp autumn air. And it's true that East Anglia is a bulge on the map so that nobody goes there without a reason, nobody passes through on their way to some other part of the British Isles.

But that is an essential part of its fascination. It is a secret world, so that becoming an inhabitant of East Anglia is like becoming a member of some distinctive sect. In recent years there has been a rapid growth in population, but even so it is comparatively rare to find anybody, other than those who have made it their home, who can claim familiarity. With its waterways fanning like veins deep into the heart of it, fens, broads, a myriad tracks leading across rich acres of wheat to timbered farms of Tudor oak, the bad lands and the forests, it is far too changeable and complex a land for the visitor to gain easy knowledge of it.

In the village where we live, the stream has cut deep into clay, gravel and sand, producing a rolling, rounded country. It is the reverse of flat, the single street dropping steeply down both sides of a valley to a watersplash, so steeply in fact you might easily think yourself in Devon – except that almost all the cottages lining the single street are timber-framed with studs of medieval oak plastered over and tumbled roofs of mellowed tiles or thatch.

The last Ice Age finished here, right in front of our house, I often feel, for the sub-soil varies all over the garden and the hills run with springs, the water brought from deep down by the gravel 'pipes' that are everywhere. But the surface of this rolling country is heavy clay, gold in summer, yellow and brown in autumn, and in winter green as downland hills, for this is the rich corn land of England where the ever-larger combines harvest ever-larger fields, and ever-larger ploughs mark the pattern of the seasons.

That little tributary of the river Brett which forms the watersplash is

The start of a new day – 04.50 on a June morning.

a winding boundary to the long and in parts narrow run of our garden, so that winter and summer we live in the company of a succession of waterbirds – snipe and rail, moorhens rowing with their necks, mallard and muscovy, strange hybrids too. I'm still stopped in my tracks every time the wild duck make their three fast flying circuits of the landing strip and then come helicoptering down, wings half closed, webbed feet extended as they guide themselves through the overhanging tracery of branches to land on the surface of the water in a flurry of spray. Or if I have a bows-on view, then the touchdown seems like that of a bosomy flying boat, but oh, so soft, and almost always that final quack of satisfaction at having successfully completed a tricky landing. Geese, too – the thrash and splash of their wings; heron that make it senseless to restock the garden ponds with goldfish, the occasional sight of a kingfisher

An example of the lateness of the spring in East Anglia – April on the Stour near Flatford Mill.

and in the summer fleets of little yellow and black balls of fluff hurrying after muscovy parents, enchanting to watch in the daytime, and at night food for the predators – only one or two of some twenty-eight successfully hatched make it into winter.

Our village is on the border between the Constable and Gainsborough countries. Most of the elms have gone now, their diseased trunks either felled or fallen, the only wagons are exhibition relics outside farms and pubs or in people's gardens, but just over the hill, a woman farmer does her ploughing with Suffolk Punches, and the skies, those cloud-galleoned skies that light both Constable and Gainsborough landscapes, have not changed. Ten miles or so to the east of us is the Dedham Vale with Flatford Mill and Willy Lott's cottage. Ten miles to the west is the old wool and silk town of Sudbury where Thomas Gainsborough was born,

Flatford Mill and Willy Lott's cottage. 'As I covered the seasons with my camera in Suffolk I became increasingly conscious of Constable and how little the overall picture has changed – the bones and the structure are still there,'
(Neville Fox-Davies).

where in the lush country bordering the Stour some of his best landscapes were painted. And we are very conscious of our good fortune, for we live here in the very centre of a twenty-mile spread of the most beautiful villages in Britain.

When we first came to East Anglia it was still something of a sealed-off area, full of disused airfields and farmers obsessed by memories of what it had been like between the wars, their sons inheriting pessimism with the land, the winter of '47 worse than anything they had known, yet the value of their land risen from ten pounds an acre in the thirties to something close on two hundred pounds. They couldn't believe it would last. There was rationing and a Labour government and country houses were under the hammer as people with money, feeling the weight of their years, looking for ease and comfort, sun and servants, fled to places like Kenya, Tanganyika, Rhodesia and South Africa, little knowing what the future held in store.

Oh, the antiques going for a song in the last of the forties! The shops were few then, the bargains unbelievable – but nobody had any money, of course, least of all ourselves with an old house that had fallen into disuse as a barn, been refurbished and made habitable for a Harrods auction in 1928 and was now suffering from the neglect of the war years. Like every young couple bounding with energy and eternal optimism we had bitten off almost more than my pen could earn, scraping the barrel of our bank balance to carry out just essential repairs, the windows all lead lights and some of them so fragile that the north-east wind came whistling in through rattling panes. An old man who helped me with the garden could remember mucking out in the room that became my study, remembered too the pricking out of the farthing stones that were such a feature of the paths and steps that help to break the garden up into what I can only describe as a series of 'rooms'. Those farthing stones were square pottery flooring slabs for the maltings pricked with dozens of air holes, the pricking done by children long before the farthing they were paid for each stone went out of circulation.

House and garden became a hive of industry, so much of neglect to be made good, the building of laid paths between the box hedges that edged the four sundial beds interspersed with interior decorating, general maintenance and the running of those two dread monsters – the old single-pistoned waterpump and the electric light plant. And somehow the books got written; *The White South* initially, and in the warmth of that first bright Suffolk summer I remember rewriting at my agents' suggestion all the middle part on board the factory ship, the book finishing up as a watershed in the development of my work, and virtually all of it done there in the garden, clacking away on my typewriter, my brain full of polar ice, my body stripped to the waist and turned almost black with the sun.

Silly Suffolk, they called it, possibly using 'silly' as a bastardisation of the old Saxon *selig*, meaning blessed, but whether because of the number

of churches – some say there were as many as 500 at the time of the Conquest, most of them wood and long since disappeared – or because of the climate, I don't know. Certainly East Anglia, like the Isles of Scilly, is sunnier than most places in the British Isles; it is also drier. And that east wind, which so often begins with the New Year and goes on and on and on, sometimes right into May, and even one year, I remember, into the middle of June, that wind which comes straight off the North Sea, straight from the Arctic and Siberia, giving the coast its reputation for harshness, also produces the champagne air that knocks the newcomer into deepest slumber and burns the skin off the sunbather's back. It is hard to convince a Mediterranean lovely that she is more likely to go down with sunburn in East Anglia than on the Côte d'Azur or the Costa del Sol. But the artists love it, that glorious light. It is the same light, of course, that inspired Vermeer and Rembrandt and all the other great Dutch painters who had the advantage of similar brightness and breadth of skies on the other side of the North Sea.

And when the dark rain clouds loom out of the west, we who live in what some call the Hadleigh'ole can virtually see them part – it seems to happen just beyond the walnut trees at the bottom of our garden. They swing south and north then, attracted by the estuaries of the Colne and Stour on the one hand and the Orwell on the other. The skies over Colchester and Ipswich blacken, storms pouring water on those two luckless towns, while we have sunshine still or at worst only a sprinkling of light rain.

But it is in summer time and in autumn, particularly in autumn, that East Anglia pays back the cost of the long, cold, east wind spring. Even when the whole of Britain has a wet, windy, miserable summer with the depressions that should be up by the Faroes ploughing eastward up the Channel, we in East Anglia can comfort ourselves that there'll always be an autumn, an Indian summer of stillness and brightness in September running into October. Always, did I say? Only recently we had the wettest October in living memory. But in general the autumns are still bright, a sun-on-mist sort of period. A cold snap in early November maybe, but then autumn running on into December, through Christmas to the New Year and the arrival of the hard, drying, invigorating winds from out of the Nord Zee. And in December when the leaves are gone, all except the burnt-leaved oaks and the russet of the beech hedges, then the willows, which are such a feature of East Anglia, come into their own, particularly the ditchside basket withies (*salix viminalis*) and hedge-trimmed white willows, the glorious red of their stems afire in the low-slanting rays of the almost-southerned sun, and everywhere the bare branches of the trees aglimmer with spring-promising buds.

On Boxing Day – and somehow I can't remember a clouded Boxing

---

A coot has six eggs, a moorhen four – those muscovy ducks well over twenty.

*Kersey Church on the hill above
the watersplash.*

*A dove's eye view of the roof of
River House, the Tudor brick
building just out of picture to the right
of Kersey watersplash.*

Day – to drive back from a party through the patchwork of fields that have got larger over the years, through the bright pargeted plaster of gaily coloured villages, the great wool churches raising square flint and stone towers to the cloudless sky, some plague-finished with brick, with withies bloodying the road's verge and the interior of the car glass-hot in the sun . . . it is moments like that which confirm one's hard-travelled knowledge that at their climatic best these islands have a beauty unmatched by any other land.

Some day, I promise myself, I'll take a year off from writing and make a pilgrimage, arm-in-arm with Pevsner, round all the churches of East Anglia; Suffolk alone has over 500 medieval churches, that's one to every 600 souls. Norfolk and Suffolk between them have well over 1,000 medieval churches, not counting ruins, and in Suffolk there are at least 300 that are of architectural importance, or in some other way special. Our own church, standing as it does on top of the valley side so that it looks down over the village, and is mirrored in the watersplash as though for the benefit of all photographers, rose on the back of the weaving industry and, like so many of the wool churches, is large for such a small population. Much of it is built of flint, the porches and the decorative surrounds of knapped flint cut square and set close so that they present a hard, almost bluish surface, a patterned contrast to the softer beige of weathered stone. In daylight or by moonlight, or when the fabric of the church is floodlit, the bold but intricate patterns of this flushwork are a constant source of wonder to me, particularly the tower that rises in six tapering steps, with chamfered corners that are really slim flying buttresses, to a crenellated top that is flint-decorated flushwork like the lower buttresses, and all up the south side the curving bulge of the spiral staircase, the whole powerful yet delicate upthrust a foil for the beautifully decorative porch below. Did they sketch it out before they built the flintwork in, or was it all done by eye the way they constructed their boats? Whichever it was, the result has perfect balance and marvellous symmetry. And there is a wonderful carved wooden ceiling to the south porch, the finest in the country for a village church.

But what I really love about it is the interior, which is very open and full of light. Again my memories are all of sunlight streaming in, and though East Anglians are not the most demonstrative of people, the strange thing is that nobody seems to want to leave after a service. Has it always been like that, I wonder? All I can say is that in the time we have lived in the village it has always had that same bright, smiling atmosphere of welcome, a warmth and friendliness that seems to pervade the whole structure. And since I have found something of the same friendliness in many of Suffolk's churches it may be due in part to the architecture of the period, to the great amount of light; also, in the case of our own church, to its position standing so high above the village. For those of us who live in the Street it is always an upward climb to the House of God. And because it can be seen from miles away, wartime

An unusual view of Kersey Church – this is why wartime fliers found it such a useful beacon.

23

pilots, returning from a mission, homed on it when they could, their prayers of thankfulness part of the church's heritage.

The present building owes its relative grandeur to the wool industry of the fourteenth and fifteenth centuries, as do all the churches of what is loosely known as the region of the Old Draperies – Hadleigh, Boxford, Long Melford, Sudbury, Kersey, Lavenham, where the Springs made their peace with God by building a crenellated chess set church of near cathedral proportions, and all the other broadcloth towns and villages. The word 'drapery' refers to the weave; it was the 'new draperies' that spread the industry to new centres and created a boom that peaked in the late sixteenth, early seventeenth centuries.

I have a told-to-my-friends outline of the East Anglian wool industry's rise and fall which I will use here; anybody who wishes can look it all up and get as thoroughly confused as I have been from time to time by royal proclamations and franchises, by the struggles between the guilds and the weavers, by taxes and cloth prices and all the mayhem of demonstration and riot that accompanies the decline of an industry. The Old Drapery story really begins in the fourteenth century when two things happened that changed the whole pattern of the wool industry in England. Until then our wool was mainly exported across the North Sea and the Channel for the manufacture of cloth on the continent, only a relatively small part of the shearing being retained for conversion to rough clothing by the people of each locality. Then, in 1326 to encourage the home weaving industry, Edward III barred all except the rich from wearing foreign cloth. At the same time he offered franchises to fullers, weavers and dyers. But this encouragement was not enough to develop the home industry, so ten years later he opened the door to immigrant craftsmen.

Quick to seize the opportunity of cutting out the expense of shipping the raw material of their trade across the North Sea, some of the more enterprising, and probably younger, Flemish weavers moved to England, to York and particularly to East Anglia, where they concentrated on the catchment area of the Stour west of Ipswich and Colchester. They already had trading contacts in these ports and only a short distance inland what we call the Old Drapery villages had a well established coarse cloth cottage industry. The very early traditional centres like Bury, Ipswich, Sudbury and Stowmarket were augmented by Long Melford, Lavenham, Hadleigh and East Bergholt, Kersey, Lindsey, the Waldringfields and others, all producing the strong, heavy broadcloth.

This was the real heyday of the South Suffolk broadcloth industry, the only real setback being the dreadful outbreak of the plague known by us as the Black Death. Reaching England from the continent in 1348, it killed off more than half the population, causing the towers of some of the churches that were building to be finished in brick for lack of stonemasons and families from the Highlands and the Western Isles to be brought down to Suffolk for lack of weavers. At that time Hadleigh and

Storm over Ipswich – looking towards the Great Wood and Hintlesham.

Lavenham were the two great centres. So important was the broadcloth industry that Lavenham, from being the fifty-second richest town in 1397, had by 1524 become the fourteenth richest in all England.

And then came the era of the New Draperies.

They were the result of another immigrant wave, the Dutch again, this time fleeing across the North Sea from Parma's Spanish armies in the reign of Elizabeth I. They brought with them new techniques that

25

had originated in Lombardy, techniques that in very loose terms meant a switch from cloths to stuffs. It was a switch from the short, carded wool that produced the 'old drapery' broadcloths to the bays and says of the 'new draperies', which were long wools, like the worsteds of Norfolk, that had to be combed and spun. It caused great bitterness, marking as it did the beginning of the decline of the Old Draperies, the weavers of broadcloth accusing Sudbury, one of the 'new drapery' centres, of producing bays that were 'little better than cotton'.

But these 'new draperies' gave great impetus to the English cloth industry, so that a big export trade developed with official standards marked by a seal much as Harris tweed has its cottage industry mark today. There were a great many different types of material produced: bays, which were then mainly blue but are still produced today as green baize for billiard tables and other purposes, says, perpetuanas, grograines, velures, mockadoes, and more than fifty others, and they could be treated in many different ways.

And just as Worstead in Norfolk gave its name to a cloth, so two of the smaller Suffolk villages produced such distinctive coloured material that their products were known by the village name – the coarse, hard-wearing blue Kersey cloth was like a serge and particularly suitable for horsemen's cloaks, and there was a Lindsey cloth. These two were what Shakespeare referred to as 'Lindsey-Kersey stuff'. I can remember wearing Lindsey socks as a boy, and quite recently I saw Kerseys advertised, not in England, but in the Maritimes of Canada, and not as cloaks, but as stockings suitable for fishermen, the name presumably having been carried across the Atlantic with the first emigrants, many of whom were from the wool areas.

The New Draperies continued to operate the domestic or cottage industry system, but after the slump that preceded the Civil War the cottagers in many cases turned from weaving to the preparation and spinning of the wool. Up to that time they had had considerable independence. Now most of them worked for a wage. Then suddenly the East Anglian wool trade went into decline, and for the same reason that some of our own basic industries today have declined – technology. The mechanical loom made cottage looms obsolete, unable to compete with those operated by power. In a few decades the bulk of the wool industry had switched to the West Country and Yorkshire, where the streams so essential for the preparation of the wool were fast flowing and able to provide power for the looms. Another century, and it was steampower, coal replacing water, so that the whole industry became concentrated in the north of England. The Old Draperies faded along with the New and in the end about all that was left of the wool industry in East Anglia was a scattering of timbered 'Gild' halls and the Old Drapery churches.

This is, I am afraid, an over-simplified version. Inevitably an industry that had been so dominant in the area for so long did not die out completely overnight. The production of bays or baize, continued at

Spring at last and the froth of cow parsley – one of those myriad small lanes that a driver in Suffolk is constantly discovering.

Colchester into the eighteenth century, though the standard declined, and as late as 1844 Hadleigh still had a large silk mill in operation. As a last resort, Lavenham switched to horsehair. Glemsford, too. I met the owner of that factory in the Army. There was straw-plaiting, and until very recently Hadleigh was producing mats and matting of coconut fibre. But it is in Sudbury that the weaver's art has lingered longest, marvellous fabric still being produced to this day, fine damasks and tapestries for the furniture and walls of public buildings the world over, even the upholstery of state coaches, fabrics that have lured us to the clacking uproar of the looms whenever we have felt the need of something special for our home. And in the same town ties and cravats.

The weaving tradition has attracted the artist craftsman of today, so 27 that there are people working their own looms to produce silk as well as woollen materials. There was a man at Thaxted wove the most beautiful scarves, the silk being vegetable-dyed in rich warm russet colours that ran from gold through brown to beech-leaf red. I recall his work in particular because on our third visit to the States we went bearing gifts of his headscarves that were crooned over by people who seemed to us, fresh from rationing, to have everything.

When we first came to East Anglia we were often in Lavenham, the Swan then a friendly neighbourhood pub, not the big hotel it is now, the Guildhall sadly neglected, its fine oak studs bravely holding out against the elements, the cold, draughty rooms acting as village hall and meeting place. In those days there was little accurate information readily available locally about the wool trade. In fact, the only thing I remember about the Guildhall then was the carved timbering and the fact that the cellars, once the town jail, had held the towering figure and personality of the Reverend Rowland Taylor for a night early in February, 1555. He was Rector of Hadleigh and a Protestant dissident, for this was in the reign of Bloody Mary. On the 9th he was taken to Aldham Common, just north of Hadleigh, and there burned at the stake. The stone marking the spot bore this simple statement: '1555 – D. Taylor in defending that was good at this plas left his blode.' The place is now more clearly marked by a monument that stands to the left of the Ipswich road.

Now, of course, things are different. There are books about the wool trade and Lavenham is undoubtedly the best place to get the feel of it, not only because in almost all its streets you are walking in the Old Drapery path, but because the National Trust now owns the Guildhall and has filled some of the lovely timbered rooms with an exhibition tracing the development of the industry locally and setting it in the context of historical events. There you can see teasels set in their cross-shaped hand tool and learn about dyeing and how the Lavenham blue was produced from woad, sometimes imported from Toulouse, how the red was produced from madder, and alum was used to 'set' the dyes. There were other vegetable dyes used, of course, including saffron, which comes from a rather leggy, violet-coloured crocus called *sativus*. It appears in the autumn and needs longish grass to prevent it from drooping untidily. At least, that is our experience. Like many of our more unusual plants we acquired it from an eccentric Irish collector, and long before we realised this was how saffron was produced. Once there were fields and fields of this crocus running north from Saffron Walden almost to Cambridge, cultivation of the bulb going back as far as Roman times when it was used as a perfume. It required about 5,000 blooms to produce

May 18th, the Stour in flood – 'on one occasion we rowed a boat across the fences'. Given a good surge in the North Sea and most East Anglian meadowlands are at risk, the high tide in the estuaries holding back the rainwater outflows of the rivers.

an ounce of saffron. Mass cultivation was abandoned, not because of any decline in demand – saffron was also used as a drug and also in cookery – but because of recurrent attacks of fungus. Fortunately it seems quite happy in our garden, though we are under attack from *armillaria* (honey-fungus).

Fulling was carried out in the backyards and the stream that supplied the water still runs under the houses in Water Street. At one time Lavenham had four guild halls, the Wool Hall that is now part of the Swan being one of them. These two halls and the house of the de Veres are the best of the timber-framed profusion of buildings that fill the town. And on the hill to the west of it stands the great wool church. The prosperity that followed upon the first wave of Dutch immigrants in the fourteenth century brought great fortunes to the clothiers, the men who purchased the wool, organised the domestic system, the cottage looms, the dyers, the fullers, and then finally sold the finished cloth at the larger fairs, sent it to London or Norwich, or exported it to the continent. The Springs of Lavenham were only one of the many wool families who found themselves able to build merchant princes' houses. These were the men who helped to finance the enlargement or rebuilding of churches and contributed to the rise of Cambridge as an educational and cultural centre, all on the back of what was still virtually a cottage industry.

The Springs' niche in history stems from the end of the Wars of the Roses in 1485. As a thank offering, John de Vere, thirteenth Earl of Oxford – the family house is the finely carved timbered building on the south side of Water Street – proposed a great church on the hill south-west of Lavenham. The second generation of the Springs, with the Branches and other rich clothiers, provided much of the finance, and though the second Spring died the following year when little more than the foundation of the tower was complete, he left a large sum of money for his son to continue the work. This son was the Spring known as Thomas the Rich. He died in 1523 leaving funds for the completion of the 140-foot tower, and instructions for his coat of arms to be repeated round the top of it thirty-two times, a considerable improvement on the merchant's mark that was all his father could stamp on the tower's plinth thirty-eight years earlier. I imagine it was Sir Thomas' ostentation that prompted another merchant prince in nearby Sudbury to turn his back on the idea of buying his way into Heaven and to have the following witty statement carved on his tomb: 'This day a Sudbury camel passed through the eye of a needle.'

With the virtual disappearance of the wool industry, East Anglia slid back into dependence upon the harvests of land and sea – and trade, of course, sea trade. The great surge of Tudor times was augmented by the arrival of Huguenots and Lutherans. Prosperity ran on almost uninterrupted by the Civil War and the Cromwellian era. The King and Bedford started draining the Fens, new systems of agriculture culminated in the precepts and example set by 'Turnip' Townshend of Raynham

and Coke of Holkham. East Anglia was rich right into the nineteenth century, the home of new ideas and new machinery, the Norfolk jacket the height of leisure fashion.

The industrial revolution that followed the Napoleonic Wars changed all that. Free trade and the growth of empire brought to our harbours imports of cheap foodstuffs from all over the world. Even after the Second World War village cottages were let for as little as 1/6d a week and there were two or three families, sometimes more, in what was really a single building. There was still the occasional pony and trap, little or no industry in the villages, and our street, where lovely curved brick gutters, like twin 'kennels' running down the valley side, emphasised its medieval appearance, was largely empty of traffic. And I kept horse hours for a time, dawn bringing the clop of heavy iron-shod hooves as six or seven great round-buttocked Suffolk Punches went off to work, pausing briefly in the watersplash to drink their fill. And then, as dusk fell, or the long summer day began to pale, back they came, the clop of their hooves silenced in the splash, the jingle of their harness the only sound as they drank. From my study window, working there with my typewriter on my knees, I could just see them ranged shoulder-to-shoulder below our

Hadleigh's old Guildhall, which is a stone's throw across the graveyard from the church and the Deanery Tower.

The fifteenth-century Deanery Tower, Hadleigh – it bears some resemblance to the moated entrance gate to Oxburgh Hall.

willows, beautiful, powerful animals, and an earnest of the unchanging nature of the countryside.

Unchanging? A few years and they were gone, replaced by the ubiquitous tractor, costs and wages mounting, and the farms becoming denuded of life, human, horse and cow. And in the sixties, the pace of change increased dramatically. Gone were our brick gutters, replaced by urban kerbstones, town pavements lining the Street. They would have bridged the watersplash if we hadn't raised an outcry. But I suppose they were right about the pavements, for suddenly in the sixties our part of Suffolk became the fastest growing area of England, the population exploding – Hadleigh, from a sleepy little market town no bigger than an overgrown village, almost trebled its population in a decade and a half – cars proliferating as oil became cheap and the numbers of those in retirement increased, traffic so thick in the Street on a Sunday afternoon that it was

Hadleigh Show – always held in May and notorious for rain. The scene is typical of these junior and very local versions of the great county shows of East Anglia.

difficult to drive down the hill to the watersplash and our own gates.

Children's voices loud in the sun, parents calling as their kids wade in the splash or feed the ducks, laughing at the mallards and muscovies with trains of ducklings holding up the traffic. Sometimes there are Morris dancers. Always there are photographers crouching to catch the

church's reflection, the steep hill leading up to it mirrored in the water, a medieval snap that shimmers with the movement of ducks and children; such a winner of a picture, with the single street and the medieval timbered cottages climbing steeply to the towering grey flint mass of the church, that in one single year it was the cover of no less than three of

Nayland and the Stour . . . It is difficult, driving across the bridge here, to realise that this river was once the great southern barrier to the heart of East Anglia, an area of fen and swamp. There is still a Fen Street, next to this view of the little alleyway leading to the church.

the major tourist brochures. It was there, in a box by the splash, that a lot of the money was raised to re-cast and re-hang the bells. But when we had done that we found the tower was unsafe and would have to be reconditioned before we could hang them, and that meant raising a lot more money – a massive task for a parish of little more than 300 souls.

The preservation of East Anglia's churches is a major problem with many parishes smaller than ours and most of them lacking the tourist attraction of a largely medieval village and a great wool church reflected in a watersplash. We worked at it hard for the better part of a decade, the August flower festival a huge attraction, and with this record of self-help I had a good story to tell when it came to a television appeal. Self-help is the key to outside support, but even in other wool villages it is becoming difficult (nearby Boxford needs £170,000), which means, of course, that raising money for churches off the tourist track is now very difficult indeed.

However, just as visitors to our village were enormously kind and generous when we were in difficulties, so I think people have now come to appreciate that the churches they visit for historical interest and the pleasure of architecture and furnishings have to be maintained by the local community. But the old wool villages do have a great advantage since, by the sheer number of visitors, it is obvious people are now very conscious that in all Britain there is no area, except possibly the Cotswolds, so rich in villages of exquisite beauty – and the Cotswolds have none of the pattern and colour that makes this southern part of Suffolk so architecturally enchanting. The Old Drapery towns and villages extend from Clare and Cavendish in the west, through Brent and Monks Eleigh, Chelsworth, Bildeston, Stowmarket and Needham Market, to Ipswich in the east; from Bury St Edmunds in the north through Lavenham, Groton, Boxford, Stoke-by-Nayland and Nayland to Colchester in the south.

This, of course, was our social catchment area, so that bit-by-bit, in all weathers and in all lights, we discovered its attractions and always it seemed there were new roads that we had not travelled before, so that sometimes, exhausted with writing, I would take Dorothy on a mystery tour, the game being to find another road we did not know within a radius of ten miles. And because of the multiplicity of remote farmsteads there always is another, though I have to warn you it often deteriorates into a potholed dirt track, sometimes finishing abruptly in a gaggle of geese and dark oak beams beside the remains of an old moat.

It is on these by-roads that you stumble upon those Dunsanian relics that house pure manifestations of the supernatural. Borley Rectory, of course . . . lying back from the Sudbury-Long Melford road, on the edge of the lost country of the Belchamps, it is barely ten miles away and the poet who once owned the place described how he was pestered by would-be ghost killers, some dangerously trigger-happy and heavily armed. He had purchased a great cast-iron water heating stove from us,

Exotic shrub and medieval timbering in startling contrast.

Elaborate pargeting close against the churchyard, Clare.

and claiming that his hands were too delicate to help me trundle the thing out to his vehicle, regaled me with a vivid account of being woken in the night and going out to find a group of magnificent young men without their flying machines perched on a wall with a Bren gun and a searchlight ready and willing to riddle any grey ladies they saw with bullets. We went there later with a journalist friend to find the poet living in the coach house. The rectory had been burned down and from the charred timbering of the roof he had constructed, with his own delicate hands, a whole range of mushroom sheds, which was why he had bought the stove. No ghosts walked, but there was a definite chill about the coach house. We would none of us have dreamed of living there among the fungi, and nobody had for a dozen years and more last time we saw it.

The same applied to a mouldering Tudor manor house near Sudbury we had explored when house hunting, its timbered gloom vaguely disturbing. I have often wondered about that house. Was there a ghost, and if so what was its response when the whole building was jacked up and mounted on wheels to be moved a few hundred yards up the hill because an industrial estate had been built virtually at its front door? And Polstead, of course. But not the Red Barn, where Maria Marten's remains were unearthed. That has long since gone, burned to the ground. And not the molecatcher's cottage where she lived with her mother. Nor at the home of the man convicted of her murder, who was publicly executed at Bury St Edmunds in 1828, his skin flayed for the binding of a book, his head pickled in a jar at the College of Surgeons. No, the Polstead haunt is at the Rectory, a haunt that appears to be all things to all people, varying according to the occupants, the last Rector to reside there leaving in a hurry because his wife couldn't stand the activities of what was described as a poltergeist. There are also stories of monks seen walking the dark, treed tunnel of the hill past the Rectory gates in the dusk, quite visible through the car's windscreen, but no longer there when peered at through the driving mirror.

This is something we have never experienced, though we drive that way very frequently. But whenever we go into Polstead church we both sense an atmosphere, and I don't think it is because of the very striking brickwork of the Norman arches and the clerestory windows above, though it is unique, being all twelfth-century and built of bricks that are supposed to be the first made in the country after the Romans had left. I think perhaps the church was built on the site of either a Roman or an earlier pagan temple. But that is pure guesswork. All I know for certain is that I find it one of those churches that has a very definite strangeness about it, not hostile, but something that causes my mind to stray back down the records of man's search for God, to strange deities encountered in many lands.

A friend of ours who has lived at the Hall there for many years has the church facing the front door and a close-up view of the remains of

The church of St Mary at Langham. Nearby, Constable found his favourite viewpoint for paintings and drawings of Dedham Vale.

The cloud-galleoned stump of Stoke-by-Nayland Church – a favourite Constable subject.

the great Gospel Oak under whose branches St Cedd's Saxon missionaries are said to have preached more than a thousand years ago. There is almost nothing left of it now, but in its last sad desiccated state it was thirty-six feet round. Its progeny now stand like three disciples, and so the legend is perpetuated, and you can stand beside them in a park that falls in a green sweep to a stream and the hill beyond that climbs up past the rectory to the huge 120-foot square tower of the church of Stoke-by-Nayland, one of Constable's favourite subjects. Just to stand there on a summer's day, drinking in that green and pleasant picture . . . this is all of England that I have ever dreamed of, at sea or in far distant lands. And then to walk down through the churchyard to the pond, where fishermen sit under big green umbrellas, where witches were swum in the days when there was no electricity and people feared the dark, and on across the little bridge and up through thatched gables 37

Only ten weeks separate the Maytime view of the flat vale of the Stour near Dedham and this harvest scene in a field a little further upstream.

and timbered walls to the village green where the road goes off to Polstead Heath and Polstead Blacks were the most succulent cherries you ever tasted.

Coming from London, this is our way home. So many, many times we have turned off the A12 at Colchester in Essex to cross the border into Suffolk at the Stour and drive through Nayland, Stoke-by-Nayland and Polstead to our own village – the same road countless times, and yet it never palls. Coming down the long hill from Colchester to the sluice and the bridge at Nayland, the pub and the lock-keeper's cottage that is now a house, the world seems changed. And not because with the crossing of the Stour we are on the final homeward lap – something much more, a sudden magic, the quintessential of an English landscape miraculously materialising before our eyes; cottages clustered round the church in a luminous pattern of colours, plaster on stout oak frames and mellow-tiled roofs that are spattered in summer with the bright yellow of our native sedum thriving in the dry air. Willows blue-grey by the river and on the hills beyond the drilled ranks of a neat little plantation of poplars.

That is the moment, driving down from London, that I feel a sense of renewal, the beauty of it like a balm. And it is always the same, this lift of the heart as I cross into Suffolk, though my nature is Scottish and I was not born here.

Why? Why does it affect me so?

Is it the knowledge that the ribbon of water I have crossed runs down to Manningtree and on into the estuary to join the Orwell at Harwich and so to the sea that was England's great highway till they built the motorways? Is it the knowledge that I am feeling at that moment what the inhabitants of this watery land must have always felt, the sense of being in touch with foreign lands? Or is it just the beauty of it all, the same that Constable saw – the great stump of Stoke church standing on the hill, the thatched cottages and old wool merchants' houses tumbling over the brow, massed with roses? More roses by the bridge at Polstead, and still in autumn they stand bright against the stubble or the first brown patchwork of the plough. Even sometimes in winter, with the bare tracery of the trees against the green of winter wheat, mist softening the hardness of the light and bonfires smoking.

It is just seven miles to our home then and I am enchanted, though the road twists, spattering mud from the sugar beet fields, and I am tired.

And it is the same when we come back from our travels. I do not hanker after other parts of Britain, or indeed any other place in the world. Those seven miles beyond the Stour – the villages, the land, the river meadows, the soft grey glimmer of bat willows – seem to say it all. I am not a poet, though there are occasions when I kid myself I get a little near to it in my descriptive prose. But when Angus Wilson, editing an East Anglian writers' book, asked us both to contribute on the theme of the traveller returning, I found I needed verse, not prose, to explain what I felt. I feel the same need here, and by repeating what I wrote then, I hope I can convey a little of what this part of East Anglia has meant to a writer whose work has always been closely connected with foreign travel.

I titled it 'The Wanderer':

In Papua or the Gibson Desert, or beyond the snow-capped ramparts of the Rockies,
    The Wanderer soaks up richness of experience,
    Behind him always the security of his own hearth,
    The security of a land that was old when the Vikings landed –
    Old in history.

In the dark hour watches of the night, star-studded or wracked with storm,
    Dreaming dreams that the world may some day read,
    Water breaking and spray cold on the skin,
    The security of that land guards against creeping fear,
    Familiarity a shield.

In a canyon in New York City, remembering old timbered houses,
    The single street falling to the watersplash,
    And Kennedy's voice broadcasting his Cuba message,
    God let me not die – not here among these concrete cliffs
    But in my own familiar place.

Animals seek their burrows, so the human animal his,
    And when the weariness of travel becomes a satiation of experience,
    Or fear obtrudes, of forceful elements or hostile people,
    Then the mind sees far-off places for what they are –
    The grass no greener.

So the Wanderer returns, enriched in knowledge and experience,
    To discover that nothing changes and a village old in time
    Has all of life within its grasp,
    Laughter and hope and copulation,
    Birth and death.

Constable, Gainsborough, those wide skies and stubbled slopes,
    The painter's palette colouring field and cottage;
    This is my England, my home, my deep, deep love.
    And here I will lay myself to rest when the time comes –
    But not yet

Not before I have said my say about the slaughter of the elephants,
    And seen the Andes and the Pacific once again.

The Stour dripping with all shades of green in June and the elder in flower.

3. Digression to some timbered inns

Sir, there is nothing which has yet been contrived by man by which so much happiness is produced as by a good tavern or inn. SAMUEL JOHNSON

Before I sailed so energetically or got myself so deeply involved in forestry, or had a base in London, our East Anglian social life took us further afield. But always, it seemed, northwards, seldom south across the border into Essex, and mainly to Georgian rectories sold off by the Church or timbered houses, farms and cottages, only very occasionally to a town house.

But an author has other needs besides a social life.

The physical side of writing – by that I mean the actual business of putting words on paper – is a somewhat enclosed existence, long hours are spent locked in on myself in the confines of my study. At times this has the mental effect of making me what the Canadians would call 'bushed', a state of mind where I feel so isolated I really don't want to face the outside world or even go beyond my own gate.

This is not good. It seldom arises now because I have too many other demands on my time and I can always get out of my shell by driving to London, which has become a short two hours away – provided we leave after dinner in the evening and from London on the return journey not later than 06.00 in the morning! For this we have to thank the booming docks of Felixstowe, the A12 having been gradually upgraded to a major truckway. But in the early days, when London was a much longer drive, the need to break out locally was very real, and not just because of that sense of being bushed. There have always been moments in every book when I grind to a halt, feeling boxed in, mentally in a rut that too long and too deep a concentration has dug for me. It is story, always story – never a writing problem.

At that point I need a change of scene, a drink, perhaps a meal out, the last two incidental to the real need which is to talk the problem through. Here my wife is marvellous, a sounding box that somehow over the years has never failed to lift me out of momentary depressions, her own very considerable writing talent contributing a new angle or a shaft of illumination, usually of character since she was originally an actress,

The Bull at Long Melford. The lit timbers look very well and in keeping, yet well over four centuries separate the old from the modernised.

43

something at any rate that starts my adrenalin running again and renews my enthusiasm for what I am trying to write.

And, oh God, how one needs enthusiasm to write anything worth while, particularly a book of a hundred thousand words that will be two years in the writing. And so we searched out the inns and eateries of East Anglia, gravitating almost automatically to those houses that matched the period of our own home. And then we talked and talked – or on these occasions perhaps I did most of the talking. However it was, Dorothy would surely have contributed something to the book by the end of the evening, so that I and my readers would be the richer for her bright, constructive mind. Anyway, that was how we came to know the inns of this part of England.

At that time the extraordinary growth of population and industry along the Suffolk-Essex border had not yet reached the stage where the renovation and improvement of even the smallest pub became a profitable exercise. More to the point, inflation and the new inhabitants, plus contracting out and the consequent reduction of labour on the farms, had not yet emptied the pubs of large numbers of the older East Anglians with their rich vocabulary and very marked accent.

Nowhere in the world have the old travellers' inns survived so well as in Britain, and if I were a stranger seeking the best of them, I would be glad of the advice to head for Colchester and beyond. Colchester was one of the great centres of Roman occupation in Britain, and it is to the Roman occupation that we owe the origin of the English inn. Also the idea of an inn sign.

Driving their long, straight roads through the length and breadth of the land, places of refreshment were essential, for virtually all travel was on foot. These staging points were marked by an ivy bush on a stake, ivy growing everywhere and its appearance not unlike the vine itself.

The equivalent of our inns uncovered at Pompeii show a chequered sign and the Romans almost certainly used that same chequered sign in England to mark those 'inns' substantial enough in their fabric to carry a mural design. In most cases it would be painted on wood, which explains why the only chequered sign I have seen still in existence was painted on a stone doorpost. But there are still quite a few inns and pubs called the Chequers, at Feltwell for instance on the edge of the Fens, at Great Dunmow too, and most of them are probably named, not for any game, but because they are on the site of one of the old Roman staging points.

In those days Colchester, which under Cunobelin had been the capital of a kingdom that included all of south-east England, was an important Roman administrative centre with 'paved' roads leading to it from all parts of the country. The wine served at all the 'inns' along these roads had to be brought in, which is why there is a Vineyard Street close under the walls on the south-eastern side of old Camulodunum – a street, incidentally, travelled by all the books going to and from the large

Architectural example of the east side of Long Melford's main street, one of the longest village streets in England, stretching virtually from Long Melford Hall, that lovely red brick turreted Tudor house, to the turn-off to Borley Rectory, that 'most haunted' of places.

modern library, and by me when I am giving a talk there. This is close by the point where old houses stood on top of the Roman wall. Quite a lot of this wall still remains. It was massive and enclosed over a hundred acres.

The metalled highways that linked centres of occupation in Roman Britain radiated out from Camulodunum as the main centre before the system linking Londinium to the rest of Roman Britain was constructed. Stane Street, the east-west highway, eventually crossed a whole series of East Anglian roads running north-south – at Marks Tey, Braintree, Great Dunmow, Bishop's Stortford. It is at these intersections that the more substantial resting points bearing the chequered sign would have been constructed. The same applies to the intersection points on the Icknield Way that runs diagonally slap across the whole bulge of East Anglia.

The route of these Roman highways was continued through the development of wheeled transport, so that coachroads and turnpikes used long stretches of them, and motoring through East Anglia today on the main roads you are as often as not following the line first laid out by Roman military engineers. Thus, the Roman chequer-mark staging posts and ivy-bush-posted refreshment points, emerging later in all their glory as Georgian coaching inns, have been in almost continuous use for the same essential and refreshing purpose right into the present day, the inn sign there for all to see, sometimes hung on gallows right across the road – one of the few remaining gallows signs is the Magpie at Stonham on the Ipswich-Norwich road.

A very obvious example of a coaching inn with its roots in the needs of the Roman legionaries and administrators is the White Hart at Braintree. The present inn is only four and a half centuries old, but it stands right on the Stane Street intersection with the north-south Roman highway. Did that site once carry a chequer board sign, or is the sign of the White Hart merely a modern version of the ivy bush that once welcomed the thirsty centurion and his men after they had slogged the first fifteen miles out from Camulodunum on their way to St Albans?

The other great historic centre in East Anglia is Bury St Edmunds. Here the inns are monastic in origin, going back to Saxon times when the shrine of St Edmund was one of the great pilgrimages. The Suffolk in Bury was originally the Greyhound. It goes back to 1295 and is referred to as 'le greyhounde' in 1539. The Angel may well have been originally under rival ownership, for the knightly organisations that emerged during the Crusades had their own inns and the Knights Templar certainly used the sign of the Angel.

Pilgrimages, the Crusades and continental wars, together with the economic growth of the country, encouraged travel, and by the late 1300s, and on into the following century, some of the most picturesque of today's inns were being built. It is a timber period, particularly in the south where the great oak forests covered so much of the country, the

Very much a part of the East Anglian scene – the pub name and the ale. The Lord Nelson is at Southwold.

At Burnham Market: like the Admiral he served under, Hoste was the son of a Norfolk parson, ending his naval career as the captain of the King's yacht, the Royal Sovereign.

A nautical touch at Wivenhoe.

47

Two styles of hotel, rural and seaside – The Swan at Southwold and The Crown at Framlingham.

material ready to hand and used as sectional building frames, much as we now use steel girder frames, the panels between being filled with wattle and daub (chopped straw, clay, lime and cow dung). At that time you could walk almost from the Wash to London without ever leaving the forest tracks, and it is here, in East Anglia, that you will find the greatest concentration of these old timbered inns.

I suppose Dorothy and I have become spoilt, living here in a sixteenth-century timbered house in a village that is still almost entirely sixteenth-century, but we now take it for granted that when we feed out locally it will be in the same almost medieval atmosphere. We have, in fact, the choice of innumerable such inns and ancient houses converted to restaurants within a radius of twenty miles of us. The timbering of these old inns has hardened over the centuries to a metallic consistency, the oak studs as strong, and often almost as black, as iron. Seen against the background of town and village, where much is of similar construction and period, the effect is a charming pattern of honey or coloured plaster, silver-grey, brown or black timbering and red tile roofs piled in steep gables.

Our first introduction to the East Anglian coaching inn was in winter. It was December and we were moving into our present home, a local builder patching up what was absolutely necessary, dust and plaster everywhere, and ourselves working from dawn to dark, helping to repair the worst of the wartime neglect. When we finished in the evening, tired, dirty and feeling almost despairful at having perhaps been tempted into something more than we could cope with, we still had ten miles of narrow, complex lanes to negotiate. No moon, the narrow, twisting lanes dark with frost, and the car, over eight years old, had spent the war on bricks.

On those dark drives Poe's *Tales of Mystery and Imagination* would flash through my mind as a solitary thatched cottage, the ruins of an old barn or the gaunt skeleton of a dead oak raised shadows in the night, and the sudden looming of a church tower so dark and squat it might have been Childe Roland's own. But when we had finally made it to the Bull at Long Melford, and the car was safely tucked away in the old coach yard, what a marvellous sense of relaxation!

The night, and that winding, eerie road were gone, our room oak-beamed, comforting in its timbered solidity. And then to go down to a table set before a huge oak-bressummered fireplace with logs blazing on the floor of it. And there was whisky when whisky was still rationed. And food, God knows how he did it! Mine host was ex-Indian army and his curry was superb. And there was wine waiting for us on the table, the colour of it ruby red in the leaping flames.

Oh yes, we had money for that. When you're broke there's no point in stinting yourself. It was our final splurge until I had written a new book. But would I be able to write in my changed surroundings? So much needed doing, the water to pump every day and that damned

A fine example of an inn sign at Hoxne.

49

electric plant to cope with. In the oak-beamed comfort of that splendid hostelry, warmed with drink and the heat of that enormous fire, anything seemed possible – the cold, and the strangeness of the night in a strange and backward part of England thrust into the background of our minds. 'Suffolk goes very medieval at night.' Yes, even now, with all the changes, Dorothy can still say that.

Go north-east out of London, and in a month of one-night stops you need never sleep in a room that did not exist *before* the first Elizabeth was on the throne of England. It was the railways and the industrial revolution, the huge sprawl of London, that finally made it an unfashionable part of England, the Cockney East End spreading into Essex and East Coast resorts being developed for the masses. Only Newmarket, Frinton, perhaps Sheringham, remained in fashion, and of the new rich, few of them settled in East Anglia, apart from City men, particularly Lloyd's underwriters, who found it convenient to walk to Liverpool Street and catch a non-stop express home at the end of the day. Long Melford, which gave its name to a boxing term, still had the longest and widest street for its size of any village in the country, but the Bull was a relatively undiscovered inn, largely passed over since coaching days. The same applied to the Swan at Lavenham. Only the Red Lion at Colchester, of the three inns we chiefly used, retained anything of the bustle of coaching days.

The Red Lion is probably the finest example of an old coaching inn in East Anglia. It was certainly one of the most important. It was also one of the few that Dickens seems to have ignored, his *Pickwick Papers* carrying no mention of Mr Pickwick ever having stayed there; (this

The entrance to the yard of the White Lion at Eye – not high enough for a post chaise, but of sufficient clearance for the baggage wagons taking the riders' gear in for the servants to handle.

marvellous character of fiction was in and out of a number of the East Anglian inns). In 1756, in the *Ipswich Journal*, one James Unwin, late coachman to Mr Hills in Colchester, purchased advertising space to 'inform the Publick that on Thursday, 9th March, he sets out from the Red Lyon Inn at Colchester, with a STAGE CART and able horses to be at the Bell Inn at Leadenhall Street, London, on Wednesday by one o'clock.'

This really was travelling economy class. Just on a week to cover the distance that we now drive in less than an hour and a half. By express coach it was a good deal better. Here is an advertisement in the same journal five years later:

On Monday, the 11th instant, will set out THE FAREWELL POST-CHAISE with good horses and careful drivers from the following inns at sixpence per mile from London to Colchester and Colchester to London in 8 hours. To set out from the RED LYON at Colchester at Seven, and from the GREEN DRAGON in Whitechapel, London, at Eight every morning in the week, for the more quick and easy convenience of such as do not choose travelling in Stage Coaches.

This was certainly first class, and the fare each way was twenty-five shillings and sixpence. The mail and many of the important coaches used the newly-built Three Cups opposite, now the George.

Horses and cocks and barefisted fights all seemed to belong together, cockfighting common to many of the inns. At the Suffolk in Bury, for instance, the invitation to a big match in 1725 reads: 'To show thirty-one cocks on a side, for two guineas a cock and twenty guineas the odd battle ... Gentlemen shall be accommodated with a glass of excellent wine and care taken to prevent disturbance by the mob.' And on the coast, of course, smuggling went hand-in-hand with the business of building, owning and running ships. The Crown at Woodbridge was owned at one time by the shipwright family of Pett from the Chatham and Deptford area of the Thames.

In our early sailing days this, like the Maybush above the anchorage at Waldringfield and the Red Lion where you turn off for the estuary, was a haunt of ours, the dark wood restful after a day's sail, or a day working on the boat at Whisstock's yard when we laid up for the winter and fitted out again at the start of the season.

But the inn I know best is the Swan at Lavenham, having traced the development of it through its long history and having been a constant visitor long before its enlargement and rebuilding in the late sixties. A book on coaching inns that I had revised, and from which so much of my knowledge of the background and history of the English inn stems,

One of the most elaborate and spectacular of timber inns – the Red Lion at Colchester. The equal, almost, of the Shakespeare at Stratford.

The gallows inn-sign at Little Stonham, one of the few still spanning an old coach road, which is itself on the line of an earlier Roman road.

The cold, hard winter clarity of an east coast estuary – this is at Waldringfield on the Deben.

was in fact a book about Trust Houses. Not the big hotel-owning company that has spread its net around the world, but the original, very limited concept of 'philanthropy with five per cent'. Earl Grey's leasing of the first public house trust inn in 1904 was not universally popular, particularly with the liquor trade! For at least six centuries the English inn had been as much a part of the fabric of social life as the manor and the church, but then in a short twenty years steam and the railways emptied the roads, and instead of hostelries and coaching inns they became little more than grog shops, centres of drunkenness whose proprietors found it more profitable to dispense liquor than hospitality. To deal with this problem Grey initiated a scheme for the acquisition of inns to be run by salaried managers who would get nothing out of the sale of liquor, but would earn commission on food and accommodation.

How he would have appreciated the present day, when words like pub food and inn food, good food and snacks, bar and restaurant appear on boards outside almost every country inn from Land's End to John o'Groats! With the vested interests of the liquor trade and the powerful temperance group against him, his scheme was not an immediate success. But it was an idea that gradually caught on and spread out from the original Wagon and Horses at Ridge Hill near London to other counties, so that by 1920 Trust Houses had developed their own architectural department which was to become expert at incorporating and adapting the original features of old inns to modern usage.

One of their architects was James Hopwood. Just before he retired he was instructed to design and organise the enlargement of the Bull at Long Melford. Unfortunately, he was on a tight budget and when it came to the facing of the wall that looks out on to the street of that long, long village he could only afford flint, the cheapest material natural to East Anglia. Then a few years later he was made an offer by Trust Houses that brought him out of retirement to redesign the Lavenham Swan Inn – they gave him *carte blanche*; within reason he could do what he had wanted to do with the Bull, which was to use oak so that every new addition or alteration would match the existing fabric.

The reason he was given a free hand was that Trust Houses in 1962 had made an outstanding acquisition backing on to the Swan. This was the old Wool Hall. They had also acquired a greengrocer's shop and a storage building that I believe had once been a smithy. These linked the inn and the Wool Hall on the Water Street frontage, while a large garden fronting on Lady Street added greatly to the land area involved. They had the whole block now, including the dentist's house adjoining the old entrance to the yard on the High Street, and somebody had had the good sense to realise this could be a gem of a hotel.

It was a decision very much in line with the development of England's old inns to meet the changes in social need. That, at any rate, is how I saw it at the time, having watched the rebuilding and been subjected to the infectious, almost boyish enthusiasm of the septuagenarian architect in charge. In fact, the story of the Swan is for me a microcosm of the English inn. When we came to East Anglia the yard was still there and we dined before a roaring fire in what had once been the stables, the whole place dark with timbers that had been felled and adzed when 'old drapery' Lavenham was emerging from the primeval oak forests that surrounded the site.

Oak is such a wonderful wood. The texture of it, that close, slow-grown grain. It was the Navy's tree, the tree that built those great ships of the line. In the end, the construction of a 120-gun three-deck man-o'-war required around 8,000 tons of timber. That meant the felling of at least 4,000 trees, equivalent to the clear felling of over a hundred acres of prime oak forest. God knows how many acres of oak were felled to build Lavenham, but walking through it in the dawn, when the old streets are deserted, is like walking through a petrified forest where every tree has been fashioned by man.

Lavenham's Water Street, the Swan on the left and, unbelievably, water still running underneath the houses as it ran all those centuries ago for the treatment of wool.

Thomas the Rich's great cathedral of a church, all pale gold in the floodlights after dark, the tower seeming higher, the intricate tracery of crenellations etched black with shadows, is the only stone edifice. The main street curves down from it to the Swan, then up and over another hill, an avenue almost of timbered houses and cottages standing shoulder to shoulder. The other main street, Water Street, running east from the Swan is timbered buildings again with the Earl of Oxford's house, the doorpost carvings wonderfully preserved, on one side, and the Wool Hall on the other, its solid, silvery corner post delicately carved. Up Lady Street, at the top of the hill, is the old Guildhall. I don't know of any timbered building finer than this, the carving still so sharp and clear. Indeed, the whole of Lavenham is unique, for there is no place in England where you can walk through such a medieval world of oak-frame buildings all wonderfully preserved by the dry East Anglian climate.

Lavenham's Wool Hall, so nearly rustled by royalty.

All of us who have worked in oak with our own hands have a feeling for it. It is such a virile wood. It planes and chisels so robustly, yet with an almost silky texture when carefully smoothed. It is a very sensuous wood. Every carpenter loves it. And the pleasure of watching it age! As soon as we could afford it, we had those lead light window frames that were not already oak replaced. The pale new oak we painted over with a slaked lime wash. It seemed such desecration, but having been given a desk of limed oak from Heal's as a wedding present by my mother I had absolute confidence in the result. Old rafters newly exposed were treated the same way, leaving the lime wash to burn its way into the oak for several months. Now you can hardly tell new and old apart, all are pickled to a faded, silvery grey, and the new wood is already hardening.

When we stripped the bulging plaster from the back of a timber frame cottage of ours close by my study we found the wattle and daub wall beneath in absolutely perfect condition, the straw and dung that keeps the slaked lime supple clearly visible. Once, on this same cottage, we treated the plaster panels between the oak studs with a real Buxton lime-wash – you add to the brew of slaked lime a proportion of melted tallow grease, a little vinegar, cochineal to colour according to choice, and for the real purist a shovelful of horse manure; it lasted two or three times as long as modern protective coatings.

If I were able to do a Rip van Winkle and return to the Swan a hundred years or so from now, I wonder whether anyone would know for sure what is old and what is not? It is already becoming difficult.

The Victorians, of course, had a different view of oak. The vandalism of today is nothing compared with what the Victorians did in the name of progress, their love of steam, iron and brick leading them to discard anything they got their hands on that was made of old-fashioned materials, oak in particular. They seem to have developed a pathological hatred of this aristocrat of timber trees.

Two oak pieces we value greatly in our own village church are five painted panels, all that is left of the Tudor rood-screen, and a most beautifully constructed lectern pedestal found on a rubbish dump at the end of somebody's garden. And in Lavenham the Swan's timber framing, its plaster and its gables that now have the soft glow of a Dutch painting, was discreetly hidden behind a modern brick façade.

Though a part of the fabric of 'old drapery' Lavenham, the Swan is hardly likely to have been built as an inn. To support an inn, as opposed to a rough tavern, there has to be traffic and there could not have been enough of that in medieval times. Yet by the 1600s it was a well established inn. The first time we dined in the old stable block I remember sitting just below the framed facsimile of token coinage issued by the keeper of the Swan, one John Girling. Innkeepers regularly issued their own local 'money' because the small cost of beer required small change, and there was usually insufficient small coinage available or none at all. The date of this particular token was 1667.

The fine Tudor doorway to Little Hall, now reconditioned and the headquarters of the Suffolk Preservation Society. It is on the east side of Lavenham's Market Place, and on the south side is the superb Guildhall, shown overleaf, one of the finest timber-frame buildings in existence.

My own guess is that the Swan as an inn dates from the 'new drapery' period and that the building was originally a wool merchant's house. This was certainly the case with the Bull in neighbouring Long Melford. Originally built as the home of one of the richer clothiers, with its yard outbuildings, later to become the stables, housing his looms and workshop, it had become an inn in the reign of Elizabeth. The carved posts giving the initials of two members of the Drew family and the date 1649 probably record later additions to the fabric.

The High Street in Lavenham would then have been no more than a dirt track. Later it would have been 'metalled' and may have had the brick gutters that look so much more attractive than the hard kerbs necessitated by the influx of cars. In those early days men and women stopping at the inn would have come by horseback or wagon, in winter splashed with the mud of the forest tracks, in summer dry with the dust of travel. The arched entrance, which now leads into reception, was never high enough for a coach, but it would have taken baggage wagons and it was through this entrance to the yard that we used to walk to the bar. The bar was on the left. It is still in the same place, the bricks on the floor the same bricks that would have been brought back in ballast by the wool ships, and the central supporting post shows how much of it was built out into the yard, for the post originally supported the open gallery leading to the bedrooms above.

But though the entrance arch was only high enough for wagons, the Swan was a stage on the coaching run from Bury to London. Bury New Post Coaches left from the Greyhound every morning at seven o'clock, stopping at the Swan and the Bull on their way to the Saracen's Head in London. That was in 1793. But the Lavenham Machine had run a direct service to the capital thirty years earlier at a charge of eleven shillings, which shows that travel is still a lot cheaper in real terms today and explains why so many East Anglians never journeyed outside of their own village except on foot. But for that period the Lavenham Machine was a flyer, making the journey three times a week in a time of thirteen hours – if God permit, the posting notices added.

In 1830 the Swan was sold by auction. It then had stabling for fifty horses, and because we knew about this we were always conscious in some strange way of a different feel about the dining-room, as though the horses had left their presence imprinted on the walls. There was housing for chaises, a barn for feed, a brew office and a plant for eight coombs or brewing vats. The description of the inn itself was 'a capital old-established FREE PUBLIC and POSTING HOUSE' containing no less than six parlours, an assembly room, two kitchens, a bar, four cellars, twelve bed-chambers.

Then the railway reached Lavenham and the Swan's yard died,

An interesting example of how easy it is in timber-frame construction to remove or add windows or alter doorways. The overhang of the upper storey is typical of the period.

Three further examples of the use of oak in the construction of medieval buildings.

emptied of horses, the once busy inn little more than the local pub. Its rebirth began between the wars with the arrival of the automobile. When the old Trust Houses acquired it in 1933 the Victorian brick façade was pulled down and once again it was serving meals. World War II brought new and very thirsty customers, men, and women too, from all over the western world, for the flat tablelands of East Anglia that now grow such an abundance of wheat then spawned concrete and Nissen huts, bombers and fighters, particularly bombers, crowding into more than eighty airfields and the number of Americans increased steadily as D-day approached.

They left cap badges as mementos and those that still adorn the black oak beams give some idea of the range of units stationed in the neighbourhood. They also left signatures scrawled on the plaster panels between the oak studs, now preserved behind glass, and there was the figure of a naked lady painted on the ceiling by an artistic enthusiast lying flat on his back on top of the bar. It wasn't at all a bad picture, but then some prude thought it wasn't quite nice and disappeared it in the subsequent redecoration. They said the ceiling disintegrated, but one day perhaps it will be uncovered and an expert with a sense of humour will perhaps attribute it to the work of a wandering friar exorcising his frustrations, which is not too much of a flight of fancy since fairly recently, in a shop in Hadleigh, murals have been found that are believed to have been painted in bits and pieces by itinerant friars giving a return for their night's lodging.

There are also hand bells in the bar designed to match the bells in the church and it was on these that the ringers used to practise every week. Before we raised the money for the bells of our own village church to be restored about the only ringing anyone practised was on hand bells. My parents were alive then and at Christmas time, when we had a party, mulled wine or punch and the hall with its oak beams all candle-lit and the central staircase with frog banisters sweeping up to the dim outline of the upstairs balcony, suddenly the bell ringers would arrive. In the candle-light and the blaze of oak logs, the bells all silver, and that little group of villagers ringing out the carols. Then the guests would take a hand, my mother, who was musical, really enjoying herself as haltingly the numbers were followed and the simple changes rung, and the beamed hall resonant with the strong Suffolk accents.

It's odd how tastes alter. It is only a few years back that everything Victorian was denigrated as being over-elaborate, even vulgar. Now, with fewer craftsmen, and their time so much more valuable, the very intricacy of Victorian workmanship is admired. The beginnings of a swing

Anything goes in these old Suffolk cottages, every period of door or window – remember it is only just over thirty years ago that one-up and one-downers like these were let for as little as a shilling and sixpence a week.

away from Victorian functionalism began quite early in the century, and one of the first manifestations of it was the cannibalisation, even the rustling of old timber-framed buildings.

As I stand on the lower lawn of my garden, at the point where the old covered-in well from which I used to pump all our water has produced a slight hollow, I look across to the *pisardii* and the willows beside the road, wondering how it would have been when this lawn was the yard of a timber-frame Elizabethan house called Bouttells. The house is gone, but not destroyed. It lurks under another name in Bures just over ten miles away.

Other houses were spirited away from the wool villages about the same time. Lavenham in particular suffered, one of its timbered buildings finishing up most incongruously on the front at Clacton. And then in 1911 the lovely Wool Hall was raided for its timbers, which were being taken to Ascot for an extension to a cottage belonging to Princess Louise, the timbers being carefully numbered for re-erection on the new site. The man who stopped this vandalism was the local Rector who, having failed to obtain any information from the contractors, hired cyclists at his own expense to follow the timber lorries to their destination. And that was how it became a home for women who cleaned out railway carriages, for the Princess was so appalled when the Reverend Taylor told her what was happening that she ordered all the timbers to be returned and the Hall rebuilt as a convalescent home for female railway workers.

It was the re-erected Wool Hall that Trust Houses purchased in 1962, the numbering on some of the timbers still clearly visible. And it was this unique building, with its quite different function and design, that Hopwood had to marry into the inn on the High Street. How he did it is for visitors to discover for themselves, but the thing that fascinated me, when he took me over it during the final stages of building, was the way he slid from the main assembly room at the Wool Hall, which he had retained while converting the rest of the place into bedrooms, through the great new dining room with its minstrel gallery and lofty king-posted roof, to the old Swan and its yard stabling, merging it all most beautifully by the inclusion of a little cloister garden overhung by the tumbling roof slopes.

And the timber work is quite something to the touch, for he had found men locally who still had an instinctive feel for traditional building in oak. The thing he was proudest of in the whole building was the little back stair that leads up to the Wool Hall bedrooms. The treads are solid blocks of weathered oak, the difficult rising curve fashioned on site, hand-tailored to fit the space, everything done by eye without reference to any drawing, just as the barges and other East Coast boats were once built.

In recent years the timbered inns have been augmented by an absolute rash of small restaurants. Hadleigh is full of them, Colchester too – the rash runs right through the old wool towns and villages, timbered inns refurbished, weavers' cottages knocked together. All through the catchment area of the Stour you can feed among medieval beams. There is a fine little huddle of hostelries, including the Talbooth, on the banks of the river where it runs into Dedham Vale at the foot of Gun Hill, and a scattering of timbered inns all through the old forested areas of Essex, one of the best the White Hart at Great Yeldham. And in Needham Market the tradition of timbered inns and fine carpentry has been transmuted into the construction of olde English pubs for foreigners and thrones for a sultan heavy with gold leaf.

But north of the wool villages the timbered inns and feeding places gradually thin out. North of the Crown at Woodbridge, for instance, and another Crown at Framlingham, the Fox and Goose at Fressingfield, the Bell at Thetford, a line that runs pretty much west from the coast at Southwold to join the Suffolk-Norfolk border – north of that line, and stopping dead at Brandon close by the Fens, there is little in the way of timbered inns or eateries. All is brick and flint after that, right up to the saltmarsh chill of the North Shore.

The reason is simple, a matter of the availability of materials and the problem of transport in medieval and Tudor times. Forests of good oak did not grow in Broadland or in the Fens, or on the sandy soil of Breckland or in that great swathe of rounded chalkland hills that runs south-west across parts of West Suffolk and through Cambridgeshire. And in those early days, when merchant princes were building homes fit to be converted to coaching inns, the only way to transport enough shaped oak studs and beams any distance was by water.

In fact, outside of Norwich and King's Lynn, the best of all the timbered inns that I can think of this far north is the Fressingfield Fox and Goose, and that chiefly because of its setting; also the fact that it was once a guild-hall and so earlier than most. On the north side its oak studs have noggings of brick between set in a herring-bone pattern, the dark of the oak and the red of the brick in warm contrast to the delicate grey mass of the church opposite, the two buildings facing each other across the graveyard.

I think I would like to stay a night at Fressingfield. Or better still, I suppose, at Dennington, a little to the south, the church there being so full of wonderful wood carving, and the Queen's Head, like the Fox and Goose, right there beside the churchyard. But then, there are so many little villages in East Anglia where we would like to stay if we were not so fortunate as to have our home here. And, in so many of them you can eat and sleep amid timbers that were cut and adzed and erected as a frame before ever Columbus sailed his *Santa Maria* to the Caribbean islands of Cuba and Haiti.

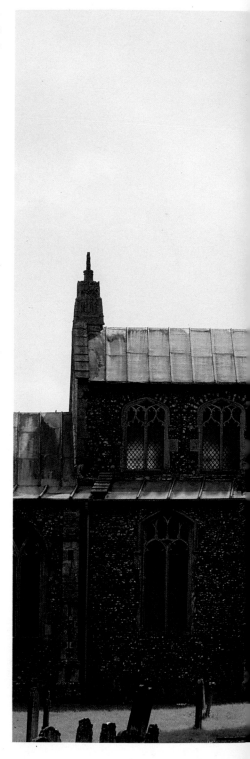

Fressingfield's flint church and the brick-hoggined timber inn, the Fox and Goose, face-en-face across the churchyard – the back door so convenient if it was a hellfire and brimstone sermon. 63

4. The unrelenting sea

At the moment of our arrival in East Anglia my dark Celtic imaginings turned to Dorothy's kinsman, Walter Scott, slaving away, book after book, to meet speculative publishing debts incurred to finance the building of his house at Abbotsford. And so in the first months, when I wasn't desperately trying to coax some life into the electric plant or persuade the one-cylinder monster to pump water from the well, and with builders hammering around my ears, I went at a new book, *The White South*, as though the bailiffs were already at the door.

Once that was done, the book finished and a film in the offing, then the sea, so much a part of me and creeping into virtually all my books, began to exercise its fascination, drawing me to the coast. Nobody living in East Anglia can sensibly ignore the great watery incisions that run deep into the land, starting at the Blackwater, which I regard as the natural and obvious southern boundary of the great East Anglian bulge, and continuing north-east with the Colne, the Orwell and the Stour, the Deben and the Alde, then anti-clockwise through Broadland waters, the saltmarshes of the North Shore, finally the Fen rivers running north into the Wash.

There is no part of England, or indeed the British Isles, so deeply affected by water, so influenced by the sea. This may come as a surprise to those more familiar with the claims of the West Country and the Western Isles, but I am not exaggerating.

I have no affection for the North Sea. It is shallow, silted, awash with the mud and effluent of several large industrialised rivers – the Elbe, the Weser, the Rhine, the Thames. It is a cold, inhospitable sea, open in winter to winds from Siberia and the Polar regions, subject to great surges that can overwhelm coastal defences and inundate vast tracts of the low-lying lands that surround it. But when the east of England was almost solid forest from Epping to the Fens, with only the chalklands and the heathlands to lift travellers out of the mud and swamp of forest tracks, that shallow sea was already becoming a great highway, those estuaries the branch lines running deep inland. And not just for the movement of goods and people up and down the country. The North Sea was the 'open sesame' to the continent of Europe, the boats that sailed from inland ports, after crossing a hundred miles or so of sea, could reach far into what are now the Netherlands and West Germany. They brought back ideas as well as goods. They brought a new attitude

Ipswich – this sets the mood of East Anglia's estuaries, a tradition of sea trade through the centuries, and now the striding pylons of the nuclear age.

to Christianity and a strong sense of independence.

Go back 8,000 years, to the aftermath of the last Ice Age, when so much water was locked up in arctic ice that the North Sea was a great plain through which the Rhine flowed northward, this then was the route by which the early settlers from Germany came to make their home in the sandy, sparsely treed area of Breckland. Here they found flint for weapons and tools. They were the people who dug those holes at Grime's Graves in what is now Thetford Forest, who began the flint-knapping industry which was to continue through eight millennia until the last of the Brandon flint-knappers ceased operation only a few years ago.

In anthropological terms this is all quite recent, of course. Back in the Middle Pleistocene period there is a great time span, from roughly 400 to 200 thousand years ago, that palaeontologists refer to as the Clactonian culture. It was the Great Inter-Glacial period and the ape-like Neander-thal Man spread north-westwards from Europe leaving examples of his distinctive flint flakes in the Thames valley and an undoubted industry at High Lodge in Suffolk. These 'people' of the Clactonian Stone Age culture are thought to have been the very first inhabitants of Britain.

All sorts of curiously shaped flints have always been turned up by winter frosts in my Suffolk garden. Whether any of them are worked or not I have no idea, but their presence, the great variety of the soil, together with the fact that Clacton is only a few miles to the east of us, allows me to look out of my study window and see in my mind's eye the edge of the Mindel glaciation in retreat, the last of that Ice Age gleaming white and Clacton Man sitting there striking a flint on an anvil stone and leaving the flakes that I shall later pick up. Pure fantasy, of course, but it keeps my feet firmly on the ground and in touch with my origins, and I have no doubt that it was dreams of Clacton Man, as well as my voyages in the eastern Mediterranean, that led me to experiment with an anthropological novel I set in Greece and called *Levkas Man*.

Those Celtic people, known to the Romans as the Belgae, seem prosaic by comparison. They were part of a steady movement of people from continental Europe that began about 2,000 BC. Our knowledge of them is confined to archaeological deduction, for this is still pre-history. We are out of the Stone Age now and into the Bronze. They came by boat, and from further afield the Phoenicians of the Mediterranean appeared as the first true merchant adventurers. The sea is no longer a barrier, it is a highroad unencumbered with forest and swamp; soon, as well as trade, it is carrying invaders, into a land that had progressed from simple husbandry to quite an advanced culture – indeed, very advanced in mathematics and geometry if current beliefs about standing stones are to be accepted.

Dolmens, stone circles, megalithic graves, these are all absent from

Parkeston Quay, just up the estuary of the Stour from Harwich.

The High and the Low – the two lighthouses that contribute so much to the Harwich skyline seen in silhouette against an early dawn sky.

East Anglia for the very simple reason that, other than flint, there is no stone anywhere ready to hand, only sarcen and similar boulders brought down in the moraines of Ice Age glaciers and unearthed in gravel pits. But there are burial mounds, some of them much older than the eleven barrows of Sutton Hoo. There is a whole range of these older burial mounds between Ipswich and Felixstowe. The Seven Hills interchange by Nacton at the northern exit to the bridge over the Orwell is in the middle of the largest of these groups, hence its name. There are in fact fourteen of them, not seven, and a further eight in a huddle to the east. All are of the Bronze Age period, as are those by Ingham just outside Bury St Edmunds and further north at Brettenham in Norfolk. Oakley says that the final stage of the Stone Age reached Britain around 3500

PRINZ HAMLET

HAMBURG-HARWICH

BC, so that most of these burial mounds, which are dated between 3500 and 4000 BP (Before the Present) would be early Bronze Age.

Visiting the Nacton group, just after the bridge over the Orwell had been opened, Dorothy complained that what we needed was a truffle hound to pick them out. Far more prominent than the barrows were the gravel piles left by the contractors. As usual the burial mounds are best identified from the air, but those that have remained sufficiently proud of the ground to deter ox and horse-drawn ploughs are still marked by coppice, scrub and bracken growth.

This new bridge over the Orwell, opened in 1982, means a lot to us, for now the Ferryboat Inn at the entrance to the Deben is only half an hour from our door, where before all of Ipswich stood between us and our favourite estuary. And aesthetically it is a good bridge, as good, I think, as that superb example of bridge building in concrete, Waterloo Bridge.

That day we first saw it the sky was clear and bright, not the hard east-wind brightness, but that softer radiance which comes with a westerly that, having crossed the whole country, has almost run out of moisture. It was mid-December, the road swinging through banks of

Harwich, start of the North Sea races, with the old naval ratings' school,
HMS Ganges, opposite on the Shotley Peninsula.

This is also the depot for painting and servicing the innumerable buoys that mark the offshore banks.

*Felixstowe Ferry and the Deben
entrance at the year's end.*

clean new-green grass and there, suddenly, were those eighteen spans rising in a great curved arc of concrete, a white humpback in the sun's winter-slant. It is the same approaching it from the north as from the south, the white sweep bursting upon you suddenly and at an angle, so that you never see it end-on, the whole upper curve of the bridge always gracefully displayed.

And at Felixstowe Ferry, where the wind was bitter cold, the sea lay flat like pewter, the tide low, the shingle banks standing wet and brown like earthworks. Two miles out on an underwater bank an 8,000-ton ferry lay on her side where she had capsized minutes after a collision with another ferry, yet a further reminder of the narrowness of the dog-leg channel leading into Harwich. It was the first time I had ever seen just the half of a big ship lying flat on the water, its mast touching the surface and perfectly horizontal, and over the next three months salvage history was made as a huge work barge armed with winches, anchors and chains hauled the storm-battered remains of the *European Gateway* upright so that a patch plate could be gun-bolted on to the long gash in her side preparatory to pumping her out and towing her into Harwich.

Walking that day to the King's Fleet by a tide-drained gut full of wrecks and old walk-the-plank houseboats all nestled into the low water mud, I was on the dyke that holds back the sea from those flat green meadows of reclaimed marsh. But in my mind's eye I saw it as it must once have been, the mud of the Fleet cradling wooden galleys all leaning drunkenly on their sides in the slanting winter sun to rise with the incoming tide until they swung to the stone-weighted hawsers in a broad inland sea that covered all the land from Walton Castle to Kirton.

The Romans, coming by way of the narrower Dover straits, made Camulodunum, at the crossing of the Colne, a major colony, the chief attraction of the place being undoubtedly the shelter the Colne and neighbouring East Coast estuaries provided for their ships. Their Germanic frontier on the Rhine was just across the sea with equivalent shelter in the river mouths, the Rhine itself a water highway running into the heart of their European conquests.

Colchester was ideally situated, even though Boadicea and her Iceni were momentarily powerful enough to sack the place. And when the Romans finally pulled out of Britain, those same estuaries that had sheltered the Roman galleys and merchantmen became the arteries of longship raiders, Saxon, Angle and Jute. Indeed, in the last stages of Viking dominance, England and Denmark were temporarily one kingdom under Canute whose northern empire finally reached beyond Scotland to Norway.

The Danes, and the Saxons before them, starting out as raiders, stayed in the end to settle. They have left a whole host of village names, most of which derive from the name of an early settler whose land it was – Coddenham, for instance, is Coda's property, Garboldisham is named after Gaerbold. A favourite of mine, Kettlebaston, was the *tun* or home-

The fine curve and elevation of the bridge over the Orwell seen on a typically misty Guy Fawkes' Day.

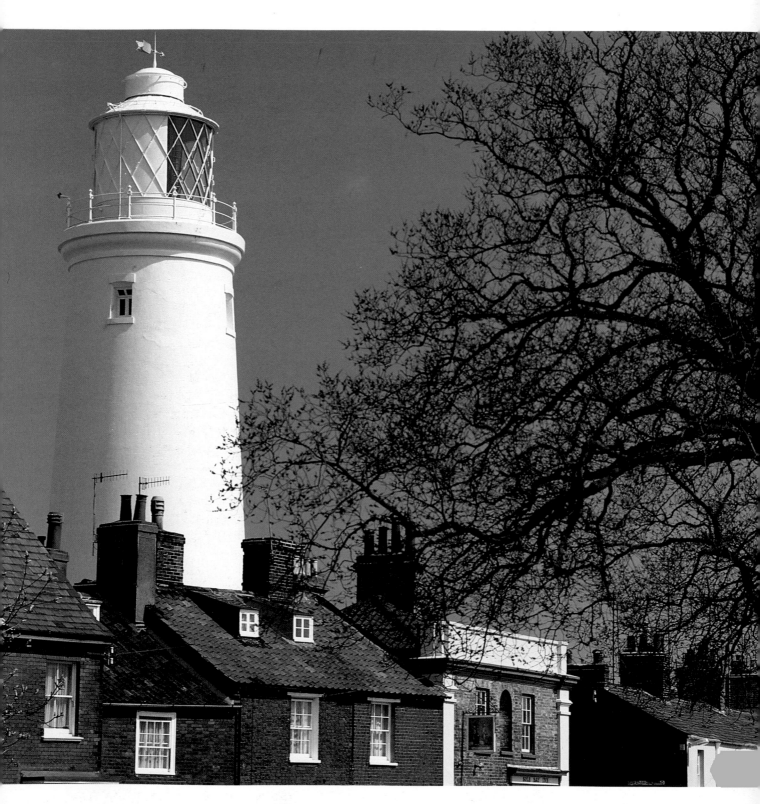

72   *Southwold's lighthouse, right on the top of the hill and in the middle of the town, and still working.*

stead of Ketelbeorn, another odd one, Swefling, belonged to Swiftel's people. With such tongue-twisting origins it is hardly surprising that later descendants, country folk who could not read or write, should have simplified the more difficult names. Thus Garboldisham became *Garblesham*, Hollesley *Hosely*, Wymondham *Wyndham*, Hunstanton *Hunston*, Happisburgh *Haysbor*, and so on, with the addition of strange pronunciations, like *Grawt'n* for Groton, but Stiffkey is only *Stuky* when talking about cockles – *Stuky Blues*. The spellings themselves were very variable. Take one of the most important of the Hundreds – Thingoe, which includes most of West Suffolk, was called by some Thinghogo and variously referred to in Domesday as Thingehow, Thingehoge, Tinchou. These are all corruptions of the Saxon word for Hill of Assembly and obviously derived from the same root as the Manx Tynwald or Parliament, which is not a Viking word I am ever likely to forget since the millennium celebrations included a tall ships race round the island in which I had five hours helming the replica of the *America*. Defoe, referring to the origin of the name Kelvedon, says, here was begun the massacre of the Danes by the women and thereafter it was called Kil-Dane – 'but it wants confirmation'. Something with which Saxon language experts would agree since they now attribute it to the more prosaic Cynelaf's valley. Other names, like Fressingfield, meaning an area of furze, or Stoke-by-Clare, a dairy farm by a gentle stream, have a descriptive origin. But settlers' names predominate and it is these people who endowed their East Anglian kingdom with the characteristics of their own race – the long head, the reserved, very independent, somewhat unimaginative and dogged nature, with an offbeat sense of humour and a very developed sense of integration, and of course that utterly distinctive accent and way of phrasing that is to most people like a foreign language.

Unlike the Celtic Welsh on the other side of Britain, you need to be very close to a true East Anglian to get a smile or a greeting out of him first. That would be giving something away without surety of some return, yet there are no more dependable and warm-hearted people, the men very talkative, some of them. Give first and they will give in return. I always remember my first encounter with the man who built *Varna*, the fastest Dragon of her day. Ernie was difficult, they said, and I wanted a mooring from him. He always worked with his hat on, and being the craftsman he was, his concentration on the job in hand was absolute. This was something I could understand. You only had to stand around until he had finished whatever it was he was doing and he was the nicest, most accommodating man in the world.

The Vikings were the last to invade England by the North Sea route. Ever since the Normans came by way of the Pevensey inlets the invasion threat has been from across the Channel. But there has been much peaceful penetration, so that the influence of the North Sea has been, and remains, considerable. And, of course, physically its impact on the coastal areas has been at times quite disastrous. Indeed, because of its surges, and the persistent downward tilting of the land, all the reclaimed marshes and low-lying ground around the estuaries from the Thames northwards to the Broadland river mouths remain to this day in mortal danger, a fact of life made abundantly clear to any visitor flying over London who looks down upon that extraordinary winged barrage erected across the Thames at shattering cost.

To get the full impact of a land under constant attack you need to go to Dunwich and see the old brown bones of the dead poking out of low, crumbling cliffs, and if the day is rough, listen for the tolling bells of churches fallen into the sea. The name Dunwich derives from the old Celtic *dubno*, meaning deepwater, to which the Saxon *wic* was added to indicate a town or port. By the thirteenth century it was a very thriving port, building its own ships, with rich merchant princes sending them on longer and longer voyages. As early as 1235 the galley fleet alone numbered eighteen vessels. For the king at that time they could muster, and spare, no less than thirty ships, one eighth of his entire fleet. Even the pirates from Friesland and Flanders had been subdued. But the great inundation of March 23rd, 1286, destroyed two whole parishes and drastically reduced the size of three others. Then in January 1328 disaster struck again, only two parishes left intact, the other four reduced to a mere handful of houses, the rest rubble or swallowed up completely by the sea. Worse even than that, the Haven mouth was gone. It was the end of Dunwich as a great port, the harbour disappearing, shingle closing the entrance gap so that the shoreline was straightened out to become roughly as it is today.

The coast everywhere is on the move, particularly along the crumbling cliffline of glacial clays, sands and gravels on the north-east coast of Norfolk. Between Happisburgh and Salthouse one town and three villages have virtually disappeared, and about all that erosion left of old Eccles was the church's ruined flint tower that stood for years like a huge sperm tooth on the foreshore. At Sheringham, in 1829, the depth of water in the harbour – yes, it had a harbour then – was twenty feet at a point where in 1781 there had been a fifty-foot high cliff with houses on it. The cliffs along a forty-mile front have in places been swallowed up at rates averaging as much as twenty feet annually over long periods and because the moraine silts and gravels of an old ice age included flint, all along this crumbling coast Stone Age implements are constantly being exposed.

The drift southwards of sea-eroded detritus still continues, an everlasting process of which I became very conscious as soon as I had a boat. I kept it on the Deben and every year, before making the first foray out to sea, I enquired about the state of the bar and how far the bar buoy had

North Sea fishing boats in Lowestoft harbour, many of them now employed as standby boats for North Sea oil rigs and gas platforms.

had to be moved. The scoured passage seaward changed each year, often quite drastically as more and more silt and shingle was banked up close offshore by the winter storms, the line of it extending from Felixstowe Ferry towards Landguard Point off what is now Felixstowe Docks. Farmers who fly their own planes, and those pilots returned for a second tour of duty at our nearby Wattisham fighter base, have for years been warning of the build-up of an offshore bank. This shingle build-up is very clear to anybody viewing the Deben entrance at low water after a few years' absence, the bar buoy and the shore markers moving steadily southward. And further out, the long, northward-groping fingers of Thames silt with names like the Gunfleet, Sunk, Shipwash, Galloper and Kentish Knock, though not with such a dreadful reputation as the Goodwins to the south, are a very considerable hazard, always on the move. It is no accident that the Trinity House flagship *Patricia* is stationed at Harwich.

Trinity House, which has been responsible for lighting our coasts since Elizabeth I extended the duties of her father's Guild of Shipmen and Seamen to the provision of sea-marks, is now responsible for some 800 lit buoys. Of these about half are on the East Coast. Of the twenty-five light vessels positioned around our shores no less than eighteen are on the East Coast. Some of these are unmanned, Trinity House having learned by experience that the servicing of these vessels can be done quicker than the Large Automatic Navigational Buoys (LANBYs), which were introduced in the belief that costs would be decimated. In fact, engineers working inside these huge buoys tended to become disorientated.

The first unlit buoys were laid by Trinity House in the Thames around 1538. They were, in fact, baulks of timber with a mark on a staff. Now the smaller buoys, numbering many hundreds, mark every estuary mouth and inlet, all the shoals and wrecks, the drilling rigs and platforms, and the majority of them are in the North Sea. The rocket life-saving apparatus was again a North Sea product, invented by a schoolfellow of Nelson, who in 1823 was granted by Parliament the very large sum for those days of £2,000, his rope and mortar equipment having by then saved 229 lives.

I remember how scared I was when I first sailed my boat down-Channel into the Bay of Biscay. Having taught myself to sail and navigate on the East Coast the thought of rocks as the natural hazards instead of banks filled me with dread. West Coast sailors, on the other hand, accustomed to rock hazards that, though hard, are mainly visible, do not like facing the hidden dangers of the North Sea banks which extend, not only to the Scroby shoals and Smiths Knoll off the Norfolk coast, but also occur with considerable frequency on the Belgian, Dutch and Friesland coasts. It was on one of these, the North Hinder, that I once lost my mast in force 6 on the North Sea Race from Harwich to the Hook.

Saxtead post mill seen against a wild March sky.

Lady's Smock (Cardamine pratensis) on Saxtead Green.

77

To see the tide making over the wet-gleaming back of an exposed bank, to sail close along the edge of it when it is covered, watching the wave pattern change as the tidal current sweeps around and over it, or in a near-gale to see drifters rolling their guts out as they fish the banks, only then do you begin to comprehend the latent deadliness of this hostile sea. Further north, of course, most people are conscious of it to some degree, every mishap to a drilling rig occasioning the reminder that they have been built to withstand winds of 120 knots and waves of ninety feet and more. But over the centuries it has been in the southern part of the North Sea that the loss of life has occurred; and not at sea, but on land.

When you are on the coast of East Anglia, particularly in those many parts where the country back of it is low-lying and protected by sea walls and dykes, or there are salt marshes with a line of dunes between you and the sea, try looking at it with the eyes of people who have homes in the neighbourhood with a view of the sea from their bedroom windows. So lovely on a fine, sunny day with coastal flowers and the birds wheeling.

But what would it be like if you were one of those householders and it was January 31st, 1953?

That was the date of the last great surge, and it was one of the most destructive for centuries. Had Dunwich still existed in 1953 as the great port it was in January 1328, there is little doubt that the whole of it would have disappeared in that one terrible night. I was away at the time so did not witness the devastation, only the aftermath, which was visible for years in damaged sea defences, scattered concrete blocks and the silhouettes of drag cranes and other earth moving equipment working on coastal skylines.

The details of that disaster are appalling enough – 307 lives lost and over 85,000 hectares of land inundated by the sea. But if the rivers had been in flood it would have been infinitely worse, indeed London itself, with sections of its underground railways and sewers, could have been overwhelmed. As it was, East Anglia bore the brunt of it, the surge coming on top of a spring tide. At King's Lynn, Norfolk's north-facing 79

Wingfield Castle, built in the fourteenth century and the home of the de la Poles; they were the Dukes of Suffolk whose political involvements were not always of the most sensible.

port on the Wash, the *predicted* water level at the top of the spring tide was 22.9 feet above the dock sill. *In fact* the level was 31 feet. Thus the surge factor was 8.1 feet. The effect of this on the coast near Lowestoft was described by an official who regularly surveyed the area. He recorded that a 30-foot cliff was cut back 30 feet in a matter of seventeen hours and a 7-foot cliff a short distance away by eighty-six feet.

Inundation on this coast has four causes: heavy rains, of course, that raise the water level of the rivers and flood from landwards; the state of the moon which, at the full, causes 'spring' or high tides; the direction and force of the wind, which produces the surge factor and the high seas which attack the coastal defences; and the rotation of the earth, which gives the tidal movement a westerly impetus. Except for heavy rain and rivers in flood, all these factors were present on the night of January 31st, 1953. Full moon had occurred two days previously. There were winds of

hurricane force blowing out of the north between Orkney and Moray, so that the resultant build-up of water in the lower North Sea carried a large surge, the tidal movements northwards being blocked by the fury of the wind.

Surges move along the coast with the tidal crest and at roughly the same rate, so they are really a tide with an extra height of water on top of it, in this case 8.1 feet. Now, if you happen to be along any of East Anglia's most vulnerable coastal areas at the top of a really big spring tide – anywhere from Hunstanton round to Salthouse in the north, in Southwold or Dunwich, or from Aldeburgh down to West Mersea – just look around you and think what it would be like with another eight feet added to the tide level. Picture it at night with a gale blowing and a big sea running, and yourself in mortal terror of your life, and the lives of your wife and children.

I often wonder how yachts would fare now in a repetition of that night? So many more of them in all the estuaries, and marinas like those at Levington and in the saltings at Woodbridge, which was the old tide mill basin, all built since the 1953 disaster. Would boats be hit now the way caravan dwellings at Jaywick suffered then?

Sea defences are costly and those in authority get lulled into a false sense of security when the time between one disaster and the next is too long. And that, of course, goes for house hunters searching for a home with a sea view. It requires a signal feat of the imagination to visualise on a summer's day how it could be in winter, at night, with an onshore gale and a very high tide topped by a surge, how hazardous and utterly terrifying.

Extreme conditions like that may happen only once in a lifetime. Perhaps you can occupy a home on the coast and never experience it. And anyway, the top of the tide is of short duration, since once it is reached it starts to fall. But one single hour in those circumstances can seem a lifetime, and like the freak conditions of that dreadful 1979 Fastnet Race, you only need to experience it once. Talk to the Dutch about the night of January 31st, 1953. The wind for them was onshore and averaged fifty to sixty knots for a period of six to nine hours with gusts of over ninety miles an hour. What the east coast of England suffered was as nothing compared with Holland, the loss of life so much greater as coastal defences were overwhelmed and vast tracts of low-lying country inundated. It was one such disaster, back in the reign of Henry I, that brought the earliest Flemish weavers across the North Sea to settle first at Worstead, then Norwich, bringing with them the new drapery technique of combing instead of carding the wool, thus producing a much longer staple which Norfolk people called worsted cloth because, as far as they were concerned, that was where it originated.

I have written about the 1953 disaster at some length because it is important that anybody coming into East Anglia in summertime, with perhaps memories of some smooth ferry crossing to a continental holiday, should understand the nature and potential of the North Sea. It is shallow, and from southern England appears to be virtually land-locked, the Netherlands and Germany to the south, Denmark and Norway to the east. But it is wide open to the north. And it is from the north that the dangers come. Looking out from Blakeney Point, the northernmost part of the Norfolk coast, there is no land anywhere to act as a windbreak between you and the great ice fields of north polar regions.

However, the hostility of this mudbank-littered sea is more than balanced by the advantages it has brought, primarily as a trading highway. The first sea book I ever looked at was a late Victorian history of the Lifeboat. It belonged to my grandmother, and when we stayed with her at Eastbourne, which then had an old rowing and sailing rescue craft on station at the Wish Tower, I would pore over the pictures, terrifying woodcuts of men in open boats pulling through huge seas to the dark-glimmering wreck of a ship with its sails blown to tatters in a storm. Most of those wrecks were on the shores and banks of the East Coast.

The eccentric brickwork of this Victorian townhall is the sort of subject Cavendish Morton, twice Mayor of Eye, enjoyed painting.

All London was at one time bunkered with coal brought by sea. It came down in 'cat-built' barques from the Tyne, and for that reason was called sea coal. These 'cats' originated in Yorkshire. Cook used Whitby-built 'cats' exclusively in those three great voyages of discovery that began in 1768 and covered the last ten years of his life. Traditionally a large number of the coal trade ships laid up for the winter in the neighbourhood of Ipswich. The estuaries of the Orwell and the Stour were particularly suitable. Defoe, writing before the 'cats', at the time of Cook's birth, observed that the conditions for laying up were so good that 'perhaps two hundred sail of ships of all sizes lie as safe as in a wet dock', the masters living 'calm and secure' with their families from Michaelmas through to Lady Day. This increased the population of Ipswich during the winter months by upwards of a thousand men 'for as masters, so most of the men, especially their mates, boatswains, carpenters etc'. They and their families were all doubtless God-fearing people, which may account for the fact that Ipswich had fourteen churches at that time – though that is a small number compared with the fifty named for Dunwich at the height of that port's prosperity.

Defoe, who managed and partly owned a tile works at Tilbury, claims that in 1668 when he first knew Ipswich there were over a hundred vessels actually belonging to the town. Accurate reporting by an eight-year-old is perhaps doubtful, particularly as he would have been too young to differentiate between those owned locally and those merely wintering there, but clearly there must have been a good few ships that were locally built and owned, ships 'so prodigious strong' that they would last half a century.

The Dutch wars were responsible for what he described as the 'decay' of the town. The English had captured a good number of enemy flyboats and these were eventually made free by Act of Parliament. Instead of

Reed, thatch and pantiles, plaster and brick – examples of cottages and their gardens at Ufford, just north of Woodbridge.

going home, a lot of them entered into competition with the local ships. They were faster, more manageable and carried more cargo, so that the same thing happened here as had happened in the estuaries further north where the local square-rigged vessels were superseded by the wherry rig. In the end the Dutch flyboats took over the trade until the 'cats' arrived. That the 'cats' also wintered in Ipswich is probably indicated by names like Cat Hard, Cat House, and I have even heard it said that the wooden bridge over the Stour at Manningtree called Cattawade replaced a fording point for the crews of ships berthed there in the mud. It may also explain that legendary oddity, Dick Whittington's cat.

Now, of course, the erosion of the land, the constant drift of sand and shingle has shallowed and silted most of the estuaries that carried the trade inland. It is not only that the coast is everywhere on the move, and the land tilting downward at the rate of about a foot every 200 years as the weight of the northern icecaps decreases; it is also the marked changes that occur with every gale. Each winter, for instance, the changes to the entrance of the Deben estuary are matched by the movement of shoals offshore of the steep, shingled entrance to the Alde, so that just as I would never go into the Alde, those who keep their boats at Aldeburgh are equally reluctant to enter the Deben. In your own estuary, of course, you have local knowledge to help you and the first traverse of a tricky entrance is seawards, but to make that initial traverse in reverse entails a considerable expenditure of nervous energy!

But though this is not a nice sea, and never has been, the way the lower part of it is half ringed with land gives to the East Anglian coast one great advantage from the yachtsman's point of view. I do not think there is any other part of the whole world where, in a matter of four days' sailing, you can reach out to eight different countries – Norway, Sweden, Denmark, Germany, Holland, Belgium, France, Brittany; I always count Brittany as being an entity on its own, just as Wales is an entity. Each of these countries has its own separate language, its own architecture and distinctive scenery, and the people entirely different, with their own racial characteristics.

My dream, you see, was already grown as I stood for the first time by the Ferryboat Inn at the entrance to the Deben, looking out past the martello tower, out across a wet waste of shingle to the bar buoy, and beyond to the Roughs and the Cork and the hazy line of the horizon, thinking of Erskine Childers and his little *Vixen* probing the sands and siels of Friesland, of Davis and Carruthers and his *Riddle of the Sands*.

The North Sea coast between Lowestoft and Southwold where the bare beachland seems to go on and on.

5. Estuaries and boats

Mud is beautiful. That's something most people only appreciate when they fall in love with an East Coast estuary. The most beautiful is the Deben. To make a flat statement like that is to invite fierce disagreement from lovers of other estuaries, but the Deben has so many advantages over the others. Woodbridge, for instance.

Woodbridge lies at the head of the estuary, a marvellous little Georgian town with Tudor undertones that owe much to Thomas Seckford, a lawyer at the court of Elizabeth I. Apart from being a little overwhelmed by traffic, it is not so very much changed from the timber and shipbuilding port and market town it was in the days when practically everything not supplied by farm and forest came in by water. To this day it boasts something you can do in very few places in the world – you can still come by rail and step virtually straight out of the train and on to your boat, provided always the tide is right.

I remember the first time I came to Woodbridge it was by train and I could hardly believe my eyes, the platform looking straight out on to the gun-metal gleam of mud, and boats lying at all angles, the sort of boats I used to draw as a kid, old 'clung-bungs', gaff-rigged and clinker-built, a spritsail barge and the hull of a large yacht looking as big as the old 'Js' I had once seen racing in the Solent, both serving as houseboats, and all sorts of funny little motorboats, some of them ship's lifeboats, all with crazily built-up topsides, mostly home-made. A young man's dream of a place with the dark wood shapes of boat-builders' sheds leaning against each other along the Ferry Quay, and towering behind them, the gaunt, decaying shape of something equally unusual, one of the few remaining tide mills in the country.

Back of the tide mill was the saltings. And on the far side of the tide-bared mud, beyond the silted remains of the harbour and the wooded sandy bluff of the far bank, something else that is unique to Woodbridge and the Deben estuary – the eleven barrows of Sutton Hoo where the greatest treasure ever unearthed in Britain was discovered.

It was on the Ferry Quay at Woodbridge that I purchased my first boat. Poor *Sonia*! Woodbridge was one of the few places in the country to have a boat auction and I bought her right there beside the level crossing because I was desperate to get afloat. She was almost twenty feet, an open clinker-built motorboat that had been given a stumpy mast and a gunter rig. She didn't take kindly to sail and was as wet as wet could be. But that was how I came to love the Deben, going down the

'Mud is beautiful' – and that's how the swans at Mistley find it.

tortuous channel called Troublesome or just plain Trouble, which at low tide can only be negotiated by those who kid themselves they can walk on water, down past the lines of moored yachts at Waldringfield and the yellow sand bluff called the Rocks, swinging past the shallows with the current sluicing, and on by Ramsholt with its pub and the church with an egg-shaped flint tower that has its sharper point facing into the prevailing wind and may have originally been a Saxon watch tower standing high on its sandy ridge. After that the shores are flatter, mud-flanked shallow dykes, until in the last straight run past the Horse Sand buoy the tide carries the boat to sight of the sea. Bawdsey Manor to port, the house where boffins working for the RAF first created radar, Felixstowe Ferry to starb'd and the current gathering speed again between banks of wet-gleaming shingle.

This was as far as I dared go in *Sonia*. And it was there, sitting in a boat that couldn't go to sea and gazing out to the waves breaking on the bar with the horizon a faint line beyond, that I dreamed of a vessel big enough to poke its nose out into the North Sea and carry me from one estuary to another, estuaries that at the moment I could only visit by land.

Early morning, and in the evening, that is when the estuaries are at their best – the stillness and the brightness, the gentle murmur of the current as the tide makes or falls, light slanting on the water, the banks mirrored in its surface, the silver flash of a fish jumping, ripples widening in a circle. But more than anything else, I think, it is those wide, uninterrupted skies, so sparklingly clear and blue in the morning, the cloud galleons forming as the sun warms the land and then at evening the skies clearing again. And the curlews, always the curlews.

Drinking beer on the Maybush lawn at Waldringfield, face burning after a day in wind and sun, relaxed at the end of a good sail – an hour to savour, it is so quiet, so beautiful. That onshore south-easterly breeze funnelling up the estuary, which often blows as hard as force 5 on the quietest of North Sea days as the land sucks cold air in from seaward, is dying to a zephyr now. There is not a ripple on the water and everything is very bright and still in the evening light, the moored yachts tide-rode to their reflections. And then, comes a friend in his little blue-painted yawl, gliding up on the making tide, tanned sails just drawing, everything reflected and no movement, like a beautiful painted canvas, the yawl's progress almost imperceptible, the bows sliding through the water without a sound, and a young woman standing there on the foredeck like Boadicea with a boathook in her hand, still as a statue. Now the boat is motionless, its masts and sails no longer moving against the green backcloth of the further bank. The tide has turned. They are not going to make it to their mooring, not under sail. The boathook is discarded and suddenly there is action, the stillness shattered by the plop of the anchor and the rattle of the chain running out. A seagull rises. Then all is quiet again and the evening stillness returns. The luminosity of the

Waldringfield on the Deben – this was where we moored our boat long before there was a marina at Levington.

The Tide Mill at Woodbridge, now reconditioned and working again. The saltings behind it have been dredged to form a tidal basin for yachts.

dying light gives a strange, ethereal quality to everything, the sharpness still there, yet somehow softened, and the yacht quite still and painted bright upon the water as it rides bows-on to the gathering ebb.

Where but on this strange East Coast of England can hardness of light so combine with the dying day to produce an hour of total magic? And when the dusk is really falling and the first owls are hooting, to paddle the last mile to Woodbridge through Troublesome's tortuous reach with mud banks grown tall on either side, not a breath of air. What an intriguing, ghostly way to go to dinner at the Crown, the first of the flood gurgling round the dinghy, reaching pale fingers of moon-reflecting water into every hollow scored by the keel of some previously grounded boat, into the mudholes of straining gumboots, and the bottom of the river seeming to clasp you in its mud-banked arms.

It is a moment then to reflect on the burial of that thirty-eight-oared longship up there in the great barrow beyond the trees nearly fourteen hundred years ago. Never mind which king it was that took the Sutton Hoo treasure to his grave, or even that he was a king. When the mud banks close around you it's all one, the age and the stature of man immaterial. A fish jumps. An old boot glimmers in the brightening moonlight, a bucket with a hole in it, and some mollusc is blowing bubbles in the mud so close you can almost reach out and touch it. For a moment the world is strangely eerie. Then a beacon looms above, its upended triangle sharp-etched against the stars, the last bend is rounded and there is Woodbridge full of lights.

Half an hour later, in the bar of the Crown, the world has become ordinary again, the moment when past and future merged and the ghostliness of mud banks was the reality banished utterly from the mind. I have never experienced quite that sort of strange, primitive enchantment anywhere else, except perhaps in the Morbihan, a strange, lost inland sea on the Biscay coast. Rocks do not have the same earthy magic. Only the proximity of mud and water seems capable of taking the mind back to the simple beginnings of things.

There is one place above any other on the coast where I prefer to lie the night, and it is not on the Deben. It is in the neighbouring Orwell, the estuary that leads from Harwich up past Pin Mill to Ipswich Dock. To find it I had to wait, of course, until I had a real boat, and like any fool of an inexperienced sailor, instead of buying some simple craft I could handle myself and creep like a mouse from estuary to estuary, I let enthusiasm and my urge for foreign places run away with me. I got myself a 10-ton ocean-racer that had been sailed for Lloyd's before they had their own *Lutine*. She was as beautiful as her name, which was *Triune of Troy*, and whether we were outward-bound or returned from foreign parts, we always cleared through Harwich, and if possible we always lay the night, or what was left of it, at the same spot – inside Shotley Spit, upstream of the old Thames barge anchorage in the Stone Heaps, close inshore and just clear of the marks for the underwater telephone cable.

I can't remember now who it was that first told me of this spot, but for me and a few others it has all the ingredients of that stark East Coast beauty. To bring a stranger in on the top of the tide and watch his face as he comes on deck to relieve himself in the dawn . . . and not just a stranger, for it never ceases to amaze and delight me. The last of the light, shore marks dark silhouettes and barely visible, sounding with a lead to be exactly sure. Then the anchor down and a moment more on

The tide ebbing, and all the Woodbridge Quay boats dug deep into the mud.

deck to check a telephone pole against a skyline council house to be sure she's holding, and after supper a final drink on deck with the lights of Harwich and Felixstowe glimmering, buoys winking white and red, a ferry heading seawards in a blaze and the water, ebbing now, slapping little wavelets against the far-off bank.

An East Coast dawn is nearly always something rare to see, so clear and hard, the air crisp and everything standing very sharp. But under Shotley – formerly HMS *Ganges* where so many Naval ratings had their education – the piping of the curlews brings everyone on deck with the first glimmer of light. And there they are, like so many bos'ns hurrying about their business right alongside, hands in the pockets of their tails, heads bent, long, curved beaks ready like spears to drive into the mud after some poor wretched morsel of marine life.

Yes – MUD.

The stern and all one side of the boat is right against a gleaming, glistening brown bank of it that curves steeply down towards the keel. Shoreward there is no water. None at all. It is all mud, gleaming like pewter, and not far away the skeletal rib-remains of an abandoned hulk stand exposed like some weed-green tombstone crying the death of all ships. And to the south-east, there is Harwich.

Now, there is nothing beautiful about Harwich, even if most of the ferries and container ships are well away from the town at Parkeston Quay a little way up the Stour estuary. There is a small pier, a jumble of half repainted buoys at the Trinity House yard, an old lighthouse, and some of the older streets are narrow and somewhat ugly. Yet, viewed from our anchorage, the Harwich skyline, so sharp, so clear, so very Dutch dyke-top in its crouched silhouette with only the spire of the church and the round blunt tower of the lighthouse standing with phallic emphasis against the steely cold of the dawn sky – and to the left of it the open sea shut off again by Landguard Point . . . No, beautiful is not the word. Dramatic, certainly, like a clearly defined statement. You feel as though there is nothing else to be said about the East Coast. It is all there, caught frozen in the dawn. This is it, this is East Anglia.

And in from Landguard Point, where the crane that lifted the flying boats out of the water once stood in massive isolation, lie a line of roll-on and container ships with a dredger moored close by, for this is Felixstowe Docks, the most successful and thrusting port in Britain with its close trading links with the Dutch Europort across the water.

At the western end of the long waterfront quay there is a wood-piled gap leading to a small rectangular basin flanked with granary buildings. This is the port as it was, and when we started ocean racing this is where we and some of the other East Coasters would lie the night before the Hook Race. It was still an air-sea rescue base then. But all one sees from the anchorage behind Shotley Spit is the low profile of Harwich hard-etched against the dawn and the chunky, lantern-masted shapes of lightvessels in for servicing. And I can never look at that scene without

thinking of Pepys, whose duties as a naval civil servant, and also briefly as the town's Member of Parliament, took him there periodically so that there are almost more references in his Diary to Harwich than to any other seaport. It was not a journey he relished, particularly if the day was cold and the east wind blowing. You can just picture him there on the waterfront, in the company of James Duke of York, ships of the line anchored off, boats coming and going, and these two men working to lay the foundations of a navy that would dominate the oceans of the world for the next two centuries.

There is almost nothing left of the Navy in Harwich now, but in those days, and until relatively recently, it was a naval port, for the North Sea has always been regarded as a potential route for invasion. It was the Napoleonic threat that sent our greatest admiral, the Norfolk-born Nelson, reconnoitring in the frigate *Medusa*, first Boulogne, then Flushing; he was at Harwich and in such haste to look at the Belgian ports that he beat a contrary wind by having the local maritime surveyor pilot his frigate out over the Naze shoal where no ship drawing more than fourteen feet had sailed before, hence the name Medusa for the buoy that now marks this passage.

Harwich and that wide-skied view, the smell of bacon cooking, curlews piping on the mud alongside and the soft beginnings of the flood tide gurgling, the breeze coming in with the sun – the breeze and the tide, it is time to fetch the anchor, caked now with good, dark Orwell mud. A small tanker heading up towards Ipswich on the tide passes as we tack out slowly under sail. Shotley Spit buoy marks the junction of the Orwell and the Stour, the Harwich approach looking wide now. But much of it is shallows and the deep water channel runs close along the Felixstowe quays, container cranes gaunt against the sky, which is no longer so cold-looking, but a hard blue.

Mares' tails are beginning to show high out to sea and the names of the buoys are Bench End, Rolling Grounds, Platters, St Andrews, Rough. It was here that Arthur Ransome had his kids lying in thick fog in *We Didn't Mean to Go to Sea*. Like Childers, he flew the burgee of the RCC, a club founded in 1880 by a small group of sailing men who believed in living aboard their boats and working them themselves, something quite novel for yachtsmen in Victorian times.

Living and working on board was the norm, of course, for the cargo carriers of the East Coast, those lovely spritsail barges with their tall topmasts and brown-dyed sails. Once, sailing *Triune* out from Harwich past The Naze and south down the Wallet to West Mersea, we counted no less than nineteen of them, and only one was a yacht barge. They were streaming through the shallow gut of the Spitway between the Gunfleet and the Buxey sands, all of them heading for the Colne entrance,

Shotley Gate, looking across to Parkeston Quay.

and every one of them was under sail, one of the grandest sights I have ever seen on this coast, or any other. That was before Pauls of Ipswich, the grain merchants, sold off their fleet, which was the largest single group of barges then left.

Fortunately that wasn't the end of them. There are no *real* working barges now, but slowly, almost painfully a few of them have been reclaimed and restored, as sailing houseboats, yachts, reception rooms afloat, for charter, for sail training of youngsters, and for racing. Yes, for racing. There are races in the Thames estuary, off the Blackwater, and from the Orwell, where they start from Pin Mill, heading seaward past Harwich to the Roughs Tower, the Cork Sand buoy, the Medusa or the Gunfleet.

Pin Mill is the place to see them, or in Ipswich Dock in the week between the race up from Gravesend and the start of the Pin Mill match. They call them matches, not races, for that's how it all started, skippers boasting of the prowess of their great oak-and-canvas loves, betting they could beat the others in the days when boxing was a bare-fisted match. And they still play it pretty rough. On the last barge match I was on we sailed level with another of our own kind. Going down the Orwell it was a luffing match, the two skippers treating their great cumbersome craft like 12-metres fighting it out for the America's Cup. 'Give way,' our man calls, edging to windward away from the shoal water and the riverbank to port. 'Mast ahead! Give way!'

God knows who was right, but their skipper didn't budge a wheelspoke and ours continued to close, and then everything became inevitable, for by the time the two of them had finally panicked, it was too late. Two vessels of that size travelling at six knots make an expensive crunch when they collide. Our big clinker-built tender, which was hanging in davits on the starb'd quarter, was stove in, but we carried on with the race; the other barge had some of its porthand standing rigging carried away, and with the topmast unstayed was forced to retire.

Two years before I had seen *Ironsides* lose her topmast carrying too much sail out by the Medusa buoy, tops'l and stays'l tumbling down like the last wild flapping of a dead gull's wings. That was the year we watched those two greyhounds of the barge world, *May* and *Edith May*, come tacking through the double line of moored yachts in Butterman's Bay, bowsprit to bowsprit off Pin Mill and not a figurehead between them as *May* took the gun. *May*, incidentally, was at that time the only cargo-carrying spritsail barge left. She was built at Harwich in 1891 and, astonishingly, was shipped to Canada as deck cargo one year to sail the Great Lakes. *Ena*, the one in which I was sailing, was a Dunkirk veteran.

These cottages on the quay at Wivenhoe are within biscuit toss of freighters entering the thriving little port upstream towards Colchester.

East Coast barges moored along the old quay at Maldon. Once the main inshore cargo carriers, these vessels, now mostly in private hands, will quite possibly have a life of well over a hundred years.

Pin Mill is one of those very special places that tend to get a little crowded at times in the summer. The south side of the Orwell here is quite high for an East Coast estuary, so that the landward approach is down a steep hill, and on match days and holidays it is difficult to find anywhere to park. The waterfront pub is the Butt and Oyster, a straightforward name which has not been bastardised like the Ostrich at the head of the estuary, originally named for the Oyster Ridge visible at low water. It is at the Butt and Oyster that the match prizes are given and throughout the year there are usually several barges moored stern-on in mudberths just downstream of pub and hard. But the hard is short and it is for mud that Pin Mill is notorious. For that reason I have never moored there and my only experience of mud-floundering at Pin Mill was after an old friend of ours had bought a converted day boat called *Florence Edith* on the Deben and had her converted to ocean racing at Whisstock's yard by the Ferry Quay at Woodbridge.

This was Francis Chichester and *Florence Edith* was the first of his sailing *Gypsy Moth*s. He and his wife were staying with us, having parked the boat at Pin Mill after a rough sail back, I think from the Hook Race. Sails and clothes and everything were wet and in the morning we went down to dry things out, but inevitably Francis and I stayed too long on board so that the tide was out beyond the end of the hard and we had a filthy wade to get ashore, carrying of all things the ship's battery for recharging.

The date of the midsummer barge match is carefully fixed so that the tide will be ebbing fast at the start, which is usually between 08.30 and 09.00. This is to ensure that all the barges, and there are usually somewhere around twenty, get safely out of the river even if there is little wind. More often there is wind, and a pretty cold one as you stand waiting for the barge's tender in the grey of early morning. No yachtsman's gear here. It is all cloth caps or woolly titfers, smocks and jerseys, that is for the true bargemen and the older hands. But however cold, there is a tremendous feeling of well-being and anticipation as you clamber up the black-coated side by way of the big leeboard and go below into the half empty cargo space to mugs of tea and coffee, great slabs of bread, bacon, sausage and egg.

And then suddenly the table is emptying, the windlass pawls clicking as the anchor comes in and you are up in the cold wind again with the deck beginning to move, hauling on a hard, raw rope to get the fores'l up. Somebody has let go the brail of the main, others are hauling in the mainsheet. The shore is beginning to move. The anchor is up. Somebody sets the mizzen and you're hauling, hauling, hauling with the ring on the big timber horse that spans the ship slamming across as the mains'l bellies in the wind. The engine is cut. All is suddenly very quiet, just the wash of water displaced at the bows, the gurgle of it along the barge's sides, the staccato rattle of chain as the starb'd leeboard is dropped. There is a heel to the deck now, and glancing up, the great brown

The home of the Aldeburgh Festival, seen from the bank of the Alde. There are swans in almost all the rivers and estuaries of East Anglia.

expanse of the loose-footed main is full of wind, and above it, above the long spar of the gaff, the tops'l is drawing, the tall topmast bending crazily.

And everywhere around you, every way you look as you balance on the slanting deck, there are barges on the move, great towering drifts of brown and white canvas. The whole estuary is full of them, and how, you wonder, how on earth can a thing so clumsy as a barge appear so beautiful?

There is usually one other barge present at these matches, strategically moored down-river as a spectator. This is *Thalatta*, one of the two barges preserved and owned by the East Coast Sail Trust, a charity committed to the sail training of youngsters. *Thalatta* is a 'mulie'. There are Spritties,

Mulies, Boomies and Stumpies, the two first being the largest. Some, like *Thalatta*, were built for the Channel trade and ventured as far west as Cornwall for cargoes of china clay, even to Ireland. *Edith May* is another, and old as she is, they think nothing of sailing her round the coast of England to Liverpool. In length and breadth they are almost the size of *Endeavour*, first of the 'cats' selected by Cook for his three great voyages of discovery.

Ena and *Thalatta* were both built in 1905, the same year as the supremely fast *Edith May*, not at Cann's, but at McLearon's old naval yard. These two sister ships, both of 150-tons burthen, are the barges I have enjoyed sailing in, the schoolship *Thalatta* owned since 1966 by Kempie of Maldon (the diminutive, so often used in East Anglia, bears no relation to the man's height – and it is never used of a woman). He would still, I think, regard himself as an amateur, and certainly he is no racing bargeman. But of all the owners and skippers around today he must be just about the most knowledgeable, and to get the feel of what it was like to be a barge-mad boy growing up among the last of the old cargo working skippers, also to get a heady, tangy draught of hard North Sea air, read his *Fair Wind for London*. This, for instance, as the young John Kemp takes his first lone trick at the wheel of a barge with the one-eyed skipper Nelson:

'We ought to come, Skip,' I called.

'No we never! Keep standing in. There's plenty of water here,' Nelson shouted up the companionway.

'There ain't you know,' I said, in a mild panic. 'The leeboard'll be

The Northern Sinfonia orchestra in rehearsal for the evening concert with the cellist Paul Tortelier.

on the ground directly . . .'

'Keep standing in, I say!' was the uncompromising command from below. But I took no notice, I put the wheel hard down. 'I'm coming round!' I shouted. 'There's no water at all under us here.'

Nelson's head appeared in the companionway. 'All right then, if you know better than me, why ask? You can let go your own bowline this time; I'm havin' me bit o' grub. And next time you ask me I shall tell you wrong again, see?'

But better than reading about it, go down to Pin Mill hard on Match Day; who knows, somebody may ship you for a lark! And that would be as near as you will ever get now to the essential East Coast of cargo days.

Thalatta's winter home is Maldon, that lovely little Essex town perched on a hill at the head of the Blackwater. Here members of the same family have been dehydrating sea water for generations and for those of us hooked on the flaky, crystalline Maldon sea salt there is no other. Downstream of the oddly-triangular tower of All Saints, and the site of the Saxon-English fort, is the old quay, usually with a barge or two alongside. Either there or at Heybridge Basin, which is sometimes so crowded with craft of all sorts that it reminds one of Wroxham. Maldon still has enough shipwright craftsmen and sailmakers to maintain and repair the East Coast barges, and they do need a good deal of upkeep now, for most of them are nearing the end of their first century afloat.

Most years, around the end of June or early July, *Thalatta* moors up under the tide mill at Woodbridge, and, incredibly, her topmast, with pennant streaming, seems to dwarf the mill building. This is the best opportunity for looking over one of these vessels as she is open to the public then, no kids on board, but Sea Cadets and other uniformed youngsters at the gangway to collect what they can for the maintenance of a lovely vessel in remarkable condition. At other times she is very fully occupied about her business of giving youngsters, Barnardo boys in particular, a glimpse of what it was like sailing this coast a century ago.

Another and much more unusual place to find a barge moored, is by the Maltings at Snape. To come out of an Aldeburgh Festival concert in the interval and stroll across the grass in the moonlight, past the huge hole-in-the-body Henry Moore statues, and to stand on the quayside looking down on to the deck of the charter barge that is often moored there with its bowsprit almost touching the bridge . . . such a beautiful sight in the still of the evening, its towering mast seeming to touch the stars, but the thing you marvel at then is how the skipper, with a bunch of rookies on board, is ever going to get it turned in such a narrow little reed-fringed gut?

The roof of the Maltings, being of wood, has superb acoustic qualities; it was probably where that early fire started.

Anchor and tide, of course. These barges, loaded with upwards of seventy or eighty tons of grain, stone, cement, gravel or clay, were often handled by just the skipper and a boy. I followed one once, hatch covers almost awash she was so heavily laden, making up to Ipswich through the litter of yachts off Woolverstone, just two men on board and the wind against them, so that they were tacking back and forth, the tide doing all the work, and the way they handled her she might have been a dinghy.

The northernmost of these long Suffolk estuaries and the least visited is that of a river that changes its name according to whether it is Aldeburgh or Orford people talking. Also, the nature of it is quite different from the Deben, the Stour, the Orwell and the Blackwater. Aldeburgh has a shingle strand, which blocks the Alde from flowing seaward, so the river turns sharp right, heading past Slaughden for over six miles, paralleling the sea and only separated from it by a shingle bank. Shingle is not the easiest walking, of course, and as usual the need of some sort of craft is soon apparent with the long vistas of flower-bright flats and distant villages all on the other side of the river.

On one occasion I had *Thalatta* as my viewing platform, joining her in the early morning of a bright June day, the wind cold out of the east. Anchored off, a little downstream of Slaughden Quay, she looked quite small against the flatness of the land and the vastness of the pewter-grey sky. But once on board, with the topmast bending to the sails and youngsters heaving on the sheets, she seemed as big as ever. The sun glimmered as the overcast thinned and the flat lands that stretched westward to Iken, and even as far as Snape, glowed with the colour of ground-hugging coastal plants in flower.

So many times I have driven through the forests to Orford, parked on the quay and looked at the boats, then gone to eat oysters at the Butley-Orford Oysterage. But to see it from the river, it looks quite different then, so very much more of a fortified port, the castle there to protect it from raiders coming by water. The estuary takes a near-horseshoe loop past masts that are standing like spears against the houses and the church on the rising ground, and now the river is the Ore and one shore is Havergate Island where the avocets first nested again in 1946. The sea is close here, little more than a biscuit-toss away, as it was at Slaughden when we started. A shingle bank again that continues for four miles, then a turn to port, shingle closing in on both sides, Hollesley Bay (pronounced Hosely) and the sea straight ahead. This is a place to visit when the last of the ebb is running furiously out through the shingle gates and all the underwater hazards are laid bare in gleaming humps of sand and pebble. Then you understand why Deben people are wary of taking their boats into the Ore.

That day we turned south past Shingle Street, hugging the Suffolk shore, sun blazing on the sails of boats off the Deben entrance waiting for the tide to make over the bar, on the martello tower at Felixstowe Ferry and on the distant cranes that marked the docks. Down past the

*Beach huts and boats on Aldeburgh's
shingle shore – the colour of the
water is typical of the North Sea.*

The clean sweep of Aldeburgh's pebble beach looking north towards Thorpeness.

Aldeburgh lifeboat, still a slip launch from the beach.

Roughs, Platters and the Rolling Grounds, ploughing across the Harwich entrance to the little Pye Sand buoy and the narrow tide-sluiced channel through the mud that leads into the Walton Backwaters. Hamford Water, Horsey Island, two villages suffixed with the words le-Soken, this was Arthur Ransome's 'Secret Water', playground of his sailing children. The wind was blowing fresh over the marshes when we anchored there, Walton and the Naze a distant huddle of houses looking small in the bright light. But once in the tender and heading into the shallows our view was instantly restricted to the mud of the banks on either side, and it was suddenly warm with almost no wind.

Stealing through a weed-grown channel between banks of gleaming mud with a bunch of children, silent now and suddenly awed at the strangeness of it all, it wasn't difficult to imagine oneself engaged in a game of pirates. Or looking back down the narrow ribbon of steely water to the black-hulled barge, the thought that comes into one's mind then is that this was how it must have been when men like Harold Blood Axe landed, the black hull a longship and our boat a Viking skiff with all on board bent on plunder and ghastly mayhem once we were through the mud and ashore.

The shore-going here was a strange one, for we had a girl from the BBC on board and she was being met. Barefoot, and with our trousers rolled to our knees, we waded through the mud, feeling for the landing's stepping stones with our toes and desperately trying not to fall headlong in the brown, black, beautiful goo, and there, as we topped the bank, was not only the man who had come to meet her but, parked on the grass-grown track below, a low-slung vintage sports car. Whole areas of the Walton Backwaters are reclaimed grassland so that it really is possible, in June with the grass fresh mown for hay, to drive along the dyke tops almost as far as Hamford Water.

With a little effort, some sharp map-reading, and a good pair of walking shoes all the half dozen or so of the sea's inroads into Suffolk and Essex can be explored from the land. Early morning and late evening – those are the magic hours when the long sheets of bright water are at their most luminous, the birds active and the wind usually fallen to a wonderful hush. But once in a while beg, borrow or hire a boat, then for a moment you can believe yourself a part of the East Coast scene. Better still, time your visit for some event – the blessing of the water at Waldringfield on the Deben, the carnival at West Mersea, the Old Gaffers' race on the Blackwater. The Gaffers started holding their East Coast meet at Stone Street because it is the only stretch of the estuary free of mud and on the occasion I was there to present the prizes upwards of a hundred boats were gathered there, all of them gaff-rigged, and most of them ex-working boats, bawleys and quay punts, crabbers, shrimpers and smacks. To stand on Bradwell Quay and watch them all stream past as they headed out to the Gunfleet and the Buxey Sands, and then in the late afternoon coming back on the tide; it was almost as good as a review of all the inshore boats that worked the East Coast a century and a half ago when sail was the motive power.

Some of those boats we had seen still working when we first went afloat. The Harwich shrimpers, for instance. These were bawleys, essentially a Thames estuary boat, rather like a mini-barge, half-decked and clinker-built, no sprit and no leeboards. The northernmost limit of their use was Harwich and many is the dawn we have seen them coming in, the broad

This symphony of seaside architecture is typical of the development of this coast, the oldest of the buildings being the marvellous Moot Hall which stands right on the beach.

deck steaming with the bubbling shrimp kettle and trays of shrimps, all pink and cooked, laid out to dry. A pint of them in an old tin cost next to nothing then, but now it's mostly too much trouble. Another we saw still working was the Essex smack, the smallest of which were used for dredging the oyster beds of the Colne, the larger for sprat netting – there were several at West Mersea.

Further north there was a Southwold beach boat and the Yarmouth shrimp boat. The East Coast sailing drifter, like the billy-boys, was at one time everywhere on the east and south-east coasts, each of them having variations, at Lowestoft where the drifter was called the Lowestoft sailing drifter and in the Humber where the larger version of the billy-boy was called the Humber sloop. Both vessels were clinker-built workhorses, the drifter for fishing, the billy-boy for cargo, its mast stepped on deck in a tabernacle so it could pass under bridges and reach deep into the river estuaries.

What a marvellous cluster of masts it must have been on the East Coast when herring and coal alike came in by sail and ships by the thousand crowded ports and estuaries. Now pictures in books and museums are about all that is left to us, except that there are still masts and boats by the thousand, but yachts, not working boats. And when one has seen all of these great estuaries in action so to speak, all crowded with yachts in summer, and some of them in the mainstream of our maritime life, with tankers, coasters, container ships and ferries coming and going, then it is time to go back up the coast beyond Dunwich and take a look at Walberswick, where a half-in-ruins church almost as big as Lavenham stands high on the skyline above the marshes.

Walberswick men and Dunwich men hated each other's guts. The two ports were bitter rivals, Dunwich virtually at the Haven mouth, Walberswick some three miles away to the north at the head of what six centuries ago were sheltered waters lying between Kings Holme and Dingle Marsh. Now Kings Holme is all one with the remains of Dunwich and cattle graze in the old harbour. Walberswick, unlike Dunwich, is still a port and still flourishing, the tide-scoured estuary of the Blyth flanked by wooden stages chock-full of fishing boats whose owners fish more for pleasure than for profit, and what is left of the old village crowded down to the piers of Southwold Harbour and living off the tourist. There is a nice old inn, the Bell, and across the tide-rushing water Southwold church and lighthouse stand high on a hill with the town huddled round. Southwold and Walberswick, both on high ground, are safe from flood, but in the low ground between, and in all the marshes round, the surge of '53 took a terrible toll.

It is in these marshes that the thatchers who keep my study roofed

Cat ignoring notice –
by a well-known beach artist?

This fisherman has the bones of long-dead seafarers protruding from the cliffs
behind him, his bait probably lying in one of the drowned parishes of Dunwich.

ESTUARIES AND BOATS

This was the first polygonal keep and is all that remains of Orford's great castle, built by Henry II to check the ambitions of the Bigods of Thetford.

In the marshes of the Blyth estuary: this is the sort of East Coast 'residence' that is at risk when the North Sea surges.

and dry cut their reeds. They do it in the three worst months of the year, starting in January. Very cold work, but at least there is some shelter from the north-east wind down among the reeds. The cutting that used to be done by hand is now done by a broad-tyred machine that bundles the reeds as it cuts. Seems it's no bad thing to be the owner of a reed marsh for it yields just about as much per acre in profit as a field of wheat without the landowner lifting a hand, nature doing it all for free year after year. Provided there are men willing to cut it, of course, and the demand for expensive reed-thatched roofs continues.

Offshore in the summer quiet of June volunteer divers search the seabed for the remains of Dunwich, in particular the old Roman fort that was thought to have been built at the Haven entrance; also for the remains of the *Royal James*, a 100-gun ship burned and sunk by the Dutch in 1672. This was at the battle of Solebay, which is the old name for Southwold's bay. But the North Sea is very different to the Solent and the success of the *Mary Rose* is unlikely to be repeated here. The Roman fort, on the other hand, and the recovery of medieval artefacts from the lost port of Dunwich, is a possibility.

There is also another port on the coast here that vanished even more completely, a great shipbuilding place called Goseford. It has vanished so completely that the name has gone from any map that I have ever seen. It goes back to the shallow-draughted longship days when the Saxons settled in what became the Colneis or Cole Ness Hundred. This area included the mouth of the Deben estuary, then unreclaimed salt marsh which they named Goose Ford. Hemley, Ramsholt, Kirton, Falkenham and Trimley – all well inland now from the dyke-constrained estuary – were settlements on the edge of the marsh, and the marsh, with its hidden waterways, was ideal for the building and hiding away of their traditional craft; King's Fleet, in particular, with its creeks providing watergates or landings for the settlements that grew up around the castle of Walton.

Incredibly, the Deben was more important than the Orwell and the Stour. In fact, Gasford was the most important centre for miles. The nature of the ships made it so. It was visited by kings, sailed ships as far as Iceland and in 1338 sent fifteen ships in support of Edward III against the French, and eight years later thirteen to the King's fleet assembled off Calais. Two centuries later, the ships getting bigger, the land being reclaimed and the river flowing fast and deep between its restricting banks, the shipbuilding and the commerce gradually shifted to Woodbridge, and suddenly there was no trace of Goseford left. It had disappeared as effectively as Walton Castle, the ruins of which lie offshore of Felixstowe Ferry.

Now the Deben is given over to yachts, a peaceful ribbon of water that for me, and for many others, including several round-the-worlders, has been a sort of 'yellow-brick road' leading to the enchantment of foreign lands. And on return, the sudden embrace as we cross the bar, of quiet waters, and of a land as beautiful as any we have ventured into.

But to reach the shelter of those friendly waters was always something of a struggle, even after we had built *Mary Deare*. Coming in from continental ports, it usually seemed to work out that it was dark when we passed the Sunk and entered the Sledway, which was the home straight, all eleven miles of it, a home straight of banks and wrecks and a confused mass of lights. We cleared Customs at Harwich, lying alongside *Patricia* if we could. She is the Trinity House flagship and always kind to the amateur sailors who do their best to drop newspapers and magazines off to the crews of the lightvessels.

West Mersea, where Colchester oysters grow and ocean racers moor alongside old fishing boats.

All of these lightvessels are named after the banks they guard – the *Sunk*, the *Cork*, the *Galloper*, the *Smith's Knoll* off the Norfolk coast, the *Kentish Knock* down to the south. Some, like the *Sunk*, were pensioned off, to be replaced by the large LANBY buoys, something I am reminded of every May when we dine on the night of the Royal Cruising Club's East Coast Meet in the bowels of the *Cromer* lightvessel, now a clubhouse and bedded down behind the enclosing mud walls of the Suffolk Marina on the north bank of the Orwell. As you might expect of such a salty gathering some unexpected glimpses of the East Coast emerge; one of the most bizarre that the head of Cromwell was in the possession of somebody living quite near, and that it was in pretty good condition, and somebody else had the head of one of the Suffolks. Having no historical heads hidden away in old biscuit tins, Dorothy and I began to feel a little deprived, but perhaps it was all a figment of the lightvessel atmosphere, the steel walls of the cavernous hull coated with a sound-deadening and sweat-dampening layer of white plastic 'porridge'.

Fortunately, there are always habitués of the *Cromer* to keep my feet firmly on the ground, for not only was the whole marina virtually built by North Sea racing friends of the early days, but our meal is cooked and served by the family of a local man who was doing his National Service as an officer on the LCT that finally got me to St Kilda when I was researching *Atlantic Fury*. Another of these retired lightvessels moored itself to the banks of the Wensum at Norwich; in fact at one time you could pick up a lightvessel for the price of a small car. Parking and maintaining it is, however, a different matter, and almost certainly more costly!

No habitual East Coast sailor could fail to develop an affinity for these flare-bowed ugly ducklings with their top-heavy lanterns rolling and bucking on the edge of the banks, and for the men who man them. To hear them on VHF – 'Kentie Knock – Kentie Knock, Kentie Knock . . . OK bor, got you clear now. Wot's in the galley, eh? We got bangers again, bangers and mash . . . yeh, she's rolling a bit and the forecast's not good . . .' – and then that wonderful feeling as the *Kentish Knock* comes up over the bows, just where she should be. On the home stretch now, for where on most European coasts it is the islands, headlands and rocky outcrops that are the markers for arrival, here in the North Sea it is the lightvessels, then the buoys that are one's landfall. This is why one so often arrives in Harwich tired and with salt-bleared eyes. The pilotage is intricate, particularly at night. There is a mass of lights, and if one has come up from the Channel, through the Downs and across the Thames estuary, then the navigator has already had a busy time of it.

Westbound across the North Sea, from Holland, Belgium or Germany, the landfall is again an invisible bank, the Galloper most likely, or perhaps the Sunk. But the lightvessel I remember most vividly of all is the *North Hinder* off the Belgian coast, rounding it at night in a tight pack

Parkeston Quay, viewed at night from Shotley Gate. This, with Felixstowe Docks and Ipswich port, all entered by the old port of Harwich, is the fastest growing and most successful port area in the country.

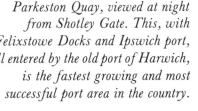

of yachts, all racing and the wind force 6, spinnakers billowing in a crazy kaleidoscope of intermittent, lantern-lit colour as we all changed to genoas for the beat northwards, and the red steel plates of the bucking lightvessel so close they would have skinned our hands if we had reached out for them. A little over an hour later, at the other end of the bank, was when I lost my mast.

The *Galloper* lightvessel was our home marker on that occasion as we motored back mastless to Harwich, and it was the *Galloper* again on the even more memorable occasion when I brought *Mary Deare*'s bare steel hull across from Holland, where it was built, for completion in Whisstock's yard at Woodbridge. She had no mast, no sails, nothing but an engine and a loo, and it was early in the year when we left the Amstel river in worsening weather. I had told the designer I wouldn't risk the North Sea crossing without his engineer on board, so there were three of us. But it turned out that the engineer was a sick man and before we were halfway across it was blowing a gale. Nothing for it then but to run for the Hook of Holland and get the engineer to a doctor. 'If you had a mast,' the designer said to me, 'you surely wouldn't insist on a chippy aboard before you'd put to sea.' I didn't argue, and after a stormy night in the Hook, we put out again.

It was at the end of this crossing that, for the first and only time, I sailed my boat between the two great concrete supports of the Roughs Tower. These flak platforms off Harwich are as much a feature of the coast as the more recent gas platforms of the Leman field further north by Lowestoft, but they have led a much more chequered life since their wartime function ceased, as pirate radio stations, even as self-declared independent states with tax haven enthusiasts boarding and reboarding them in dead-of-night scrimmages. All of which is fairly natural to the East Coast scene, smuggling having been a clandestine industry more widespread than in the much-publicised south and west.

It was three years later that we sailed *Mary Deare* down the Deben for the last time, bound for the Straits of Gibraltar and the Aegean. We took our departure from Woodbridge and as we passed Waldringfield it was with a catch in our throats that Dorothy and I saw the landlord of the Maybush raise a loaded tray of drinks high above his head in farewell and watched the familiar marks slip by – the Saxon tower of Ramsholt church, the Horse Sand buoy, the Ferryboat Inn and the depleted huddle of radar masts standing high above Bawdsey Manor.

That was my last sight of the Deben from my own boat, so now I can be accused of nostalgic bias. But I don't think it's that. Helford in Cornwall has a reputation, but sailing into it on a run down from Scotland via the west coast of Ireland I was disappointed. It just does not compare with the Deben, where so much of history and physical change adds fascination to beauty, so that in travels around the world I can literally say this is still the loveliest, the most fascinating, and my favourite estuary.

Dance of the swans at Manningtree – the Stour estuary has one of the largest bevies of swans in East Anglia.

6. Broadland

Most people come to the Norfolk Broads for the first time, as I did, by way of Norwich. This way you come on the water suddenly at Wroxham, which is the 'capital' of Broadland's leisure image. It is full of boatyards, ships' chandlers, stores for victualling boats, charterers, everything in fact to do with leisure and tourism, also the residences of people who run these facilities. Here the strangeness of the area is not immediately apparent, being a sort of mini-Maidenhead. But coming up from the south, that is something different, the riverine beauty of the Waveney valley soft contrast to the fen-like farms and arboreal dereliction of The Saints. There was a time you could get hopelessly lost in The Saints. Even now, with its new signposts, the thirteen saintly parishes, eight of them South Elmhams, can be confusing, and with a North Sea murk blowing in from Broadland, this is owl and ghost country, each saintly village possessed of an unkempt green or crumbling church, every copse a neglected ivy-clad jungle of rotting trees, and dung dumps looming tall as ancient barrows across flat, featureless prairies of farmland.

It is best to have an objective in The Saints, otherwise you may feel trapped in medieval sanctity. There is, near St Margaret – or is it St Cross, or perhaps St James (all roads at one point lead to St James)? – an eleventh-century minster that stands like a small piece of Burgh Castle, a rectangle of old flint rubble walls set in a great earthwork square full of witch-like trees. And near it is a nice sixteenth-century farmhouse that was supposed to have been built as a summer residence for the Norwich bishops. It has a moat and the ruins of what may have been an earlier chapel. I won't say more to guide you there, except that there is a little brook and the minster ruins are owned by a most pleasant farmer whose telephone calls him on cordless radio wherever he is about the farm.

Pale as death the snowdrops lie, waxen in drifts throughout The Saints, the country so desperately flat you feel all the time you are on the verge of falling off the edge of it. So, mostly I take the Waveney valley route, from Diss through Homersfield with its bridges and crescent of modern reed-thatched cottages, through Bungay to the chain ferry at Reedham. This wonderfully antediluvian contrivance is, in fact, the only means of crossing the Yare between Norwich and the river's outfall to the sea at

Horsey Mere, the most north-easterly of all the open water stretches of Broadland.

Great Yarmouth. It is also a way of stealing up on this marshland country, but even then it is still a good eight miles before you reach the Broads proper at South Walsham.

Just when they started digging those broadenings of the Norfolk rivers that constitute one of the strangest and most remarkable areas of Britain nobody is very sure. But dug they were, most of them, laboriously and over a period of six centuries, by the North Folk who from the ninth century onwards were stacking and drying the dug peat to provide warmth against the winter's bitter north-easterlies. The population was high for the England of that period, which is why the peat diggings are so extensive.

Eventually the slow tilt of the land and the changed tidal levels caused the dug areas to be flooded. These are the sheets of water we now call the Broads. There are altogether forty of them varying in size from Hickling, the largest, which has a surface area of 148 hectares (366 acres) to tiny little meres no bigger than a hectare (2.47 acres).

Most of these 'broads' are linked together by a network of rivers and channels. These provide 120 lock-free miles of uninterrupted sailing, so that in all it is an aquatic playground of at least 200 miles. The surrounding countryside is a wetland region, most of which is really very extensive grazing land, and it is this ecological complex that is generally referred to as Broadland. It covers an area of 570 square kilometres (220 square miles), and it is the whole Broadland region that is unique and in such great danger, the waterways cluttered with too many motorboats, the whole area faced with a summer influx of people that is too great for it to cope with, and the price of wheat destroying the old grazing pattern. But the further broads and less frequented parts of the rivers still have that strange feeling of a world apart, and in those quieter reaches, particularly on the Waveney, Yare and Bure, the first indication of a river's proximity remains as often as not a disembodied sail or the top of a cabin roof moving sedately through flat meadowlands.

The whole Broadland area is triangular in shape with its apex at Norwich and a long coastal base that runs from Lowestoft in the south through Great Yarmouth and Breydon Water to Horsey Mere and Sea Palling in the north. And whether you're afloat, or visiting the Broads by land, the impact of this strange amalgam of water and land never palls. The instant I am across the bridge at Acle, or through Wroxham, with its boatyard sheds standing shoulder-to-shoulder in the curve of the Bure, and on to the small roads leading to Barton, Hickling or South Walsham broads, I have that feeling of having been transported into an other-worldliness where all worries are sloughed off and nothing but the next stretch of water has any importance.

Once, waiting to appear on Anglia TV, I stood on Foundry Bridge over the Wensum at Norwich, the Nelson on one side, that splendid 'baroque' railway station on the other, and below me a small cabin cruiser motoring leisurely past a moored lightvessel, under the bridge

and into the treed stretch beyond. It was November, a cold snap in the air, but the sun was shining and the trees were golden. There was just that one boat, nothing else at all moving on the river, a man and a woman standing by the wheel and not a breath of wind. I thought then, how lovely! So many things to do in life and no time, and yet here were these two – they had made time, and though the nights would be chill and the days short, they would have the freedom of all the magnificent miles and miles of channels with hardly another boat to be seen.

It always surprises me that more artists have not concentrated on capturing this strange world. Peter Scott, of course, but only incidentally as the habitat of his bird pictures, and since he was occupying one of the two ornamental lighthouses at the exit of the Nene into the Wash his background was more often the Marshlands and the Fens. Seago has probably caught the atmosphere of the Broads better than anyone, but though he lived at Ludham close by Womack Broad and Potter Heigham he certainly did not confine himself to the Broadland scene. And Cavendish Morton, in all the years he lived at Eye, was always more a Suffolk than an East Anglian painter. In fact, I can't think of any painter who has done for the Broads what Constable was able to do with just a proportion of his work for Flatford and the Dedham vale.

The heart of Broadland with the greatest concentration of broads is the River Bure around Wroxham. Belaugh and Bridge broads upstream of the Norwich road bridge, Wroxham and Salhouse broads, the two Hoveton broads, then Decoy, Broad Waters, Ranworth, South Walsham and any number of small offshoots and meres, all on the Bure between Wroxham and the point where the Ant comes in from Barton Broad in the north. South Walsham Broad and Ranworth Broad, I think these are the two I like best when coming by road, but less for the atmosphere than for the scenery with tall trees enveloping Walsham's two churches and greensward running down to lakeland scenes that might be the setting for Malory's *Morte d'Arthur*.

Some of the broads, like Burntfen and Alderfen, Crome's, Upton and the great expanses of Ormesby, Rollesby and Filby, are virtually cut off as far as boats are concerned, the last only connected to the Bure by Muck Fleet, which is hardly a gin palace highway. But, one way or another, all the broads, from that wild north-eastern grouping of Hickling, Horsey, Heigham and Martham, so close to the sea that, snugged down by Horsey Staithe in a gale, you can hear the waves pounding beyond the dunes, to Surlingham, Rockland and Hasingham broads and the Flitton and Flixton decoys in the south, all drain into two rivers, the Bure and the Yare. The Bure with its tributaries, the Ant and the Thurne, and the even more extensive reaches of the Yare-Waveney system,

Something I shall never forget, my first experience of wind whining in the halyards was on Horsey Mere.

constitute most of the 200 miles of navigable water.

At some time the whole of this catchment area drained out through the once-large herring port of Great Yarmouth. Now Oulton Dyke takes some of the Waveney water out through Oulton Broad under the swing bridge of the other once-big fish port of Lowestoft. But still the Waveney makes a great loop past Oulton Broad, flowing north-west to the New Cut junction, then finally north-east to link up with the Yare, the two of them draining into Great Yarmouth's tidal basin of Breydon Water. This joins up with the Bure just below the railway bridge to flow south into the sea behind a vast deposit of sand and shingle. Once this two-mile long commercial gut was full of trawlers. Now it is the flat-iron shape of supply vessels to the offshore rigs of the Leman Bank and other gasfields that are chiefly moored there.

From a pilotage point of view, exploring the Broads by road is almost as much of a lottery as it is by water, so many apparent highways leading to dead ends. This is particularly true of all but the mainest of roads leading down to the Bure and the Yare. There are ferries marked, but they are mostly for passengers only. The one at Reedham is the only car ferry. Operated by chains stretched across the Yare's muddy bed, the number of cars it takes is limited so that there is usually a tailback. The pub here is very handily placed and those with time to spare can relax and watch the slow passage of the boats as they play an endless game of dare with the ferry's clanking chain.

But it is on the little cul-de-sac roads, some of which have a tendency to flood, that the sense of exploration becomes dominant. There is an air of secrecy about them, each patch of water, when discovered, seemingly lost in mysterious solitude. There is a feeling of timelessness, the world forgotten, a dream. I have sat for ages watching a cat trying to catch fish. Once we watched a dog watching a swan who was watching over his mate nesting in the flags nearby. And a boy all alone sailing a model boat. It looked like the ones I used to carve, and the intentness, the absolute concentration as he willed it to hold its course for the wooden boathouse opposite and not get blown into the reeds. Perhaps that is the charm of the Broads, a flashback to boyhood days, each broad a grown-up bath with toy boats and toy waves. No danger here, just a place to dream, and in the quieter reaches the enjoyment of watching others at play. That beautiful racing machine, slim as an Indian canoe and varnished to a silken gleam, and a girl in a cotton dress sitting it out as the tall sail takes her spinning without a sound across the mere and into the sunset. I remember her so distinctly, a water goddess in her sailing canoe. Was she real, or did I dream it?

Sometimes I wonder whether the Broads themselves are real. The saltmarshes along Norfolk's northernmost coast, yes. They are of far sterner stuff, a man's world, cold and bright and hard, with the sea for ever flooding and ebbing to threaten the life of any careless bird-watching visitor. But the Broads are different, a never-never holiday world – a

week, a fortnight, the boats all in temporary ownership – old hands, newcomers, laughter and the blare of radios – and in the evening when the pubs are full, then, only then a sudden hush as dusk begins to fall. But still there is a magic in the air, the strangeness and remoteness of the further waterways, and always the weather and the wind, the proximity of the sea and the infinity of distant vistas, sails and boats gliding through meadows, the ruins of an abbey or a windmill seen from afar, the shape of a bridge, cars on a road moving fast while you are on water travelling slow.

It is a strange world and I defy anyone not to sense this strangeness as soon as they have passed through Wroxham, which is the 'port of

Ranworth Broad – this is what the Broads are all about, the hire of motor cruisers.

The screen paintings are what make St Helen, Ranworth, so important; some of the finest in the country.

entry' for most holiday-makers. For myself, whenever I go that way or cross the old hump-backed bridge at Potter Heigham or glimpse the reed-shallow waters of Horsey Mere, my mind goes back to *Scamp*. All the sailing Dorothy and I have done, from Scandinavia round to Turkey, all the ports and islands, all the thousands of sea miles, began with that little boat.

A week on the Broads and in that week we learned to tack and gybe and live like gypsies in the cramped confines of a tiny cabin. A simple sailing handbook had been my winter companion, but as for so many others, the conversion of book-learned theory to practice was full of disaster and laughter. The gentle art of gybing, for instance, with the wind aft and the mains'l swinging across under control, the boat heeling the other way, helmsman ducking and changing position – you can become so obsessed with getting it right that you almost forget there is a simpler method of changing tack with the bows instead of the stern facing into the wind.

Despite the number of boats, which have always been something of a hazard on the Broads, it is still an excellent sailing nursery, better than those big reservoirs like Rutland Water on the far side of the Fens, for so much of it is river sailing with a bank handy when helm and sails become so confused that the helmsman of the moment is near to panic. If I were newly married and teaching myself to sail again, I would still opt for the Broads, because it's not just sailing, but living on board that has to be learned, and going ashore there presents no problems – indeed, it is an accidental occurrence that happens all the time!

The argument about how this unique area of Britain came into existence will continue as long as people like Blakes, who have for many years had something of a corner in the organisation of Broadland holidays, continue to issue brochures. It is probably more masochistically satisfactory to emphasise the digging of peat than the more natural causes. Until the 1950s it was generally thought that the whole area had developed from a bay in Roman times to the present half-reclaimed marsh in much the same way as the Pevensey marshland has developed since the arrival of William the Conqueror. The theory that Caister and Burgh were Roman garrison centres guarding the wide entrance to a shallow bay must have some basis. Caister was a Roman-Iceni town with its own harbour and quay, and a small boat harbour as well, which supports the belief that the Romans moved supplies by water rather than their network of roads, at any rate in East Anglia. Beginning to grow as a Roman town about the second century AD, Caister's earthwork and timber defences were later faced with stone. Later still, the great castle at Burgh on the south side of this Broadland inlet superseded it.

Burgh is another of those Castles of the Saxon Shore, bigger than Pevensey it looks, though that may be because of its position standing over the south end of Breydon Water. The day I walked there it was autumn, so that, looking out over the acres of fall-brown reedheads

St Michael, the Archangel, and the seven-headed dragon, is the most prominent of these marvellous paintings, the cost of which may have come from a will dated as early as 1419.

Every stretch of water has its own graveyard; an old wooden hulk upstream from Lowestoft in an interesting state of decay.

Downstream at Oulton – the flotsam and jetsam of coastal commerce.

edging the Yare river and the leaden sweep of Breydon, I could only dimly see the Broadland windmills standing gaunt in the mist. But down by the water, beyond the river and the cattle grazing, I counted six of them, some with sails, some just ruined stumps, all of them looking very tall in the total flatness.

The castle was originally quadrilateral, but the western wall is gone and bits and pieces of the north and south walls lie at crazy angles with no apparent foundations. Only the eastern wall remains virtually intact, so that it is more like a curtain wall 200 metres long, a great grey line of rubble concrete with squared flint facing and bonded courses of brick standing almost as high as when it was built, only the parapet gone, and four flat circular towers added on, with an open gateway in the centre of it to form the gap through which I could see the hazy outline of 'hills' and trees looking big as hills on the far side of the marshes.

Nearby is the little round-towered church of Burgh. Fritton, Belton, and Burgh all have Saxon-type round towers. St Olave's Priory, named after the King of Norway and just across the Waveney bridge from Fritton where there was an ancient ferry, is much later, around 1216, with a refectory undercroft that is something like Beeleigh – thin stone columns and vaulted arches of heavily limewashed brick. In Burgh churchyard there is a big cross of ancient design that commemorates that early saint named Fursey who was born around 587, 'laboured' in the vicinity of Burgh circa 630 and died in France about 650. Thus, if you fail to cross into Broadland by Reedham Ferry, and if you can shut your eyes to the sprawl of Belton's housing estates, then Burgh Castle is really just as good an introduction to Broadland. Particularly if you go on up the coast north through Yarmouth, not to Caister Castle, but to the miserable little relic of Caister Roman town half buried on a hilltop by bungaloid growth, for then you will appreciate how the tidal thrust has blocked the great bay that was reckoned to be twelve miles wide between Flegg and Lothing. All that is left of it now is Breydon Water and the rivers stretching inland with here and there a mere or lake and the swordblade gleam of drainage ditches and cuts.

It is only latterly that it has been established that very large quantities of peat were dug from the river banks in the days before ships began bringing 'sea' coal down from the Tyne. Even so, not all the 'broads' can be peat dug. Some are definitely meres or lakes left by centuries of drainage and reclamation which is there for all to see, in the way the rivers have been enclosed by banking, with ditches and drainage channels, connecting cuts, ronds, dykes and fleets. Both causes would seem to make sense, but however each individual area of water was formed, it is the preservation of Broadland as an ecological whole that is of primary importance. Having destroyed in the name of advancing agriculture the marshes of the Fens, it is up to us to concentrate on preserving the unique little marshland triangle that the farmers have left us. Already as much as a quarter of these wetlands have been drained, ploughed and roaded, the East Anglian monocrop of wheat ousting the grazing of cattle in marshmeadows that were once full of plants, birds and insects. Like most really unusual habitats in our islands, what remains is under great pressure – from too many boats, too many humans, and what seems to go with the twentieth century, too much noise and too much litter.

There are over 7,000 boats on the Broads. That's just about sixty boats to each mile of lock-free water, and most of them motor cruisers. Imagine what that does to the river banks, particularly when drivers have had a few drinks and think the speed limit is for the other guy. As for the human influx, the yearly number of holiday-makers afloat has now topped 200,000. The result, despite chemical loos, is that Broadland waters are mostly a murky brown, obscuring the light so necessary for the healthy growth of macrophytes, which is the technical name for the submerged and floating aquatic vascular plants.

And it is not just the waterborne tourists that are destroying the ecology of the Broads. Commercialisation of the boat centres of Wroxham, Potter Heigham and Hoveton, plus a rash of small residential properties of less than aesthetic design, have ruined the appearance of the more popular areas. Add to this all those who come in daily to tour Broadland by coach and car and you will begin to realise the pressures and how vital it is to preserve what remains of wild marshland.

Something else, too – the change in land use. Cattle are one thing, but as more and more land is drained and planted to wheat, it means deepened drainage channels, pumping engines – water housekeeping, in fact. It means fertilisers and pesticides which drain off the land into the dykes, ditches and fleets, which then cease to be the home of rare bogland plants. The water fern, milfoil and water soldier will disappear, together with the frogs and insects. And if the marshlands go, what about the Yare valley's wintering bean geese, or the yellow wagtail, the redshank and the snipe?

And in the Broads themselves, and along the wet peat and bog areas bordering some stretches of river, changes in land use and human requirements are having a disastrous effect. The modern bungalow or riverside dwelling, even the farms and farm buildings, use tile now instead of traditional reed thatch. The result is not only visually painful, but it also means less reed cutting. The sedge, too, since it was used in thatching for the house ridge. As marsh hay it was also used for cattle, but this, too, has now been replaced by better quality hay trucked in.

It was the regular and extensive cutting of reed and sedge that kept the peaty wetlands in good fettle. Now, the reed-beds are being taken over by wet scrub and woodland, willow mainly, which is a far cry from the natural habitat of the reed warblers, bitterns, reeve, marsh harriers and swallowtails.

But it is the change in agriculture and the high density of boats that results in the murkiness of the water. This loss of clarity has been progressive over the past twenty to thirty years, the whole marvellous

water playground becoming increasingly polluted. There is an excess of what are described as 'nutrients', which are mainly phosphates and nitrates, and the resultant algae are most apparent in the spring and autumn when the turbid appearance of the water is brownish through to an almost green colour.

In short, the Norfolk Broads are now sick with excessive use, water pollution leading to an excess of weed and an accompanying decrease in the depth of most of the broads. The river banks have had to be reinforced with wood or steel shuttering against the wash of boats, which have in some cases been wearing the banks away at the rate of a foot a year. Fishermen are as concerned as the environmentalists, for the tidal reaches of these sluggish rivers have a good stock of perch and pike, bream and roach, while trout, roach and dace predominate in the non-tidal reaches.

And, of course, where the land has been drained and turned over to wheat, it is not marsh any longer, but the sort of prairie you can see in the clays and chalklands. As I write another big area, Halvergate Marsh, is under threat, 9,000 acres of lush grazing marsh that farmer owners want to drain and convert to a naked prairie for wheat or barley. Once that is done, it cannot easily be undone, and it becomes like the other conversions, all hard standing, with spray irrigation an extra drain on the level of the water in summer. No geese or duck here, no oyster-catchers or redshanks, no Bewick swans, and no bog or water plants, the uniqueness of it all gone for ever.

I have mentioned the sluggishness of these rivers. The Yare, for instance, between Norwich and Yarmouth has a fall of only four inches in each mile. Unless a tidal outflow is added to the force of water coming

---

Barton Turf has more boats and water than its name implies. Working boats like this keep the channels open for navigation throughout the Broads.

The other face of Oulton Broad: upstream of the road bridge all is leisure and pleasure in August.

down the river, there is insufficient scouring to keep the channel open with a reasonable depth of water for shipping. This has been a problem with virtually all the East Coast ports. Harwich, with two tidal estuaries flushing out the entrance, still has to be dredged. Land reclamation in the Blythburgh marshes behind Dunwich, Walberswick and Southwold steadily diminished the tidal scour from the flats and salts. With the ports of Dunwich and Walberswick already gone, the outflow from the River Blyth was insufficient to keep the Southwold exit free and the harbour silted up. The story of Southwold is a microcosm of the perpetual conflict between landsmen and seamen, and nowhere in Britain has this dichotomy of interest been so apparent as on this East Coast, landowning greed always seeming to triumph over those whose interest is the sea.

Even Lowestoft, with its close water-links with Norwich, had its

Great Yarmouth, looking from the swing bridge down the long sand and shingle spit, which is here known as South Quay; also a view towards the bridge showing North Sea oil support ships moored alongside.

problems until Peto bought it in 1844. He was one of those incredible nineteenth-century entrepreneurs (the Houses of Parliament, the Crystal Palace, a prison, the Great Exhibition); a little matter of rebuilding the fortunes of an East Coast port and improving conditions for the export of cattle by building a specialised fleet of ships presented no problem. A decade later and the place was bustling, more than a thousand ships coming and going, over fifty thousand tons using its facilities.

Yarmouth made numerous attempts in the fifteenth, sixteenth and seventeenth centuries to keep its outlet to the sea open for ships that were getting bigger all the time. Even with the scour from Breydon Water

A sudden change in the May weather produced this early closing view of Yarmouth's empty beach, sea and pier. ▶

the extent of the silting was such that right into the middle of the nineteenth century the largest ships had to anchor in the Roads and offload part of their cargo into local vessels before they could get across the bar into the harbour.

These local boats were the black-sailed keels and wherries, once a common sight in Broadland waters, now virtually extinct. Historically they are the most interesting of all the various types of sailing craft developed locally around the coasts of Britain, for their origins go back a thousand years to the Viking longship. This was the seagoing tool that led to a maritime migration of most extraordinary proportions, and that migration led directly to the Norfolk wherry. There are now two of these vessels preserved by the Wherry Trust, the *Lord Roberts* having been lifted from Womack Broad to join the *Albion*, its timbers preserved by total immersion in mud and water.

On one of the occasions I have given a talk in Yarmouth I found myself guest for the night in the home of a Potter Heigham Thain. Descended from the Anglo-Saxon aristocrats with the title thane or thegn she had the blue eyes and flaxen hair of her race, and so had her eleven-week-old baby. Her grandfather had built up one of the biggest fleets of wherries on the Broads, some twenty vessels, one of which was

The pier entrance.

the *Lord Roberts*. But, as her husband pointed out, look up the telephone number of a Thain in Potter Heigham and you will find they are nearly all farmers, for as cargoes dwindled they turned to growing the produce they had carried, putting their money into land instead of ships. It is worth having a look at the Wherry Trust's vessels, for the hull shape is very similar to the longship, clinker-built, double-ended and wide-beamed, with a shallow draft and a good sheer. Really, all that is missing is the dragon-headed upcurve at prow and stern and the squares'l rig.

Undoubtedly the dragon heads became superfluous once settlements had been established and trading, rather than raiding, became the pattern of life; also, of course, the ships were a lot easier to handle in rivers and enclosed marshland waters without them. Surprisingly, the square sail remained till long after it had been replaced by fore-and-aft rig for the Dutch Botter and other small vessels on the other side of the North Sea. In fact, it wasn't until the last half of the sixteenth century that a sudden rush of Dutchmen seeking refuge from the depredations and cruelties of the occupying Spaniards gave the watermen of the Norfolk rivers a chance to see for themselves the advantages of a rig that did not have to wait upon the wind but could make to windward. A cautious people, living largely in isolation, they gradually developed a

The things they do to houses in search of seaside business.

new windward rig to suit their particular needs and I shall always be glad that when I chartered that little boat at Wroxham and started learning to sail, I was fortunate enough to see one or two of these vessels still plying the Waveney and the Bure.

Wherries came in sizes ranging from twenty to seventy tons. Built of local oak, they were heavy and very sturdy, yet under their newly developed rig they were surprisingly fast, capable of a sailing speed of seven or eight miles an hour. A 30-ton wherry would be about fifty-two feet long and thirteen feet broad, and even when loaded would only draw two and a half feet. There were no stays to the mast, except the forestay, and by setting the massive spar in a tabernacle, and counterweighting it with about one and a half tons of lead bolted to the butt, a child could lower it. The huge loose-footed sail was dressed with a mix of seal or herring oil and tar with lampblack to complete the almost witchlike appearance.

Here is a description from a century ago of what it was like to shoot a bridge in one of these vessels:

> On you go before a strong breeze until within 100 yards of the bridge, when the sail is sheeted flat; the man goes leisurely forward, leaving his wife or son at the helm, lets the windlass run; down comes the sail; the gaff has then to be detached from the mast and laid on top of the hatches; then, just as you think the mast must crash against the bridge, it falls gently back, and you shoot under; up it goes again without a pause, the forestay is made fast, and under the pressure of the windlass the heavy sail rises aloft, all before you have quite got over your first impulse of alarm.

Wherries and keels both traded down from Norwich to the port of Lowestoft, and back in Roman times there were doubtless smaller vessels bringing cargoes and passengers up from the coast to Venta Icenorum, a Roman 'camp' on the banks of the Tas. There is not much support now for the theory that this was Boadicea's capital, but like Colchester, it was certainly one of the tribal capitals of the Iceni. It was big for a town of that period, extending finally to some thirty-four acres with a deep ditch all round it, except where the Tas provided a natural defence.

The Romans made it an administrative centre, and though not as important as Camulodunum it had the usual Roman buildings and was surrounded with massive walls strengthened by very solid-looking round towers. Considerable excavation was carried out on the site in the early thirties, but this was filled in for the protection of what little is left. The site is at Caistor St Edmund, just south of Norwich, and 'Caistor was a city when Norwich was none, and Norwich was built of Caistor stone.' Nice oak gates with crown-carved posts lead across the eighty-foot wide ditch that guarded the town and up on to the top of the earthwork remains of the great Roman wall. There is a church here, snugged up

*Waxham, at the northern end of Broadland. This is where you can lord it over
miles of empty strand.*

against the south-east corner of the ramparts, sparsely plain with a dressed flint tower and a view down to the Tas and across arable land to the whole circle of the walls. Nothing remains of the Roman buildings, nothing visible that is, though aerial photographs are quite revealing and the actual position of the buildings can be picked out and their nature identified. The site now is very rural, very Norfolk, the valley of the Tas – like the Glem, or any of the other rivers of East Anglia – cutting gently into the country so that any appearance of flatness is gone and those who cycle have an uphill-downhill task.

I saw it last on a day of great heat which, in typical East Coast fashion,

was made enchantingly bearable by a cooling north-easterly breeze, and the whole of the town area was golden with the whiskered heads of ripe barley, oaks marking the great circle of the walls and a sparrowhawk hanging in a blue sky. And even if little of the original can be seen, it is enough to stand there in that graveyard with the humps of the old walls all round, for there cannot be many English cities of the antiquity of Norwich where you can walk the buried streets of the British-Roman town from which it sprang. And now that the great abbey at Bury St Edmunds is in ruins, Norwich is architecturally the ecclesiastical wonder of East Anglia, so that I am glad my work has taken me there more

Two night views of Norwich – the River Wensum looking towards Pull's Ferry, and Elm Hill, just west of the Cathedral.

This interior view of Norwich Cathedral illustrates the great loftiness of the nave, the marriage of wood and stone in the roof – it also shows part of the extraordinary organ which dominates the rood screen.

often than to Colchester or Ipswich, despite the greater distance and a somewhat dull and dangerous road.

Now, if I were going there for the first time, I would aim, if I could, to enter the city after dark, partly I must admit because of the problem of parking, but mainly because of the extraordinary, quite overwhelming impact made by the ingenious floodlighting of so many of the old buildings. I never saw it at night until I was asked to present my own version of that nicely evocative radio programme, *With Great Pleasure*. We did it in the Maddermarket Theatre, a reproduction of an old Elizabethan playhouse just by St Gregory's and the Strangers' Hall, on the hottest night of the year, and when we had finished the narrow lane that leads up to Pottergate and Cow Hill was empty and looking very mysterious in the lamplight, the church lit with a soft glow. We then drove round half the old part of the city searching for the restaurant where a table had been booked for us, and everywhere, it seemed, there was floodlighting, every corner revealing a new piece of flint and stone through a tracery of leaves, the side of a tower etched black in shadow or a clerestory framed in light. The restaurant was in an old stone building and across the way was another of the city's thirty-three pre-Reformation churches, also quite subtly floodlit.

But it is the cathedral that is important, for this and Durham are the two most essentially Norman cathedrals in Britain. But whereas Durham from the railway stands smoke-blackened and very prominent on the side of a hill, Norwich with its cloisters and Bishop's Palace is almost discreetly hidden behind the limes bordering that over-trafficked, largely Georgian 'square' with the fearful name of Tombland – not as you might immediately think an old graveyard, but a name derived from the Saxon word for an open air market place, the 'toom'. The cathedral's spire is, of course, visible for miles, being set very slender between four offspring pinnacles on top of one of the most elaborate and beautiful towers ever constructed by the Normans, the total height of 315 feet topping all but Salisbury's great spire. At night, floodlit, tower and spire stand like an enormous off-white exclamation mark above the old part of the city and this is the time to walk from Tombland in through the great Erpingham gateway and stroll the floodlit peace of the cathedral close, which is vast and at the eastern or lower end runs right down to the old watergate at Pull's Ferry.

Norwich is a city to spend time in and to wander, a luxury I have seldom achieved since only very occasionally have I spent the night there. So many churches, so many pubs, so much to see and the people so varied, and the shops and markets full of the produce of fen and marsh and upland estates, game from the big shoots, wildfowl from the

This is the most striking sight in Norwich at night, the great Norman tower of the Cathedral, the finest in Britain, floodlit.

The cloisters are unusual in that they are two-storeyed, with a false upper storey on the north side. Vaulting bosses occur in profusion and number almost 400.

saltmarshes and a variety of seafood from the North Sea coast and estuaries that London cannot better.

Until the last century and a half Norwich was the most isolated of cities, the Fens on one side cutting it off from all the centre and north of England, the Broadland marshes on the other, and nothing but farms and fishing villages to the north, so that the only really big centre of population and industry within reach by land was London itself, and that was well over a hundred weary miles by horse over heath and forest tracks. It was, in fact, easier and often a good deal quicker to go down the Yare to Lowestoft and take ship to Rotterdam, Bruges or Antwerp.

This quite a few of the citizens did, for Norwich, too, grew and flourished on the 'new drapery' wool industry, exporting large quantities of worsted fabrics, the city's clothiers sending their salesmen all over Europe and exporting the output from Norwich looms through Yarmouth and Lowestoft to cities as far apart as Moscow and Madrid. Defoe gives a figure of well over a thousand ships actually owned by the city's merchants. The latter half of the eighteenth century was the peak of the Norwich wool trade, even the East India Company trading over twenty thousand lengths of fine camlet, and bay-yarn being bought in from as far afield as Ireland to be worked up at Norwich, every man, woman and child fully employed.

No wonder the city took on an almost 'continental' flavour. Out on a limb, with the North Sea its most practicable route to the outside world, it developed a remarkable degree of self-sufficiency, so that even now those who live in Norfolk see little need to go to London or anywhere else other than Norwich for their needs.

Again, winter, or at least autumn, is the time to get the feel of this north Anglian city, that sense of isolation. Certainly it is the time when Broadland waters return to some semblance of the strange, remote world they once were. Most of the motorboats are tied up then and those that are still on charter moor up as night falls close to village or pub. By Christmas the whole range of wintering wildfowl have arrived and for those who are prepared to face dusk or dawn in a small boat there is still a whole world to watch. It is a shy world, but as both ducks and geese tend to seek safety in numbers flightings can still be spectacular.

It is difficult now to find a decoy that is still operating, but at one time the more isolated meres like Fritton and Flixton had decoys that were harvested like a crop to produce an income out of an otherwise useless part of the estate. The fowl trap was a curved arm or dyke of water arched over with netting on bent willow rods. About ten feet across at the entrance, the decoy pipe narrowed to a tunnel net, and it was at the end of this, in the secrecy of screens or reeds, that the keeper would do his work, silently and swiftly grabbing up mallard or teal and wringing their necks. There was a decoy dog as well as feed to attract the birds, his leaping about drawing them in through curiosity, and the decoy man would make his approach along a shallow ditch carrying a piece of

The twelfth-century castle keep on its ten-metres high mound is also remarkable for its external decoration. This view does not show the massive car park that surrounds it. Norwich has always been a great marketing centre.

smouldering peat to cover his scent.

It was indeed a very secret business, the keepers in the role of first and second murderers. But murder by stealth was ruined by the noisy slaughter of the gun, and ducks, feeding always at night, fell victim in the dawn to the gun in the reeds or the wide-scattering shot of that punt-mounted blunderbuss. How often does the wildfowler consider, waiting there in the reeds or in his punt on the saltmarshes for the first greying of the winter dawn, where the birds he is going to shoot have come from, the mystery of their flight pattern across the northern hemisphere from Scandinavia, Finland, Novaya Zemlya, from Siberia beyond the Urals? His answer is, of course, that one cold summer in the Arctic can destroy more wildfowl than he can ever kill on any number of bitter East Coast dawns. But a bird that has come so far and is seeking food in the depth of winter deserves better than to have a gun added to

140

all the natural hazards, especially now that man is encroaching so fast upon its habitat; ducks and geese can quite easily go the way of the avocet and the ruff if the pressures become too great.

Once otters were a common sight in the Broads, so bold they would sometimes eat their night's catch of pike or carp or tench on the hatch-cover of a wherry or leave their wet pawmarks on the deck of a sailing boat. Rare now, that arrow of bright water behind the dark head, the quick flash of movement by the roots of a tree, the sudden smooth splash. With up to three cubs a year, and the security of a water entrance to the tree root holt where they breed, they could probably have survived being hunted for sport or shot as vermin by keepers, but no animal as dependent as otters upon water can survive its pollution; in addition, of course, they are harassed half the year by the constant movement of motor cruisers, the noise of humans and their radios. No wonder the only certain sighting of them now is at Philip Wayre's Otter Trust at Earsham.

The Trust was originally planned for a wetland estate close to our own Great Wood. Instead, it is just over the northern border of Suffolk, and a wonderful introduction to Broadland for those coming up from the south along the Waveney valley. A couple of little round-towered churches, Redenhall's pinnacled tower standing high on its hill, and there is the Otter Trust land close alongside the river's north bank with a quarter of a mile of spacious, dredged-out otter pens, three lakes breeding carp and occupied by a mass of waterfowl that include the largest collection of bean geese in the country, and marsh, meadow and coppice for Chinese water deer and muntjac deer.

The whole of the Trust area is designed for the education of children and the breeding of otters. The otter has quite a short life, about eight years, so that breeding up of cubs is important, for the Trust and more recently for release into the wild. The two pens furthest from the entrance are much larger and barred to the public; here young pairs remain isolated for a whole year to acclimatise them to the wild before being loosed. In addition to the European otter, which is the one belonging to the Broadland habitat and to the rest of the country, Philip Wayre gives pen space to the Asian short-clawed, a tropical otter from India and South-East Asia, also the Indian smooth-coated from China and South-East Asia. These two exotics are important, particularly for children, because the European otter is a nocturnal animal, very shy, very difficult to see in the wild; not at all easy to display to visitors. In fact, the only way this can be done is by shutting the animals out of their dens in the middle of the day, and, because they need warmth, this is only possible in the summer season, which means from Easter onwards.

The year is thus divided into visitor time and a winter period when most of the work of the Trust is done, the breeding, the dredging out of pens, the despatch of dogs and bitches, the care of cubs. And something else the Trust does – the surveying of rivers and the establishment of otter sanctuaries that may involve river areas of up to six kilometres,

The lush summer look of the Waveney upstream from Beccles, and the centre of the town with its town hall and the solid tower that stands separate from the church.

depending on the degree of co-operation from local landowners and farmers. This is something very encouraging for the future since already 252 of these otter 'havens' have been agreed on eleven of East Anglia's rivers.

Having seen something of the natural Broads life that is now almost impossible to see in Broadland itself, the actual entry into this strange flat world of land and water offers a choice – go north just after Bungay for the chain ferry at Reedham, or go on to Beccles, then north to the rail and water bridge by Fritton and one of the oldest and most exciting of those little round-towered churches that are so thick on the ground in this part of Norfolk. Beccles, with the quay crowded with boats and its long river frontage, has its fascination, but I prefer Reedham, provided I have judged it right and the wait at the ferry is not too long.

The turn northwards, away from Suffolk and into Norfolk, is by the two narrow square towers of Gillingham's churches, the one immaculately flinted, the other half ruined and ivy-clad, and then into what is surprisingly well-wooded country, until, beyond Thurlton, the narrow road can turn into what seems like a sordid lane full of water and dung. Suddenly there is a signboard with MARSH FARM painted white on black and a gap in the hedge with Broadland stretching flat green marshmeadows away to the right, to the rising ground beyond the Waveney; and to the left, past the brick engine-house and water wheel of an old pumping station, the coachroof of a motor cruiser, like the top of a double-decker bus, slides silently along a grass embankment. This is the bank of the Yare and all beyond is table-flat, the hard air and the flatness magnifying anything raised above the level of the land or in any way perpendicular. In less than a mile we are at the chain ferry, the river stretching left and right across our path and on the other side the immaculate black and white building of the Ferry Inn.

Suffolk is behind us now, Norfolk ahead, the buildings, most of them, twentieth-century brick, the villages all seeming to be poised on the edge of a void as though the floods were for ever lapping the foundations. Why is it that it always seems to be winter in Norfolk even if it isn't, the light brown reedstalks bending their darker heads to the wind, the sedge grass on the dyke tops flickering in perpetual motion? Thurlton church is reed-thatched, and so is another just beyond the village, a charming little round-towered church overlooking the Yare marshland. Reed thatch and the remains of priories, windmills standing with their four arms spread or just the derelict stump like a lighthouse in a flatness equal to the sea, a flatness that runs away to the north as far as the distant heights that mark the boundaries of Broadland.

The clanking ferry, the glimmer of a sail, cruisers waiting by the river bank and the bright ribbon of the water . . . it is all marvellously exciting, a new, quite extraordinary land. But don't look to the left, towards Cantley and that piled up monstrosity of a sugar beet factory that some fool of a planner has allowed to dominate this lovely Seago landscape.

Horsey Mere from close by the old pumping mill – this is exactly how Dorothy and I first learned to live on and sail a boat.

7. The Fens

Whenever I am in the Fens I think of Hereward the Wake holding the Isle of Ely when all the rest of Saxon England had fallen to the Conqueror. This is not so much in admiration of the last free Saxon leader standing against the Normans so long after Hastings, as a deep, instinctive feeling of what Ely had once been to the people of the Fens. Before Bedford and the adventurers, all the surrounding country, north-west almost to Peterborough and south to Cambridge, was vastly different to the intensively-farmed, pump-drained, shrunken peatland it is now, and it was not until the Normans found a way across the swamps of the Ouse from Willingham to Aldreth that the last Saxon stronghold was forced to capitulate. Undrained, the whole area was one huge swamp veined with rivers and a network of water passages, the insubstantial patches of meadowland seeming to float on the water table and only the few real islands standing clear and firm.

Ely is the largest of these real islands. Like Thorney and Ramsey, and a dozen other places with names that mostly end in 'ea' or 'ey', it is formed by the occasional outcropping of the deep underlying Jurassic boulder clay. In winter, when the trees are bare, it bulks large over what is now the first of the Bedford Levels as you approach the Fens by way of Newmarket Heath or the Brecklands. There are three Levels – North, Middle and South. The North Level lies to the north-east of Peterborough, the Middle between Peterborough and Ely, and the South Level to the north and east of Ely. It is the Middle and South Levels that are the major problems. These are the lands below the sea, the peat so saturated with lime that the natural vegetation is very different to that of the acid bogland peats found on moorland.

Heading for Ely, I usually cut up via Mildenhall and the American air-base, the Breckland heathlands of gorse and wind-crooked Scots giving way to hedges, the sand and gravel-covered chalk sloping very gently down through Kenny Hill to a sudden, startling vista of flat land and infinite sky, as though this is the shore of some dead sea. Away to the right a line of poplars stands on the horizon like the stakes of an eel trap, and in the distance, to the left, still a good eight miles away, stands a most improbable castle, dark in silhouette against the sky. ELY! And

The Isle of Ely's great cathedral seen as the visitor should see it for the first time – from afar and across the Fens.

all around, black miles of flat fen, puggy with rain and drifted here and there with the pale of old silt or deposited mollusc shells where the subsoil is starting to show through. Areas of growing crops give the relief of colour to a flatness that is quite startling and only broken by the occasional rectangular grey of corrugated iron storage sheds.

Ely's silhouette is still there at the little railway halt of Shippea Hill, a big ditch to the right and bridge after little bridge, and just three and a half miles short of Littleport, a sharp turn to port and Ely is straight over the bows. One is looking then at the full breadth of the building, the lantern out of line with the west tower, so that it is like some mad fairy fortress reaching skyward in a series of levels. And as one drives towards it one cannot help wondering how, almost a millennium ago, those Benedictine monks could have even contemplated such a vast stone pile in the midst of such a wild bog of undrained peat with no suitable building materials anywhere in the vicinity.

Gradually the silhouette grows until beyond Prickwillow it is rising high in the sky – a series of level crossings, the Great Ouse bridge, and then on to the island itself and the bulk of the cathedral lost, only tower

A closer view of the Cathedral, its most remarkable feature now revealed – Alan of Walsingham's octagonal lantern tower.

The massive 215-foot high West Tower, from the top of which all the Fens from Norfolk to Lincoln, and south as far as Cambridge, can be seen.

A cannon in the grounds.

*Close-up details of the west face of
the great tower of the Cathedral.*

and lantern showing above the buildings and a scattering of trees.

I think this is a more exciting way to approach Ely than coming up from Newmarket because it usually means walking through part of the shopping area after parking the car, or through the market if it is market day. This way you enter the College, or close, by the north gate so that the towering immensity of the cathedral suddenly bursts upon you, the impact of it quite startling. And another thing, there is a little door on the north side that brings you virtually straight into the Lady Chapel. This to my mind is the loveliest piece of architecture in the whole massive edifice, so light, so white-stoned, with fan-vaulted roof, no stained glass at all, everything seeming lit with an ethereal brightness, and nice inverted Y benches of what looks like plain ash, very pale. But then, of course, there is Prior Crauden's Chapel, which was built by the same man – Alan of Walsingham, who also designed and built the incredible lantern after the great Norman central tower had collapsed on to the choir.

Naturally, the best place from which to view the lantern is the west tower. From there you can see everything for it is 215 feet high, and besides the cathedral and the College area, you look down on all of Ely as though in plan, at the gardens and the mellow tiled roofs, the green fields falling from College to river where Oliver Cromwell, who had at one time been Steward to the Dean and Chapter, trained his Ironsides. On a clear day you can see the gallops and race course at Newmarket, Mildenhall church with its little red cap of tiles on top of the tower, and west across flat miles Peterborough cathedral, the spires of King's Chapel, and north, just sometimes, the Wash. It is only then that you realise how truly Ely is the stronghold of the Fens and appreciate how god-like the island position must have seemed to those early monks as they raised their great stone ship higher and higher.

The lantern has always fascinated me ever since I discovered it was built largely of wood and fixed in place by huge oak trees. There are eight of them, great concealed beams sixty-four feet long, over three feet wide and two feet eight inches thick. The trees were cut in Bedfordshire and after being trimmed by adze to the correct size, they were brought down the Great Ouse, the combined weight being eighty tons, a reminder of the sheer tonnage of wood and stone Walsingham and his people handled. All right, it took the better part of a couple of hundred years to build the whole cathedral, and then another twenty-six to clear the rubble of the fallen central tower, cut into the fabric, install the lantern and clean everything up, but looking at the size of that lantern, walking round it, looking at the vast height of the interior – twenty-six years hardly seems very long considering that it was all done by muscle power.

The foundations of the cathedral were laid in 1083, but its origins go back to a Saxon king with the odd name of Anna. He was slain at Blythburgh and in 670 one of his daughters, Etheldreda, inherited her first husband's lands in the Fens, including the 'Isle of Eels', eventually fleeing there from Northumberland and her second husband to found a nunnery and live an austere life as the first abbess. She was made a saint and almost three centuries later King Edgar founded a Benedictine abbey at Ely. Her story can be followed in the carvings on the corbels that jut from the lantern's eight supporting piers.

Inside the cathedral it is the soaring painted ceiling of the nave and the light from the Octagon that catch the eye. Outside – and it is outside that I really like to be at Ely – the College surrounds just have to be walked, for here is what remains of the monastery. Go out from the great tower and first there is the Bishop's House, then the Prior's, incorporating parts of the monks' refectory, all mixed up with the Kings' School. It is largely a walk along a blank dark stone wall, then suddenly there is the large square mass of the monastery gate and through it, to the right, the old tithe barn.

Kings' School was founded by King Alfred. Edward the Confessor was a boy there. It is that old. Turn sharp left through the gates and there, close by the Bishop's House, is Prior Crauden's Chapel, entered by a little door that leads to a short spiral staircase and a small platform looking down on to the entrance to part of the Priory where boys in dark suits come and go. The door here leads directly into one of the daintiest and most personal chapels I have ever visited, sunshine pouring in from the clear glass in the west window, the stained glass over the altar glowing and the lovely stonework almost as pale as in the Lady Chapel. It was built in 1321 and I think the height of it makes it appear smaller and more personal than it really is, for this is the Kings' School Chapel.

Another, broader path leads from the great gate towards the sundial on the south side of the cathedral itself. To the right the green fields seen from the top of the tower fall steeply almost to the river. It is this open space and the sharp fall of the ground that makes the outline of the cathedral so particularly impressive from Isleham and all the fenland to the south-east. The wall of the Bishop's House has small blind window arches, the old refectory building behind heavily buttressed, almost like a church, and Firmary Lane, running east to a glimpse of traffic, has big blind arched windows along the south side. That walk round the cathedral confirms what the view from the tower has already indicated, that the town is circumscribed by the limits of the island's Jurassic outcrop, so that Ely faces the same problem as so many of the East Anglian villages, a place of worship quite out of proportion to the size of the community and heavily dependent, therefore, on the generosity of visitors.

Back to the tower for a moment, to look northwards from this lofty vantage point, out to where the waters of the Great Ouse, the Bedford and the Nene are carried high to the Wash between artificial banks, then to walk round the tower, carefully marking the miles of sunken flat criss-crossed by ribbons of water pale under a wide sky ... this is a patchwork of some of the most priceless land in England. And much of

The surrounds of the Cathedral, normally the Close, are called the College; the building to the right is the old grain store, now Kings' College dining-room.

Beyond the College, there are meadows dropping away towards the river Ouse.

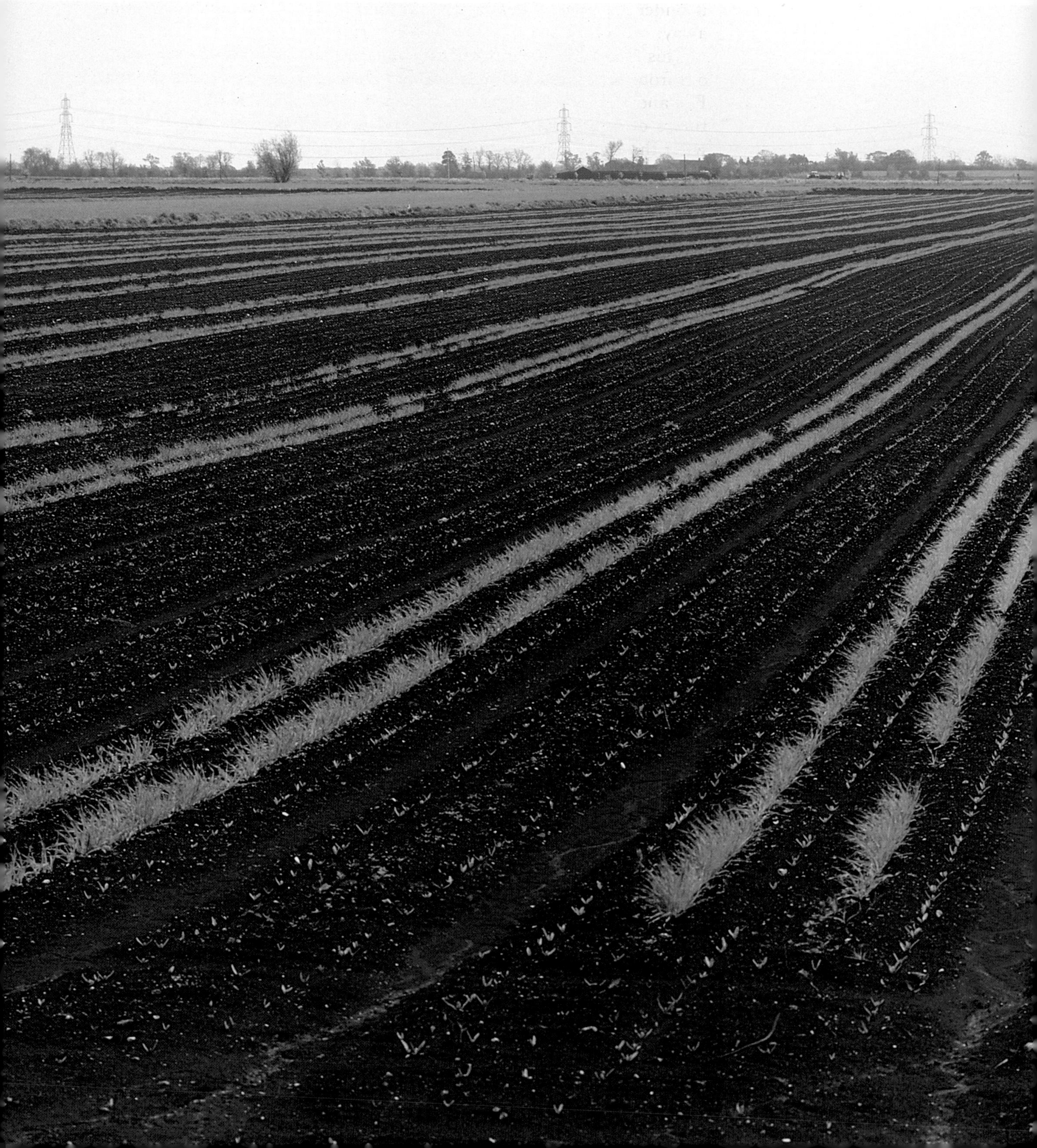

it under sentence of death, for it is land that is shrinking and wasting away.

This is not like the Broadland country, man-made waters spreading out from the marsh and meadowland of sluggish rivers. This is the real Fenland – the Black Fens – a drowned land that farmers and adventurers of capital have reclaimed. And it was done without thought of what the effect would ultimately be. Wicken Fen, which is open to the public and only a few hundred yards down a lane in Wicken itself, illustrates the danger of fooling around with the water table. This marsh, preserved in its natural state by the National Trust, is already markedly higher than the wasted peatlands surrounding it. Perhaps I should add that last time I was there the blackboard notice announced that the walks should not be attempted without gumboots!

Since this is a book of enthusiasms, it goes against the grain to introduce a sour note. But ever since I had a long discussion with the Dutch *Waterstaat* minister before embarking on a tour of the newly-reclaimed lands of the Zuider Zee, I have been fascinated by the problem of what he very aptly described as 'water housekeeping'. For the Low Countries, it has been very much a question of keeping the sea at bay, and latterly of shortening the defensive coastline by the linking of islands and the erection of barrages. The water housekeeping problems this created proved enormous, from the need for a ring of lakes to maintain the water level in Amsterdam, and so prevent exposure to air of the wooden piles that support the city, to the maintenance of a sufficient flow of fresh water to keep the sea's tidal flow at bay and the salt content of the polders at an agriculturally tolerable level.

Unfortunately, too little was known about water housekeeping in 1629 when the owners of large estates headed by Bedford cast acquisitive eyes on what they regarded as unproductive swamplands. Drained, they would produce oats and wheat for cattle and humans, flax and hemp for clothing and sails (including the sails of windmills!), and newly won pastures would fatten the beef herds being driven south for the London market. The Dutch were brought into it, of course, which would have been fine for the silt areas around the Wash, but Cornelius Vermuyden had no idea that the peat fens, once drained, would waste away.

About half the fenland country is peat and it is not just a problem of the peat shrinking as the water is drained out of it like a squeezed sponge. There is oxidisation as well, so that it goes on shrinking, though at a much reduced rate, shrinking they say the height of a man in the life of a man.

Peat itself is a product of what soil experts describe as biological degradation. Like the humus solids in sewage works it can't be degraded

Here we are in the real Fens, not the Marshlands of the north, but the Black Fen country, where the dark peat has grown such fine crops over three centuries and more. 153

further, though biochemical reduction by oxidisation will occur whenever it is allowed to dry and become exposed to the atmosphere – which occurs, of course, at the surface as soon as a crop is harvested and the fen prepared for the next sowing. Peat is just about the ultimate in crop raising material, but since retention of water is its main asset a lot of fertilisers have to be used so that farming it is almost a hydroponic operation, particularly as one of peat's most outstanding properties is its ability to absorb chemicals from water.

The shrinkage and the wasting of the peat means that the problems of drainage are ever increasing, ever more costly. It is like inflation, a cumulative disaster, with the water that was being channelled to the sea flowing back into the newly shrunken peat lands. Faced in less than half a century with what was still thought to be no more than a problem of dried out peat, horse and wind-powered lifts and pumps were introduced to get the water out of the shrunken lands and into rivers and drainage channels that now had to be banked up. At one time there were over 8,000 windmills pumping water to keep the land from flooding. But wind power only pumps water when the wind is blowing, and with the land still wasting away, there came a time, about two centuries ago, when windmills could no longer cope.

What saved the farmers then was the invention of the steam engine. Later the drainage system was switched from coal to diesel and electric power, the cost rising all the time. Covering some 1,300 square miles, the Fens are the most intensively farmed land in the country, the individual holdings relatively small in the black peat country, very much larger in the silt lands to the north where there are many more villages, and where in some places, particularly around Sutton Bridge and the King's Lynn–Sleaford road, there is considerable ribbon development. On the peatlands, however, there is no ribbon development, no urban sprawl, no factories, no airports, nothing that cannot be supported by the fragile peat; here it is only on the old island areas that there are any towns or villages, or where the 'shoreline' thrusts long, low fingers into the peatlands, as at Haddenham on the road from Newmarket to March, a vital peninsular with vistas of shrunk peat running away on either side.

Back in Saxon times, and right into the Middle Ages, this was a water world where people lived off fish and eels, game and wildfowl, a primitive, self-sufficient world where stilts were as common as walking sticks and the annual visit to some community that had a market the sole relief from virtual isolation. It was a life that did not interfere with the delicate balance between water and land. It could have gone on for ever, self-perpetuating and entirely natural.

A Norman knight, entertained by Hereward in 1073, reported back to King William that the French could sit on Haddenham field blockading Ely for another seven years so rich was the soil around the island, meres and bogs protecting it like a wall, an abundance of farm animals, wild stag, doe and goat, and in the water round innumerable eel, great 'water

wolves', pickerel, perch, roach, burbot or eelpout, lampreys, also an abundance of geese, gulls, coots, divers, water-crows, herons and duck. In short, though the life was hard, the Fen-men were well provided for, which is why they fought so hard for the preservation of their habitat.

But for a personal glimpse of what it was like to live on an island smallholding of a few acres at the time the landowners first began fooling around with the water table, I cannot do better than quote from *Ethelreda's Tale* written by Norah Lofts, who died recently, one of the most internationally successful of the many writers who live in East Anglia. She had always been closely connected with Bury St Edmunds and the majority of her novels were backgrounded on historical research and her knowledge of this part of England. The opening of the tale, which is one of six in her novel, *The House at Old Vine*, gives a heart-rending account of how it was for a girl in the Fens, around 1670, watching her father work himself to death in a desperate effort to save his island plot, the marsh waters rising inexorably as faceless landowners miles away drained their estates and directed water elsewhere.

The world Ethelreda shared with her father was one in which nature provided all basic needs on a seasonal rotation. There were common lands, strips allocated to each family, and these provided lush grazing in summer when the river levels fell. Livestock might have to be ferried there by boat, but everybody had their due share of this rich communal land which provided meat and all manner of dairy produce. And in the summer larks and plovers were netted in their thousands. There was fish, eel and molluscs in plenty, wild fowl during the difficult winter months. There was peat for fuel, reeds for thatching and rushes for the floor. And those with a few island acres had crops and fruit, nuts and berries. All except the peat was renewed each season, so that, while the living could not be called rich, it was adequate and varied, a natural cycle of near self-sufficiency.

Ethelreda had a crucifix hung on a nail in the hut she and her father shared – 'The only single thing that wasn't plainly useful. We always touched it before going fishing or snaring, or on a journey.' They called it Touchwood and it was one of their rituals. But they had others:

> On the night of the fifth new moon of the year we had the Beltane Fire and cooked a cake of barley bread in the middle of it. The fire was always made of last year's rushes and burned very fiercely; if the cake of bread was cooked through when the fire died down, then that was a good sign; if it was still doughy, then the fishing and everything else would be bad . . . When Father took the boat and threaded his way into Ely he always took a good load. There were rush mats which we

Railway lines running out across the Fens from Shippea Hill. This is to the east of Ely and shows how the rails are now above the shrunken peat lands on either side.

had woven in the long winter evenings . . . smoked eels which could only be properly prepared over a peat fire and will then keep almost for ever, and behind the boat great bundles of reeds, strung out along a rope and floating.

But he never brought back news from Ely – 'our talk was different; we used many different words, and even those that we had in common with the people of Ely and the outside world we pronounced in our own way.' And it is to Ely that she rows her boat after the death of her father and the inundation of their land.

That was how isolated people were in the undrained Fens before the Fen Tigers fought their losing battle against the farmer-adventurers and their drainage channels and windmills. What followed was inevitable, so that Charles Kingsley was writing just over a hundred years ago: 'Gone are the ruffs and reeves, spoonbills, bitterns, avocets . . . Ah well, at least we shall have wheat and mutton instead, and no more typhus and ague.' It was a spartan existence, of course, and only those with iron constitutions lived into old age, 'and yet fancy may linger, without blame, over the shining meres, the golden reed-beds, the countless waterfowl, the strange gaudy insects, the wild nature, the mystery, the majesty – for mystery and majesty there were – which haunted the deep fens for many a hundred years.'

This was the world of that mad punctuation-free primitive of a poet John Clare, whose feeling for nature and careful observation of a bird seen usually in jinking flight combined to produce this:

Here tempests howl
   Around each flaggy plot
   Where they who dread mans sight the waterfowl
   Hide and are frighted not.

'I long for scenes where man has never trod . . .' he wrote in a poem called 'I am' ('yet what I am none cares, or knows'). 'Untroubling and untroubled where I lie:- The grass below – above the vaulted sky.' That last line is the Fens just drained and cattle grazing. In a recent Fen-set novel, *Waterland*, Graham Swift writes of the Great Ouse – 'Ouse. Say it. *Ouse*. Slowly. How else can you say it? A sound which exudes slowness. A sound which suggests the slow, sluggish, forever oozing thing it is – Ouse, Ouse, Oooooouse . . .'

Some draining of the Fens began as far back as Roman days. Maybe the Saxons did some draining, too, around the great Iron Age earthwork of Stones Camp near March, for instance. But whatever in the way of

A fen murk in early July. This is very typical of the way the North Sea affects the weather in this part of East Anglia.

drainage was achieved in those days, all was allowed to revert to swamp in the Dark Ages. There is in the middle of Britain, wrote St Guthlac, founder of the Benedictine Abbey at Crowland about the time of Bede, a 'hideous fen of huge bigness, oft-times clouded with moist and dark vapours, a place of great dreadfulness and solitude . . .' In this period the monks did a certain amount of reclamation, largely to keep the islands on which they built their monasteries clear of floodwaters, but the real drainage of the Fens did not start until the seventeenth century. The Dutch came over. The Restoration was in full swing, King Charles and the Duke of Bedford the chiefest of the so-called Adventurers with Cornelius Vermuyden appointed architect of the whole ambitious project. The main canal was seventy feet wide and ran from Earith to Denver, a distance of twenty-one miles. This became known as the Old Bedford River. Twenty years later it was supplemented by another cut, the New Bedford River, which was 100 feet wide, and there was the Forty Foot Drain running east and west to act as a feeder. And in the newly-reclaimed land the adventurers raised crops of flax, hemp, oats and wheat the like of which had never been seen before.

But peatlands shrink most rapidly on first exposure to the air, so that it was not long before windmills were needed to pump the water into the new cuts, and since the country bordering the Fens was well forested with hardwoods, material for the construction of windmills was readily available. First there would be one windmill, then two, then three –

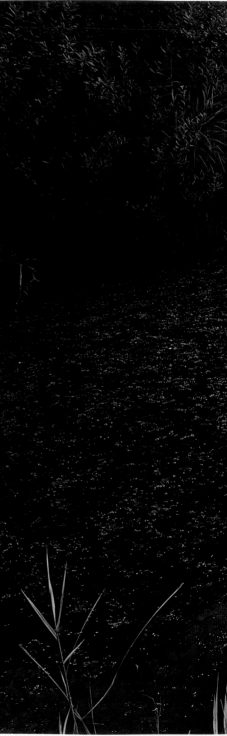

Here are two details from Wicken Fen, which the National Trust maintains in its undrained state. Caution: there be insects here!

finally banks of them, and being built of wood, they were movable. It was only after the switch to steam that they built brick engine houses, the remains of which can still be seen dotted around the Fens. In addition to the Forty Foot Drain, there was the Sixteen Foot, the Twenty Foot, and all the older drains known as *eaus* (ees), one of the largest and oldest being Popham's Eau. And as the peat shrank, in addition to windmills, a system of washlands was introduced. These were fallow meadowlands into which flood waters could be directed in periods of unusually heavy rain. The most obvious of these is the narrow nineteen-mile long strip between the old and new Bedford cuts. Here, and in all the washlands, eels thrive, growing fat on the earthworms that come to the surface when the waters flood in.

The final stage of the Fen drainage was a cut taking the waters of the Nene into the Wash, and it was finished off with ornamental lighthouses either side of the new river mouth. They look a little tired now, and so do the cottages attached to them, their gardens hidden behind protective hedges so that the effect is one of solitude in the immensity of a mud-banked waterworld where the only seaward company is the gaunt giraffe-like heads of drag cranes. The lighthouses themselves are shaped like the tapering stumps of windmills, each wearing a little circular leaden cap with a chimney pot incongruously sticking up out of the centre of it. It was the eastern one that Peter Scott leased to keep and study wild geese and, though he had never seen it, this was the spark that fired Paul

These are the two ornamental lighthouses marking the emergence of the river Nene into the Wash; we are looking south towards Sutton Bridge and the left-hand one is where Peter Scott had his first bird sanctuary. The close-up is of the other lighthouse on the western side of the river mouth.

Gallico's imagination, resulting in that little wartime classic, *The Snow Goose*, the painter a hunchback who was followed to Dunkirk by the wild goose whose life he had saved. It was a story to bring a lump to the throat, particularly at the time it was written, a sort of East Coast fairy tale that I read before ever I came to live in the land Gallico had written about. Since then, on two barge matches, I have sailed with a skipper so gnarled and weatherbeaten, so much a man of the East Coast estuaries, he has merged in my mind with the recollection of that *Snow Goose* artist.

The Wildfowl Trust at Welney does for the fenland waterbirds much the same thing as the Otter Trust does for otters in Broadland, providing an introduction to both resident and migrant populations, and for those who are sensitive to nature a greater awareness of the life around them. And on the other side of the Fens, near Peakirk just north of Peterborough, the Trust have a ringing station in Borough Fen, operating a decoy that has been in regular use for over three centuries.

In 1851 one of the iron columns taken from the Crystal Palace was driven into the peat of Denton Fen. It was driven flush with the ground immediately after Whittelsey Mere, the largest of the open waters, had been drained. Known as the Holme Post, it is still there, but you won't be bending to count the inches it now stands proud of the ground, you'll be gazing up at it, for it now stands proud by well over a dozen feet. That is the measure of the peat's shrinkage in the land of the Great Level.

Bearing in mind that the black peat soil is ninety-five per cent, some say as much as ninety-eight per cent, water, it is hardly surprising that in places the residual two to five per cent of degraded matter has disappeared altogether leaving the underlying soil exposed. And not only the clay, and strips of gravel that mark old tide limits, are exposed, or the silt of streams flooding down from the higher hinterland, but also the stark calcareous white of the powdered shell of molluscs deposited in the mud of old meres. But it was the roddons that really brought the shrinkage home to me. I couldn't believe it the first time I found myself on one of these banks that meander across the fenscape. You will find them wherever there has been an old riverbed, for they *are* the riverbed, and often they are the only hard-standing around, the river detritus of silt and gravel standing proud in a land of shrunken peat. It is the roddons that account for isolated farmsteads standing raised above the surrounding farmland, for the odd track, or a drift of yellow gravel across black peat soil. They also account for many of the undulations in fen roads, the sudden unyielding base providing a wave or hump that traffic will make worse as the peat on which the road generally rests is compacted ever tighter.

And there is another factor besides shrinkage and wastage. It is wind-blow. It happens almost every year to some extent, for it is very seldom a March goes by in the Fens without it blows bitter cold from the north-east. One March in particular, in the late sixties – I shall

This peacock seems strangely located for a bird not usually associated with water since this is Denver on the Great Ouse, where the original sluice gates to check the river's flow seaward were built by Vermuyden.

never forget that year, for I had just planted fourteen acres of Corsican pine in our Suffolk woodlands, over 17,000 trees and I lost the lot.

The ground was already dry when it started to blow from the east, and what that bitter wind did to the Great Level heartland of the Fens was as bad as anything that has ever happened in the dead dustbowl of America. This is how I described it at the time:

The wind is rising as we approach the Fens, the black rich earth light and friable in the brittle sunlight, dusty almost. Suddenly, somewhere, a particle of that soil shifts, jumps to another, dislodges that, and in a moment the topsoil is quietly blowing, drifting close to the ground like the start of a sandstorm in the deserts of Arabia. Soon we are motoring through a sepia haze, and as the dust storm rises and the soil really begins to blow, the whole surface of the land seems to be on the move.

To complete the picture, vehicles felt their way through the murk, their lights on; the lights were on at midday in the little rail junction town of March and in places the soil was building up on the roads at the rate of nine inches an hour. Drifts three feet deep formed. Men, fighting a losing battle to keep the highways open, wore goggles and war-surplus gas masks, muffled their heads in scarves, while the tide of black dust flowed like quicksilver from shovel and bulldozer blade. It lasted six days, from March 15th to March 21st, and later, when rain came, the fertiliser in the soil turned the dust to slime.

In the Great Level, and all through the fenland farms, hundreds of miles of dykes and ditches became clogged with drifts of silt up to six feet deep. It wasn't only the topsoil that blew, it was seed and fertiliser as well. No less than 30,000 acres had to be re-drilled. One big farm alone lost 200 acres of carrots and eighty acres of wheat. On another, the farmer described his fields of lettuces as bowling towards him like beach balls. One man cleared 200 tons from his drive and his wife sucked up five vacuum bags of soil dust from inside the house. Yet another, who lost ten acres of special onion seed, reported the top half inch of soil blown into the dyke – 'and on the same day I got a bill for the onion seed!'

Nevertheless, the Fens do have a leisure aspect. The slow-flowing rivers with their cuts and drains are great places for the coarse fisherman, ideal for competitions. Coming down from the north I usually break away from what used to be called the Great North Road, heading home by way of Wisbech and Breckland, or else through the Great Level flats between March and Ely down through Newmarket or Bury St Edmunds. Once I struck the lower route on the day of what I think was the *News of the World* fishing competition. I have never seen such an astonishing riparian sight, coloured and striped, but predominantly green, umbrellas set rib-to-rib for what seemed miles. The fish they were after are much

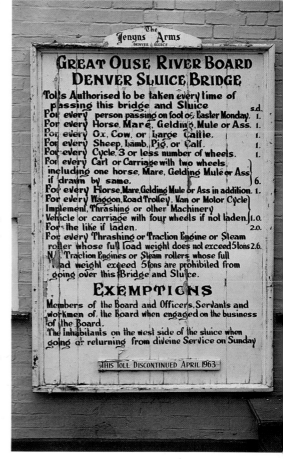

An old River Board notice at the Jenyns Arms inn. Boaters tend to gather here.

the same as those to be found in the Broadland rivers – perch, pike and carp, roach, bream and rudd. But I didn't see anyone actually catch anything and anyway it doesn't happen to be my idea of fun. Yet those fishermen, lost to the world in contemplation of their floats, had clearly discovered one of the best sedatives in the world, the marsh-reclaimed vista under its vast expanse of sky so quiet and restful, the water in front of them so still, and the rain falling gently on their umbrellas.

In June this lower route is full of elder bloom, the big white overblown heads in bright contrast to the lush green of barley and wheat, and the tangled undergrowth of the drainage system. On the banks of that system grow the inevitable alder and willow, also the green-winged orchid, and the dykes and waterways are full of milfoil, duckweed, water violets, water lilies, great yellow cress – believe it or not, but Wicken Fen boasts 267 plant species, also 72 sorts of mollusc and 212 different types of spider. There are trees here, so that it is not so monotonous as it is nearer the Wash. Nevertheless, the slightest rise in the flatness of the land is a relief, the old islands standing out like hills, but all half-concealed by the exuberance of growth, so that even Ely can be surprised coming across the Hundred Foot Drain by Mepal and Sutton. Cambridge is very close here, almost a part of the Fens, the flat ridge of farming land north of the old Roman road to Huntingdon showing very little rise above the shrunken peat level to the north.

Until recently the Fens were not regarded as archaeologically important, but the shrinkage of the peat and the use of aerial photography is now uncovering sites that go back more than 5,000 years. In just one field near Haddenham two Roman temples have been found, an Iron Age burial mound, a Bronze Age barrow and a Neolithic causeway camp – a concentration of finds probably unique.

Driving south across the top of the Fens, through Spalding and the billiard-flat silt farms of the Marshlands, I once caught the bulb country in tulip time. Hundreds upon hundreds of acres, every type of tulip, all in great bands of colour, brilliant in sun and wind. It is a marvellous spectacle, and since the flowerheads need to be picked to save the bulbs from wasting their energy in seeding, the intricate floats massed with blooms that appear at the flower parade in early May are a great sight. This parade was started in the late fifties, but I have never been in the Marshlands on that particular day. Perhaps just as well for the theme of Maritime England brought seventeen floats out on to the four-mile parade route and a crowd of over 400,000. Some of the floats were a dozen feet tall and sixty feet long, and with up to half a million tulip heads held in by wire mesh on each float the nautical images must have been of superb brilliance.

The Marshlands are not the Fens proper. There is no peat here, it is all silt land, much of it recovered from the sea by the natural build-up of river sediments and only spasmodically subject to flooding. The land is firmer and there are lots of those chunky, square-towered Marshland

The Denver corn-grinding mill is particularly fine; the best is probably at Fring.
Most windmills in the Fens were for pumping water.

churches, some of them dating back to the thirteenth century, several quite large, a mixture of ashlar and other stone with some brick, very little flint. Also, the land here is higher than the shrunken peatlands of the Black Fen country so that the huge volume of water drained by the Nene, the Ouse, the Welland and the Wissey from a hinterland that stretches almost into the Midlands is being forced to do the impossible and flow uphill. Hence the pumping stations and the high banks that stand up like reservoir embankments above the flat of the land.

It is, in fact, an Alice-in-Wonderland world and an idea of the immensity of the work necessary to control the flow of that water can be seen if you turn down Sluice Road in Wiggenhall St Germans and take a look at the colossal sluice gates and pumping station erected by the Middle Level Commissioners in 1934. This is the largest pumping station in the country and lifts the Middle Level waters into the Great Ouse. The extent of the lift can be measured by the height of the river's bank, most clearly, and most pleasurably, revealed at nearby Wiggenhall St Peters where the ruins of the church nestle right against them, the top of the roofless nave and chancel walls, all covered in wild flowers, standing about level with the top of the bank. There is another view of the St Germans Pumping Station, from the opposite direction, at the Eau brink bridge just outside Wiggenhall St Germans, and another indication of the lift some two miles to the south where the fine, intact church of Wiggenhall St Mary Magdalen is also nestled close against

The Brinks at Wisbech, stretched along both banks of the Nene, are like a Dutch painting, particularly the North Brink which contains some of the best of the town's Georgian architecture.

The Crescent in the centre of Wisbech is now virtually the cultural hub of the town with library and theatre.

Peckover House, built in 1722 and then acquired by Jonathan Peckover who founded the local banking firm of Gurney, Birkbeck & Peckover, now belongs to the National Trust.

the bank and the bridge over the Great Ouse.

There are boats, of course, on the waterways, some of them far inland. Not as many as there were, for in the days of steampower and coal every drain where there was a pumping station had to be supplied with bargeloads of fuel. Wisbech, the most superb of marshland towns and the one-time seaport capital of the Fens, is growing as a port again and some use is being made of canal boats for the heavier cargo such as timber.

Wisbech reminds me of the Nyhavn in Copenhagen with its palatial merchant houses lining the waterway. It is an old Wash seaport of sailing days and whichever way you come into the town, whether from Sutton Bridge or King's Lynn, the approach is along the Nene riverbank, so that you have a view of the Georgian architecture of the Brinks across the water. And the nice thing about Wisbech is that the centre of it all just north-east of the bridge comes together in a close huddle around the church, the castle, the museum, and the flowery little Georgian circle of the Crescent and Union Place.

There are also holiday boats in the Fens now, in appearance something between the narrow boat of our own canals and the more barge-like type developed by Britain for the Midi Canal in France. But boats are still a relatively rare sight outside of the main arteries, the fenland drains mostly ribbons of empty water that reflect the sky and in summer look as though they are in imminent danger of being overwhelmed by the lush vegetation.

The Nene, flowing under the swing bridge at Sutton and out into the Wash between those two lighthouses, has spread its silt so far that Wisbech is now almost a dozen miles from the sea. The outflow from the largest of the rivers, the Great Ouse, has, on the other hand, been sufficient to keep that river's port much nearer to open water. The Old and the New Bedford rivers flow this way, the Nar, the Wissey, the Little Ouse, the Lark, the Cam and the old West Ouse itself, also the Middle Level cut – a lot of water! Thus, the two Denver sluices (the new one was completed as recently as 1959) drain the water from almost 350,000 hectares of land. It is the sheer volume of this water, which is now carried the eleven miles from Denver to Lynn by the Great Ouse Relief Channel as well as by the river itself, and is in places wider than the river, that has kept Lynn waterway well scoured so that it has continued as an active port since very early days. In fact, it was the lamprey-eating John, who tried to cross the silt shore of the Wash and lost his baggage wagons and the crown jewels to the incoming tide, who, in 1204, gave Lynn its Charter, and you can still see it – and all the others granted since.

Unlike Ely, where virtually all the interesting buildings are ecclesiastical, King's Lynn has a considerable range of civic and commercial buildings. I always think of it as the seaboard counterpart of Norwich, the grey centre of the town packed with architectural interest, both medieval and Georgian. Developers down the ages have treated it much

more kindly than Ipswich, or Great Yarmouth even.

The priory, on which the white limestone church of St Margaret's now stands, goes back to Bishop de Losinga and 1119, St Nicholas was started in 1146, Red Mount's brick octagon dates from 1485, a wayside chapel on an artificial mound for pilgrims on their way to Walsingham – quite fascinating in its construction; there's Greyfriars founded in 1230, its tall octagonal lantern tower still standing, the Saturday Market and the hall of the Guild of the Holy Trinity, 1421, built you would think by a crazy draughts player, all chequered flint flushwork and stone in front. Medieval buildings alongside those of a later date, but all merging in a harmonious whole so that one's impression is of history unfolding in the fabric of the buildings.

The whole centre of the town, though a little severe as one would expect of a seafaring place wedged between marshland and the bleak North Shore, comes together in a way that makes it somehow different from any port one has ever been in before. The little alleyways, the glimpsed courtyards, and always the river. Almost every year it seems to flood the town. Stand in the entrance door of St Margaret's and measure the 1978 tidemark against your body, then visualise the streets and the church awash and yourself wading through it with the tidewater up to your buttocks. Look at the doors along Nelson, Queen and King streets, every doorway edged with wooden slides to take wooden slats as an attempt to hold the flood waters of a high tide at bay and keep it out of the houses.

Lynn was a port long before Hereward's defence of Ely. It grew into an international port on the back of Norfolk wool. Two centuries later 'new drapery' cloth, and the close connections it developed with the Hanseatic League through trade with Denmark, had made it so important that Henry VIII renamed it King's Lynn. The League's own sample yard, one of only four Hanseatic 'steelyards' in Britain, operated from 1475 until it was bought almost three centuries later by a Lynn merchant, and even then he bought it out of the joint ownership of the burgomasters of Bremen, Hamburg and Lubeck.

But what I think is so extraordinary, considering the shallow, sand-banked nature of the Wash, is that at this very moment it is experiencing the same upsurge in trade as those two other enterprising East Anglian ports, Ipswich and Felixstowe. And yet, like most other Norfolk towns, there are hardly any high buildings, everything huddled together and crouched close to the ground as though for protection against the north-east wind. And if anybody wants to know what the port was like in the days of sail then the little Purfleet basin behind the Custom House gives

---

Flood markers on the right of the entrance to St Margaret's show the extent by which the January 31, 1953, King's Lynn level was topped by that of January 11, 1978.

an idea. Last time we were there it was full of good old-fashioned silt and there were three open boats lying derelict against the north wall, also an old single-masted cargo boat that looked like an abandoned Billy Boy stuck there in the ooze in front of the old warehouse belonging to Peatling & Cawdron, the Lynn wine merchants.

The three great treasures of Lynn are the Cup and the Sword, both supposed to have belonged to King John, and the Red Register, which is the record of commercial transactions with their Baltic and Scandinavian trading posts and is one of the oldest paper books in existence. The Cup is the most exciting of the three – to me at any rate. In Lynn for the Festival as guest speaker at one of Christina Foyle's literary luncheons, I was allowed to hold it in my hands, and into my mind flashed a picture of that night when the baggage was lost – rain and wind, and the tide making across the shallows fast as a carthorse could move, and this cup . . . how did it survive? Or is it all just another story that has been passed on down half a dozen centuries, like the treasure of Bury St Edmunds? The style is supposed to date it a century later and nothing to do with John, but sometimes artist-craftsmen produce a piece that is in advance of their time. No matter, it is very beautiful, and also very fragile, for the translucent mauve enamel is liable to chip and flake.

The smell of the sea is in the air and the feel of the town is strangely 'frontier', the same feel you get in any northern port when the wind comes straight from the arctic ice. I have always had a sense of adventure when visiting Lynn, a feeling almost of exhilaration. Something I do not feel down there to the south in the Fens proper. I am conscious only of their strangeness and an uneasy certainty that something has gone very wrong with it. Like a plant affected by a hormone spray, the Fens are a mutation. They are also, like the Broads, unique, something not to be found anywhere else in the British Isles. These two areas, and also the saltings of north Norfolk, where the tide reaches hungrily through the marshes to lap at boat quays that are far from the sea at low water . . . no wonder so many people regard those of us who live in East Anglia as almost a race apart.

And yet, the fact that Chatteris, in the heart of the Bedford Level, could be described as the 'undisputed capital of Carrotdom', and that the flat, sunken land around it also produces vast harvests of celery, peas, onions and parsnips, wheat, barley and oats, potatoes too and sugar beet, makes it something akin to the horticultural area of Essex close east of London. But the Fens are so much more remote, associated vaguely in people's minds with seal kills and stranded whales and the loss long ago of those crown jewels. And if the Fens seem remote now, how distant and alien they must have seemed in the days before steam! A stage cart taking a week from Colchester to London in the mid 1700s would surely have taken upwards of three weeks to make the journey from places like Chatteris, Wisbech and Downham Market, or even from Ely, and that only if it could get through the clays.

A glimpse through the archway into one of those courtyards that are so typical of old King's Lynn.

The Customs House at the north end of King Street, originally built in 1683 as the Merchants' Exchange, is still in use.

In the best time of the year it was different. Between August and October in the early 1700s geese as well as turkeys were making the journey *on foot*, feeding on grass and stubble as they went, the turkeys with their feet sometimes hardened by the application of hot pitch. Defoe says that a 'prodigious number were brought up to London in droves

from the furthest part of Norfolk, even from the fenn-country, about Lynn, Downham, Wisbech and the Washes, as also from all the east side of Norfolk and Suffolk.' And he adds, ' 'tis very frequent now to meet droves with a thousand, sometimes two thousand in a drove.'

It has been said that this marvellous, inveterate traveller was too

The building with the strangely chequered front is the Guildhall erected five-and-a-half centuries ago for the Guild of Holy Trinity.

gullible. It is certainly true that East Anglians, like many country folk, take pleasure in gulling the 'foreigner'. But Defoe was a reporter, in my view an accurate one. No man would spend the last years of his life in such a compulsive outpouring unless he was a born journalist; it was in this, his most experienced period, between 1724 and 1726 that he wrote the three volumes of his *Tour thro' the Whole Island of Great Britain*. He was prolific – at least 300 publications, as well as contributing to a lot of the periodicals of the time – but he was no hack. When it is hearsay he usually says so, and when it appears he is being taken for a ride, he is probably only repeating the story because it is too good to let pass.

For instance, coming up into East Anglia from the great castle at Tilbury by way of Leigh in the early 1700s, he reports nothing for miles but the 'continued level of unhealthy marshes called the Three Hundreds' till he came to the Chelmer and the Blackwater, which he described as making a large 'firth or inlet of the sea' called Malden-Water. He then goes on to talk about fowling in those Essex marshes, the enormous number of birds sent up to London, and of the ague which the fowlers contracted, adding with wry humour, 'which they find a heavier load than the fowls they have shot.'

The ague, incidentally, was then the medical term for malaria, a disease that was prevalent in the Fens and other low-lying areas of England, a fact which often comes as a shock to those of us who have only taken their anti-malarial tablets in hot countries. And if Defoe's informants are to be believed the ague was a killer for those who were not immune. In the Three Hundreds he was told the men went into the uplands for their wives, the girls there being prettier, fresher complexioned and altogether more vivacious. This was hearsay, of course, as was the statement that an upland wife didn't last above a couple of years down in the fogs of the marshes. The man who told him that claimed to have got through about a dozen and a half wives! In the Fens proper, before the draining, the women would have been made of sterner stuff. But whether they were comely, ah, that is a different matter. And the young men, the Fen Tigers, what were they like? No itinerant daubers went painting through the Fens so the best we can do is look closely at the faces carved and sculpted in Ely and in some of the old churches and monasteries, and talk to the people who live there now, ruddy-faced and independent, some of them tow-headed as a result of the Dutch connection.

But still the Fens to me are an alien land; I could never live there, not in the bleak peatland with its drains and its furious growth. But the Marshlands, the silt soil north of the region, with their prairie-like appearance, their gas stations and grain silos, their very definite frontier atmosphere, that is a different matter. This is all sea reclaimed, a landward extension of the Wash, so that to cross it all you ever needed was the sun or the stars to guide you, and no polar airstream sending a tidal surge to overwhelm you!

A grain ship unloading alongside King's Lynn's South Quay; in a high wind the swans have a field day!

8. Those lovely, lovely churches

On a bright May evening, orchard and cottage garden luminous with the pink-white of apple blossom, the tang of a dying sea breeze in the air, we drove out to one of those little churches that seems to belong to the people whose land surrounds it, so close it stands to house or farm buildings. From the road above the gravel pit we looked across fields of rape, lemon yellow in the sharp light, to the farm's roofs just topped by the little round Saxon tower, red tiles and grey flint against the hard blue sky. The road we turned up led nowhere but to the church and the farm. The yard was spotless, machinery all tidied away, barn doors shut, and the grass new-mown.

The church was built of flint, like the little round tower. Most of these churches are flint. Flints lay in the fields and on the beaches, they were the cheapest material available. Now the cheapest material is cement and sadly a lot of the flint has been rendered. But on that bracingly chill evening of exquisite beauty nothing jarred, the grass in the little valley dropping away at our feet, long oak fences and cows grazing black and white against the green – a scene of ineffable serenity.

And then we went into the church and listened to Leclair, Beethoven, Rawsthorne and Dvorak – two violins and a viola. The church was very simple, just the tower, nave and chancel with a wood roof of course and old wooden pews finely carved, the wood acting as an absorbent sounding box. The acoustics were superb, the music swelling and filling God's house with sound, but no echo, the tones exact.

In the interval there was wine, and from the porch we looked west along the length of the little valley to a lake and a planting of poplars, the winter wheat and rape a patchwork of green and yellow with the square tower of our own church just visible through a screen of poplars marching across the horizon like soldiers in single file with fresh green banners flying. The name Scott on some headstone was a reminder that this was Old Drapery country where families from the Outer Isles had been brought down to weave the wool centuries ago.

It took my mind back down the years to another recital in another wool church; Yehudi Menuhin in the great 'cathedral' of Thomas the

The church of Thomas the Rich at Lavenham, built in the fifteenth century on the profits of the wool industry. The exterior stonework is as intricate as the carvings of an ivory chess set.

Rich in Lavenham where we had drunk our coffee in the interval sitting with the dead on damp headstones. A very different evening, the rain only just ceased, everything damp and soft, no wind, and the music of that incredible violin singing in our heads.

Recitals and concerts; the congregations may have diminished but at times the churches of East Anglia seem full of people and music. In the early years of the Aldeburgh Festival, besides the Jubilee Hall, the churches of Aldeburgh, Blythburgh, Framlingham and Orford were pressed into service, even Ely cathedral. And when the Snape Maltings burned, the Festival once again turned quite naturally to the great Blythburgh church for temporary housing of a part of its programme. In fact, Framlingham has a grand piano permanently stationed in the huge open-plan chancel beside all the over-elaborate effigies on the Howard family tombs. Serious music has been welcomed in many of the East Anglian churches, and not necessarily religious music or professional performers. A violin and cello we know come down from London each year with an orchestra of enthusiasts sixty-strong just for the sheer joy of playing together, not caring about an audience. At the other end of the spectrum there are the ecclesiastical choirs, Ely in particular, and King's College Chapel in Cambridge, now virtually synonymous with Christmas, the voices of its choristers in word and song going out all over the world.

The round tower of Aldham church standing apart from any buildings other than the farm. I often wonder whether this isolation of so many East Anglian churches was the effect of the Black Death.

178

Polstead, where witches were swum and Maria Marten was murdered – the Red Barn murder of Victorian melodrama.

This has meant that many who are not churchgoers, whilst enjoying the acoustics of lofty edifices of wood and stone and flint, have had the opportunity of absorbing the beauty and serenity of church interiors. There is no area in the country that has such an extraordinary number of churches with features of architectural importance, and because so much of it was broadleaved forest with a preponderance of oak it is in the main the woodwork that is of importance.

Nowhere in the world can you see roofs like these. Hammerbeam roofs with marvellous winged angels. And there are rood screens, some with loft still standing. But the screens have been more vulnerable to Puritan vandals, and those other, mainly Victorian, vandals of fashion and reconstruction, so that in many cases only a part of the tracery, or some painted panels, are left. But in a thousand or more churches something of oak remains, the carvings in most cases darkened by stain, but in some

Kedington – there is a crucifixion here that is Saxon, and inside, the many generations of the Barnardiston family seem gathered in petrified replica.

Boxford with its fine south porch. On the other side you will find a fourteenth-century wooden porch, very rare.

the wonderful silvery-grey of untreated age-old oak lightens the whole interior.

Outside of town and city, the old wool churches are the best known, the most frequently visited. Lavenham, which took forty years to build, should be seen from the outside. Stoke-by-Nayland, too – its splendid tower rising in steps to the four corner pinnacles, the whole bulk of it, thrust upwards on Tendring heights, a landmark as soon as you cross the Stour at Nayland; and its setting close in amongst the old houses of the village, Tudor on one side, Georgian on the other. There is a great carved door at the entrance which gives me a feeling of being transported back into the period every time I see it. Kersey, again for its setting, high above the village, its reflection in the watersplash, and a little gem of a south porch with a marvellous roof to it. Another south porch at Boxford, sadly in a poor state, but what is really interesting about this church is the old oak vaulting of the fourteenth-century wooden porch on the north side.

Nearby Groton, though much smaller and with hardly any village, is much better cared for, which is perhaps as it should be for it is from Groton that John Winthrop emigrated to America in 1630 where he founded the city of Boston in New England and was the first Governor of the State of Massachusetts. Americans still pay tribute. There must have been a whole batch of emigrants from this area of Suffolk – a close sailing friend of mine, an American, traces his family straight back to Stoke-by-Nayland. However, to my mind the finest of all the wool churches is the one we first saw – the church of the Holy Trinity standing solid and immensely impressive at the upper end of Long Melford's vast green, the grey stone a foil for the mellow Tudor brick of Melford Hall to the east, the interior of the Lady Chapel the equal of almost any of the shrines in the great cathedrals, and the flushwork everywhere of outstanding quality.

Before I try and pass on some of my wonder for the builders of these churches and the men who felled and worked and hoisted the great timbers and carved such remarkable figures, I must draw attention to a little Essex church on the threshold of East Anglia that is unique. It is the church of St Andrew at Greensted-juxta-Ongar, and it is important to see it before driving into the old oak forested lands to the north because then you know how the old Saxon wooden churches were built. This is the only one left and it is the oldest wooden church in the world. It has, of course, been restored and improved, but the dark timber walls of the nave are the same split oak logs that were used in the building of it in 845 and some of these may date back to an earlier church built in the seventh century.

Dedham, a lovely village in the Constable country where the church's flower festival became a great attraction.

The Saxon church was thatched, had no windows, only holes for ventilation, and was lit by torches. Scorch marks are still visible. Almost every century since the arrival of the Normans there has been alteration, but still the timber of the nave walls stands solid as a stockade, the rounded trunks shoulder to shoulder, all matched in size so that the impression is of a carefully selected grove of oaks felled at the same time. After being logged they were split so that they would present a flat surface on the inside. In the first church, which would have been built under the direction of St Cedd's missionaries, the timbers would have been set upright in the ground, but in the later building the Saxon carpenters tongued and grooved in order to lift the trunks off the ground and on to a horizontal timber or cill to achieve what is really a very early, very solid timber-frame building with at least some sort of foundation.

There is another church on the threshold of East Anglia, built of stone about the time that first wooden church was erected in a forest clearing, but the setting of it so utterly different, so very East Coast, that for me it has a much greater appeal. It stands on the south shore of the entrance to the Blackwater, its seventh-century nave virtually intact. Forget the bulk of Bradwell's nuclear power station no more than two miles away, turn your back on it and face seaward over the Dengie Flats and St Peter's Sands. You are looking out on a scene that has hardly changed from the time around 654 when St Cedd's converts to Christianity stripped part of the great fort of Orthona. This was one of that half circle of defence ports from Wash to Wight known as the Forts of the Saxon Shore; it had been built to guard the estuary entrance, and with the materials they erected the church of St Peter-ad-Murum right slap in the centre of the great bastioned wall, probably at the gateway. Rider Haggard, who lived at Ditchingham in Norfolk, was there four years after the great gale of 1897 which had flooded much of the land. 'Behind us lay a vast, drear expanse of land won from the ocean days bygone, bordered on the one side by the Blackwater and on the other by the Crouch rivers, and saved, none too well, from the mastery of the waves by the sloping earthen bank on which we stood.' And he goes on, 'In front, thousands of acres of grey mud where grew dull, unwholesome looking grasses. Far, far away on this waste expanse two tiny, moving specks, men engaged in seeking for samphire or some other treasure of the ooze-mud. Then the thin, white lip of the sea . . .'

Things have changed since Haggard's day, the flat clay shoulder separating the two estuaries – that 'drear expanse' – now prairie-

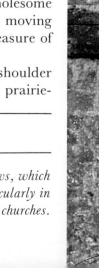

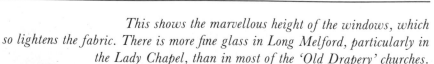

My favourite of all the 'wool churches' – Long Melford.

This shows the marvellous height of the windows, which so lightens the fabric. There is more fine glass in Long Melford, particularly in the Lady Chapel, than in most of the 'Old Drapery' churches.

184

cropped, the farms big with isolated brick houses each like a kraal surrounded by a huddle of grain silos. The track east from Bradwell village takes you past a pub with the improbable name of The Cricketers, and after that, if it's winter, you'll most likely be on your own. From the rough car park St Peter's is clearly visible, a stone barn of a place standing surprisingly high against the huge expanse of sky, the featureless land and the sea beyond.

There are oaks beside the track and in summer the green or gold of corn either side; to the left ships laid up in the Blackwater look as though they are stranded on dry land, and beyond them is Mersea Island and Clacton with the Naze just visible. Cedd came south after a successful conversion tour of the Midlands in 653, presumably by boat and presumably he landed at Orthona, the walls of which stood in a bastioned rectangle with the quay as it had been when it was a Roman port. No point in my going over the history of this place, however fascinating, for anyone visiting St Peter's will find it all there, meticulously recorded in H. Malcolm Carter's excellent booklet. I would think by now it has sold nearly 50,000 copies since it was first published in 1966, which gives some idea of the number of interested people who have made the pilgrimage to this remote headland, though it can't really be called a headland, for it stands barely three metres above the salt flats held by the Essex Naturalist Trust and known as Bradwell Cockle Spit Nature Reserve. There is even a bird watchers' house nestled in the copse just south-east of the chapel.

Despite its loneliness, the door to St Peter's seems always open, the interior as homely as the barn it was once used as – you can see where the wall was broken down to let the wagons in. Here, in the quiet solemnity of a plain stone building going back a millennium and a half, the oldest church in England, where all sorts of people from fishermen to bishops have worshipped, you can let your mind drift in thought or prayer, or, remembering the peace of it and the air of quiet welcome, the nice shape it once had with its apse, its three porches and its lofty tie-beamed roof, walk the grassy bank of the sea wall and let the mind run free in the endless space of that very exposed place. Here you are on the maritime threshold of East Anglia and looking seaward you can picture yourself one of those early Christians building their fishermen's chapel and wondering at the reaction of those Saxon barbarians across the Blackwater to the north.

Apart from Greensted and Bradwell, there are relatively few Essex churches that are really outstanding; that is, by East Anglian standards. Maldon, perhaps, for its thirteenth-century triangular tower and the way the whole town hangs on its hill above the Blackwater, Saffron Walden, which is big and is regarded as something akin to King's architecturally, Thaxted with its light, airy interior and the old Guildhall close by, and if you're coming into East Anglia from London by the A12, then it is

worth taking a quick look at Shenfield, just to see the effect of using oak

Bradwell: looking out to the ships laid up in the Blackwater, or across flat farmland to the lonely chapel by the Roman fort, enables one to ignore the modern bulk of the nuclear power station. St Peter is seventh-century, and one of the oldest churches in Britain.

instead of stone for the supporting columns of a church roof. Runwell, only a few miles to the east, has medieval timber porches, but here at Shenfield there is a great arcade of beautifully shaped wooden pillars running down the centre of the church between nave and north aisle. There are seven of these pillars, each a complete oak bole that has been fluted to receive four smaller oak pillars or shafts so that the effect is very like the intricate columning of stone seen in cathedrals, the pillars running up into massive roof beams. The walls of this church are over a yard thick and at the rear four wooden arches, very black and massive, with the curve of big ship timbers, are bedded on huge uprights to support the bell-tower.

When we were last in Shenfield it was the first warm day of the year, the door wide open and workmen sitting reading the papers over their morning tea. One of them told me something I would have expected, for the oak pillars are about the age of our own house frame, being set there around 1490 – he said the wood was as hard as iron. But then he added something I had never heard before: each of the pillars had been erected on a large block of York stone – presumably brought down either as cargo or ballast by one of the ships plying the East Coast trade – and to provide some sort of a damp course, slate being unavailable, layers of seashells had been introduced between the butts of the oak pillars and the stones on which they rested.

The name Shenfield is a mixture of Norman and Saxon – Chenefeld, the field or place of oaks. It was one of the main crossing points in the great oak forests of Essex. Indeed, the canon, who was there watching over the workmen, claimed that Shenfield was the real centre and pivot of Essex, the meeting point of the north-south forest track, now the A12 truckway, which was used by pilgrims proceeding from Canterbury to Walsingham – close by in Brentwood there are the ruins of a wayside shrine – and the east-west track connecting the centre of England with the coast at Prittlewell (Southend) where Cedd may have built a church as he did at Tilbury.

There is still another church rarity in Essex, conveniently placed at the eastern end of a group of exceptional towns and villages that includes the Bardfields, the Hedinghams, the Belchamps – and Borley. Thaxted is the first of this group, its high-spired church quite startling as you approach from the south, for its stone clerestory seems to be superimposed upon the marvellous silver timbering of the moot hall. A windmill standing almost as high balances a picture that is very Constable in certain lights, and at the top of a brown cobbled alley the churchyard appears as an enclave completely surrounded by the town's old houses and inns. Fine oak doors, fine porches, and inside an airiness that is almost fairylike, particularly in the open area of the chancel with its warm-patterned floor of amber and red tiles and its dainty squares of stained glass in windows that are clear except for a top fringe of Dowsing

remnants.

The next small town, Finchingfield, is different, a symphony in black and white that straggles out from mounds of grass and a hump-backed bridge beside a duck pond. The church, with its strong Norman tower surmounted by a ridiculous little square grey bell box, stands high above a huge green, and at the back of it an old sandpit of a graveyard lies unkempt and forgotten amongst the nettles at its feet.

Of the villages, the Bardfields are the most picturesque. They were an artists' colony when we first drove past them on our way to London, but the present bright polish suggests a richer immigration. The churches here are flint and squat-steepled, Great Bardfield's northern face entirely spoiled by a monstrous up-ended square of clock-face that leers blue and gold from the grey fourteenth-century flintwork. Little Bardfield, on the other hand, hides its flint walls and tiny steeple behind a great cedar in the grounds of the Hall, which is white with red tiled roofs and little gables.

The Hedinghams next, and beyond the great 100-foot high Norman keep of Castle Hedingham and the large Norman church with its hammerbeam roof and twelfth-century oak doors, in a maze of minor roads to the east of Sible Hedingham, are the Maplesteads and the church we are looking for. It is a round church, given to the Knights of St John in 1185 and rebuilt by them in the fourteenth century, and you come upon it, half hidden by oaks and yews, standing in its large churchyard and looking out on a vista of fields and woods. When we were first told of it, we already knew two of the four round churches still standing, the Temple in London and the church of the Holy Sepulchre in Cambridge, but the setting here is so different.

It is a real gem, for it has a tiny little hexagonal nave barely twelve feet across with six slender stone columns of intricate pattern supporting a small tile and wood bell tower. This delightful little nave is circled by an aisle and yard-thick walls, and everything inside is a virginal white. Built on to the round church is a large, very exciting chancel with a raftered roof, apsidal at the east end so that the whole thing looks like the exposed ribs of an upturned boat, the gunnels painted with little Maltese cross-like designs in silver and the ribs with emblems of red on silver. It is the only fourteenth-century example of this type of chancel in the country.

The round church is in the parish of Little Maplestead, where the cottage roofs are bonneted with rows of dolls' house dormer windows, and it is partnered by St Giles at Great Maplestead, which is again an apsidal church originally dating from around 1100. Just before the altar is a great Norman arch and the roof of the apse shows the same upturned boat-gunnel effect, but the roof itself is recessed with the rafters supported on the outer edge of the walls and a little window that gives the whole

A detail of the very striking spire of Hadleigh's St Mary.

189

a strikingly skylight effect. Victorian restorers did great harm to this square-towered muddle of a church, so that I only enjoy it for the two recumbent alabaster figures of the Deane family with their black apparel trimmed with gold, their Titian hair and little fair moustaches and wisps of beards, above all for the family crest of muzzled boars' heads, all red and gold, on which their feet rest.

There are nice little shingle steeples all through the East Anglian threshold country. Then up near the Suffolk border the square flint towers take over. All this land was predominantly forest, but in Cambridgeshire it is different, the country part chalk, part marsh. Cambridge itself is not good for churches, nothing to compare with Norwich. A handful of wool era buildings that include St Bene't's with its Saxon tower and one of the only four round churches still left in Britain; also there is St Andrew's the Great, built barely a century and a half ago and under constant threat of demolition, where there is a monument to Captain Cook, something that makes it important to me because of the years I spent following in the footsteps of the great navigator around the world for my book of his last voyage. The lack of early ecclesiastical splendour leaves one with the feeling that there was neither wealth nor energy to spare after bringing all those barge-loads of stone along the Cam and building that glorious range of colleges along the Backs. Architecturally, and in every way, Cambridge is colleges, not churches, and apart from Wren's masterpiece at Greenwich they are just about the greatest architectural heritage we have of stone in association with water. Without the Backs and the softness of the river, the whole complex would be almost top-heavy, the stone, even though a soft grey, too massively paraded. But with the weeping willows and the meadows and the slow-flowing water, punts gliding like gondolas . . .

Ah well, perhaps I see it through rose-tinted glasses, for I am fortunate in that, over the years, I have several times been guest speaker at literary luncheons held in the Garden House Hotel and afterwards Dorothy and I walk along the Backs with Queens' and King's and that beautiful dream of a chapel looming pale grey above the weeping willows and the green of some of England's best kept lawns, then Clare and Trinity, St John's, Magdalen, and all those bridges – from the all-wood one at Queens' to St John's ornately stone 'Bridge of Sighs'. But walk from King's Parade north along Trinity and St John's streets and you will see what I mean about the overwhelming effect of such a preponderance of stone, and the religious atmosphere very strong with King's Chapel at one end and St John's and the Round Church at the other, each college laid out like a cloister.

Though I was not educated at Cambridge, or any other university for that matter, through talking to the literary and travel societies, and through friends, I have slept in several of these older colleges. St John's is perhaps my favourite, chiefly I think because the Senior Guest Room, which is across the 'Bridge of Sighs' and in the cloister area bordering

the Backs, high up in what they call the 'wedding cake'; its bathroom is in one of the two octagonal towers, so that in the early hours of the morning I found myself lying in a hot bath gazing up at a very old, nicely moulded octagonal ceiling. Where else but Cambridge, or perhaps Oxford, would the private bathroom of an immense suite be squeezed so perfectly into an old octagonal stone tower?

But of old churches there is a dearth, and even the county, most of which lies to the north of the town, has very few of real note, perhaps because so much of it is drained fen, or reclaimed marsh, and therefore both wood and stone had to be floated down-river from Midland forests and quarries. However, there is one church that has a hammerbeam roof beyond belief and the lovely name of St Wendreda. It is in March of all places, the old rail junction for the Midlands traffic and once the workshop for those sagging miles of line where ballast, sleeper and rail rest on floating beds of willow bundle matting, a method of transporting heavy loads across wet peat that is still used in the construction of forest roads. The slender spire can be seen miles away, but expecting a big church, close to it appears quite small, like a beautiful model set in the midst of a large greensward lit in May with the candles of chestnut trees. Of all the great oak roofs of East Anglia this is the most spectacular, not so much for the roof itself – there are others just as good, and better – but for the angels. There are seventy of them (one counts them automatically, much as young lieutenants count the bosoms of the ladies on the ceiling of the Painted Hall at Greenwich), all carved in wood with wings outstretched, a whole host of them in full flight like geese fleeing through the air from the booming blast of a punt-gun.

A few miles south-west of Ely – Ely is in Cambridgeshire, remember – there are two more fine roofs, at Soham and Isleham, both somewhat similar in construction. Soham is hammer and tie with intermediate braced arches and angels peering down. There is a nice oak screen, too, and almost half the pews have bench-ends. Out across East Fen Common then, and into the table flat of the most easterly fens with Isleham church on the starb'd bow standing high on its island, a little red-roofed cap on its tower, grey barns here and there looming through mist like stranded barges, and on the horizon to the north-west the incredible mass of Ely cathedral standing like a fortress with the high bank of the Ouse running towards it.

Isleham I like, the little town huddled so close around the church, the Griffin Inn opposite and everyone so friendly. That is something I always feel about the Fens, the people that bit more welcoming, as though the nature of their land makes the arrival of a stranger as important as it is to a bedouin in the desert. The roof here is high and very fine, tie-beamed with arches between and face-down angels jutting from the central point of each of the clerestory windows. But despite the roof and the elaborate Peyton tomb effigies, all black and gold – almost as highly painted as those of the Norfolks at Framlingham – it is the little Benedictine priory building a few hundred yards to the south that really attracts me. It is very like St Peter's at Bradwell in both size and construction, but not so old. There is a lovely view past the priory's north wall buttresses to the church tower and the nave's high clerestory . . . and all around the flatness of the Fens.

Finally, and for quite different reasons, there is Sutton to the west of Ely. The fourteenth-century two-tiered octagonal lantern tower stands up like a huge pepperpot above the flat of the fenlands on either side the Bedford river, its model obviously the great cathedral. But what looked huge at a distance proves so much smaller when seen from the main street of the little town itself, and the distortion is reversed in the fenlands glimpsed between the houses, for they seem so far below, their flatness reaching to the horizon and giving a false sense of height to Sutton's island site.

The rest of East Anglia's outstanding parish churches are in Norfolk and Suffolk, a concentration of architectural glory and fascination that

is unmatched anywhere else in the country, or I think in the world. Again it is the oak more often than not that is the crowning glory, particularly after Laxfield's puritan devil, William Dowsing, had spent half a lifetime hammering away at saintly effigies and lovely stained glass windows so that I have more pre-Reformation glass in my home than that wretch left in most of the churches. Throughout these two counties, but predominantly in Suffolk, there are great tie-beamed roofs (some of them cambered), hammerbeams and angels as good as those at St Wendreda (though the angels never so many, never so flighty), bench-end carvings, stalls, wonderful elaborate screens, the roofs of porches, even porches vaulted with wood.

But the chalklands, heaths, peats and saltings of the north were no place for the large oaks required for splendid roofing. Thus in Norfolk there are fewer of these, but still quite enough for me to admit I probably haven't seen half of them. The finest we both of us happen to know are St Giles and St Peter Mancroft in Norwich, of course, and the churches at Necton, Cawston, Salle, Swaffham, Outwell, Upwell, Great Cressingham, and Wymondham – nobody can forget Wymondham. The Salle, or Sall, roof incidentally is architecturally interesting, the outward thrust of the nave rafters being transmitted to those of the aisles so that the weight of the roof is distributed to the outer walls. But nearby Cawston is finer, one of the finest angel roofs, in fact, and there is a woodwose, too. Altogether there must be well over a score of marvellous great roofs that people from other counties, and countries, would travel miles to see; wherever, in fact, there was forest, or else water nearby for the transport of heavy timber.

But it is in the carvings and screens, the Norwich glass, the age of the buildings, particularly some of the smaller churches, that Norfolk excels. Those simple round towers, and the typical narrow square towers, some standing remote in field and copse, and in the towns larger, more ornate towers, and most of them standing up out of the flatness of the land, as though pointing to the heavens and crying aloud their promise of safety from flood, of a place of assembly, a place of worship, where all will be secure against Black Shuck and other evils.

Because of the strangeness and remoteness of many of them, I always have the feeling that Norfolk's churches have more atmosphere than those of Suffolk, that they are more unusual, embody more oddities. It may be just that I am more familiar with the latter, and the sheep are always fatter over the border, but Norfolk certainly has more round towers – Pevsner says 119 compared with 41 in Suffolk, 8 in Essex, and barely a dozen in the whole of the rest of the country. And because of the reed marshes there are more thatched roofs, also the buildings often seem to be of an earlier date, squat like downland churches, their interiors

---

The 'pepper pot' tower of Sutton's St Andrew. Like Ely, its lantern is octagonal.

darkly medieval. There is nothing of the sunny magnificence of the wool churches of south-west Suffolk, my memory mostly of flintwork and ice-cold interiors that have a grim austerity, as though the fabric had absorbed something of the bitterness of winter winds, or perhaps it is the strong Norman-Saxon influence. The remains of priory churches and abbeys, mostly started in the Norman period, add to this impression of strength and antiquity.

Norwich, of course, has the greatest concentration of old churches in East Anglia. How many did I say – thirty-three? And all of them medieval. Over fifty at the height of the wool trade, circa 1500. Flushwork patterns are typically Norwich and there are a number of two-storeyed porches, but again what fascinates me are the roofs, particularly I think that of St Giles with its bosses and angels, a beautiful example of woodcraft. It is also important as representing an early stage in the development of the hammerbeam.

You need to spend several days in Norwich, something of course I have never done, being within two hours' drive. It is a city as full of surprises as London, as old in time as whatever little corner of it you happen to have discovered – the various gates, the back courts, the innumerable buildings of the wool period, the ferry points, the market, particularly the market, which is still big and bustling, full of canvas booths flapping in the wind.

Ecclesiastically, I suppose, the most important place to see after Norwich is Little Walsingham, though I must confess to a sense of disappointment each time I have been there. The Priory, like most of those in Norfolk, was built by the Normans, but it was the shrine that preceded it by some three years that was the origin of the pilgrimage. It was erected over a spring of Holy Water by the wife of Walsingham's Lord of the Manor, Richelde de Fervaque, who had been told of it in a dream. Canterbury, then across the Thames and into East Anglia, to the shrine of Our Lady of Walsingham, that was the pilgrim route, and the Milky Way pointed to it – the Walsingham Way – and the waters of the wells worked miracles so that the shrine and the pilgrimage became so famous it was known as the Nazareth of England. It is a wonder Chaucer did not base his *Tales* on this ride, for Walsingham was already one of the great pilgrimages a century before he was born, but perhaps he thought East Anglia's heath and forest tracks too arduous for storytelling.

The new Anglican shrine, the coach park and the tourists, give the place something of a commercial air, but nothing can quite obliterate the ancient feel of Walsingham itself, Knight Street and the sixteenth-century flint and brick houses, the little square or Common Place with the pyramid stone roof of the Conduit in the centre of it, the narrow street running west from the shrine with the precinct wall flanking it with solid flint, the Abbey, the Friary and the Harvest House. It definitely has atmosphere. And then you drive, or walk out 1¼ miles to the Slipper Chapel, which is Roman Catholic with a modern layout surrounding it,

The church with the lovely nave, the host of flying angels and the perfect town setting – St Wendreda in the Fenland rail centre of March.

East Barsham Manor should be approached from the south. It is one of the finest examples of Tudor brickwork, and certainly the most theatrical.

a new and very modern church beside the large car park, and the atmosphere is gone. The Slipper Chapel itself is small and fourteenth-century, but not comparable with Prior Crauden's Chapel at Ely.

Much more exciting to my mind is East Barsham Manor, a highly decorated early Tudor fantasy in brick that bursts upon one quite suddenly on the road from Fakenham. I do not think I have ever seen any building quite so startlingly theatrical, not in brick. And for those who travel to Walsingham, not just as sightseers, but on a pilgrimage of their own, and wish to pray, I am very much in agreement with those residents who prefer to attend St Peter's in Great Walsingham which is impressive even without its chancel, also somewhat stark out there on its hill beyond the ford, the interior brick-floored and nicely open with wonderfully carved benches in two great units fixed to longitudinal oak stretchers half the length of the nave – a really fine church.

Not far away, near Castle Acre, there is a huddle of four little Saxon churches that are plain and simple and worth losing yourself to visit. I have only seen them once, and that was in the pouring rain – they must look lovely in the sunshine.

Great Dunham is the really exciting one. A small nave, a tiny chancel that is almost a double chancel, so much of the church taken up by the great square central Saxon tower with its unadorned and rounded arches, everything simple, very solid, so that suddenly one feels the power of religion through the ages, the feel of long years of worship by a strong virile people. I came to it through narrow lanes deep in water, sand and gravel from the fields, and tractors with their ploughs on the move; a hilly, wooded country with a good deal of conifer. West Lexham, square-towered again, is half hidden by trees in the midst of a tiny hamlet of flint and brick, East Lexham has a round tower, then Newton, square and central again, very plain with a little pointed cap of a tiled roof slapped on the top of it to keep the rain out.

But of all the innumerable bits and pieces of Saxon church fabric to be found around Norfolk nothing that I have seen quite compares for total effect with the little thatched, round-towered church a stone's throw across the border at the very tip of that finger of Suffolk that runs up the North Sea coast almost to Great Yarmouth. Possibly founded by Canute, asymmetrical and apsidal, it is dedicated to St Edmund and stands across from St Olave's Priory overlooking the treed serenity of the Fritton decoy lake. Here you have to step *down* into the chancel, which is offset from the nave, an apse formation with L-shaped furnishings of dark oak, a plain little screen and three stained glass windows in arched recesses, the one over the altar of St Edmund himself, old murals too like Slavonic frescoes. The cell-like atmosphere, the dimness and the shape took me back to those little chapel shrines on Lake Ochrid in Yugoslavia where the Cyrillic alphabet was invented so that the Gospels could be written down in the language of the Slavs . . . I had the sense of cowled monks kneeling there in the dim light, going back in time to the early mysteries of the Christian faith in East Anglia.

I have digressed, of course. But then so will you when you try to tell other people of the churches you have seen in this strangely varied land, for there are so many of them. To the west, by the shores of the Wash, are the marshland churches, four or five visible at a time – the four Wiggenhalls, St Peter's in ruins, St Germans and St Mary the Virgin with fine bench-ends and carved benches, St Mary Magdalen with some excellent fifteenth-century glass. West Walton, Walsoken, Terrington, Tilney, the Walpoles, St Andrew and St Peter – it was in this parish that King John is supposed to have lost his baggage train; this and Terrington St Clement are the pick of the marshland group. They are predominantly stone buildings, and unfortunately most of them are locked.

196 Wisbech, like a number of the churches of this area, has its tower offset

to the north, and then there is Lynn, of course. In fact, right through the county you are never far from market town or river harbour. Downham Market, Fakenham, Swaffham, East Dereham, Aylsham, right across to Great Yarmouth in the east, and Wells and Blakeney in the north, there are towns serving a satellite host of small villages, and everywhere a church, so that to cover them all Pevsner was forced to split his work on Norfolk into two volumes.

There are, in fact, well over six hundred churches that are at least 250 years old, most of them medieval, an indication of the richness of the area in the early wool-exporting days and later with the development of the weaving industry. At one time Norwich ranked with York and Bristol as one of the three most important cities in the kingdom outside of London.

Then there are the ruined churches, almost a hundred of them, many of them in ruins at the time of the 1602 survey. And, still in addition to these, are the monastic ruins – far more of them in Norfolk than anywhere else in East Anglia. Castle Acre just has to be seen for the wonder of its west front and ruins as impressive as any in England – the well, the gateway, the remains of the prior's rooms above. But the priory ruin that attracts me most is at Binham close by the north shore, the towerless church standing high-walled in bright green grazing fields to the north of the village with the very extensive priory ruins to the south of it. Inside, the church is just a nave, high and narrow, the arches either side in three storeys, as at Wymondham, but here all are the rounded Norman type. Something about the position appeals to me, so much a part of an agricultural world that has the simplicity and loneliness of an East Anglian equivalent of a Biblical scene.

Wymondham itself, on the other hand, is much more of a show piece, a large abbey church with two towers, one square, the other octagonal, that give it the look of Ely when seen from far off rising up out of the trees. It is particularly interesting because it is really two churches, the town church with a big square tower with its corner buttresses like slender five-sided lift shafts, then to the east the octagon tower and nothing but ruins to mark the monks' church. In the sunshine with the shadows slanting the town tower is really something to see with its carved stone parapet, fine flushwork, and there is more flushwork on the clerestory, also a carved balustrade to the top of the lovely two-storey north porch. The nave is a truly massive example of Norman work, three tiers of arcade arches beautifully decorated, and a very good roof, bosses under the ridge and on the purlins, angels flighting as terminals to the hammerbeams and behind the altar a quite spectacular carved wooden reredos reaching up to the roof, and all of it bright gold. It is modern,

The little town of Clare is dominated by a fine church that seems to hang over the bustle of the market place.

but the solid Norman strength of the building can take it.

Better even than this, and not far away, in the little market town of Attleborough which serves the fast food Norfolk turkey and duck producing country, is a grey flint church in a neatly kept graveyard with the long line of the Griffin hotel white with a black trim running alongside. The Norman tower now stands at the east end supported by four massive pillars. There the church ends abruptly, no proper chancel, but between the nave and the altar, which is under the tower, there is perhaps the finest rood-screen I have ever seen in a parish church, the oak so warmly brown, the paint all nicely faded with a rood-loft over, the whole screen running right across the church with a very dainty traceried entrance-way to the altar. And there are mural decorations on the wall above the screen, on both sides of two small Norman archways, one above the other. The nave is ridiculously high, so are the arches supporting a very small clerestory and the pillars of the arches as slender as the tower pillars are massive. The high clerestory gives the church a hunched look, rather like Needham Market. The Norman tower was once central, of course, the College of the Holy Cross owning the choir, but this was pulled down at the Dissolution.

These two churches are as fine as anything to be found in Norfolk – outside of Norwich, of course. But then I remember that little group halfway between Wymondham and the north shore comprising Salle, Cawston, and the Reepham twins. Did the stone for Cawston really come all the way from Normandy via the Broads and the Bure river, then overland from Coltishall, with each parish on the way doing its share of the pulley-hauley? Never mind, it is the hammerbeam roof that is so superb, the screen and the carvings of my favourite image, the woodwose. Salle, on the other hand, is built of stone from Northamptonshire, an early fifteenth-century superlative, the equal of the best in Suffolk, with angels in the nave's arch-braced roof, the transept roof all fine panelling, the woodcarving everywhere superb.

Then a few miles to the west is North Elmham, site of what is thought to have been East Anglia's first cathedral, before the see was moved to Thetford for a short time in 1070 and thence by de Losinga to Norwich in 1094. The original church, and the whole area around North Elmham, was almost certainly destroyed by the Danes, probably in 866, the see being re-established in the next century, so that it is thought by some that it was here, not at Bures on the Suffolk-Essex border, that St Edmund was crowned. As a guess I would suspect there may have been a ceremony in both places, the one religious, the other political.

From Cawston it is only a very short distance to Aylsham and Blickling with the magnificent Dagworth brass and several small brasses of the Boleynes, the one of Anna Boleyne dated 1479 and prophetically with the head missing. But to get an overall impression of the medieval wealth of this large county I think I would start from the Broadland churches and work up through the glacial sands, gravels and clays to the Cromer

Southwold's St Edmund: outside, the flintwork of the tower is impressive, inside there is a fine screen with painted panels and stalls, most of the woodwork fifteenth-century.

ridge, then west into the flint country and the land behind the marshes. Ranworth was where I once started because of the painted rood-screen, which is very fine for a church of its size, then on to South Walsham which has two churches side by side, one with a tower, one without, one used, one unused. Rollesby, Martham, Somerton, Waxham – here the church is half in ruins by the dune defences and a lovely old flint farmhouse, Waxham Hall, lurks like a Pathan chieftain's tribal home behind a huge flint wall that has little decorated towers at each corner and a fine fifteenth-century gatehouse.

Sea Palling (Pawling) marks the end of Broadland, the beginning of the low-cliffed, crumbling coastal belt, and all through the agricultural hinterland there are square-towered, flint-built churches standing like beacons against the skyline. You take your choice, to be rewarded sometimes by the setting alone, sometimes by the thing you have come to see or something you discover for yourself, and sometimes by the feel of the building, just occasionally by pity for the neglect of the place. But there are so many of them, and it is flint, flint, flint, all up the coast and deep inland – so much flint in fine, attractive buildings cannot be seen anywhere else in the British Isles.

Paston is one I particularly like; thatched and square-towered, with a nice raftered roof, it stands outside the village, close by the Hall where there is a really superb and very large reed-thatched barn with a splendid tie-beamed roof. And nearby Knapton has to be seen. Tall and flinty, with a very large gilded cock on the top of its weathervane, its roof has been described as the best hammerbeam and angel roof in the county. It is certainly one of the best with seventy-two angels of unusual design on a roof that is double hammerbeam, another twenty-two angels carved on the panels between the lower hammerbeam, and there were others, I think, but the light was dim when I made my count. And to the south is Worstead, where the Flemish wool-combers, driven out of Flanders by a North Sea surge, settled in the reign of Henry I.

It is characteristic of all this wide-skied north-east of the county that, however prominent a church may be from a distance, you lose it in town or village, often to the extent of having to ask where it is. You can stumble over medieval churches and Norman ruins anywhere in Norfolk, but for me this north-eastern part is best of all for church-gazing, most of them so easily spotted from a distance, a few, like Stiffkey, half hidden away, all of them interesting, one or two superb, and vestiges of Saxon and Norman stone and flint work everywhere. And all through Norfolk there are superb brasses, 215 according to one leading authority, including some rather gruesome ones in Norwich that one day I really must search out.

Suffolk also has 215 brasses of note, Essex 237, figures that are only surpassed by Kent, which is a clear indication of the predominance of wool and cloth as the source of wealth, most of the great brasses being of the fourteenth and fifteenth centuries. But for the great oak roofs of

Blythburgh's magnificent church stands just clear of the village overlooking the marshes. The flushwork decoration of the exterior is particularly good.

The superb, massive timbered roof with the screen rising towards its faded paintwork. Blythburgh church is one of the settings for the Aldeburgh Festival.

DRUNKENNESS

A closer view of the faded
paintwork of Blythburgh roof
showing in detail how
the angel wings are grouped
around the central bosses.

Finely carved bench-end
interpretations of the Seven
Deadly Sins.

202

SLOTH

SLANDER

East Anglia, it is Suffolk, not Norfolk or even Essex, that is supreme. 'No county is richer,' Pevsner flatly declares, and he is right. There are so many hammerbeams, double hammerbeams, carved wall plates, tie-beams, arched braces that I hardly know where to begin, and even in the tiniest village with the dullest church one can often be rewarded as soon as one raises one's eyes to the roof.

Apart from the wool churches, the greatest concentration of really breathtaking parish churches lies along the coast and its hinterland from Ipswich northwards, the sea trade merchants taking over from the clothiers as the main providers of funds. Southwold just has to be seen for its exterior standing high on Southwold hill close by the lighthouse, its 100-foot tower faced with worked flint, an unbelievable flurry of flushwork the like of which I cannot remember seeing in any other church. And opposite it, on the other side of the Blyth outfall, is Walberswick, half in ruins so that the make-up of its fifteenth-century flint and rubble walls can be examined in detail. Like Southwold, it stands high on a ridge, its 130-foot tower visible for miles. But the pick of the Blyth trio is Blythburgh itself.

Coming upon it from the south, it stands on a sort of headland jutting out into the marshes, a delicate monument above the silted remains of the old Roman port and lands that Edward the Confessor once held. The exterior of it always reminds me of Lavenham, though it is not quite so rich or so gracefully chess-like, and the interior is simple, a very open plan, where the old oak planks of the benches, with their carved ends, form austere parallel black lines against the warmth of brick flooring; overhead the painted timber roofing is faded to pale grey and there are angels flighting.

Despite the roof, despite the bench-ends, which include carved arm-rests or finials depicting the Seven Deadly Sins, this is again a church that is at its best seen from the outside and from a little distance. But down the road a few miles, at Dennington – now here is something to drive a thousand miles to see. Better than Framlingham with its gaudy Norfolk tombs, better than Lavenham with its Spring family chantry,

| AVARICE | HYPOCRISY | GLUTTONY | PRIDE |

better than anything in Ipswich, Hadleigh or Sudbury, better I think than almost any parish church of its size in the county. Its interior is full of priceless carved bench-ends, there are parclose screens that are quite fantastic surrounding the north and south chapels, a marvellously delicate tracery carved in wood, and where the paint has faded, the oak is a soft silvery-brown like the Blythburgh roof, and inside the south chapel the figures of Lord Bardolph who fought at Agincourt (is this where Shakespeare got the name?) and Lady Bardolph, who lies on his right side because it was from her he obtained the title. At his feet there is an

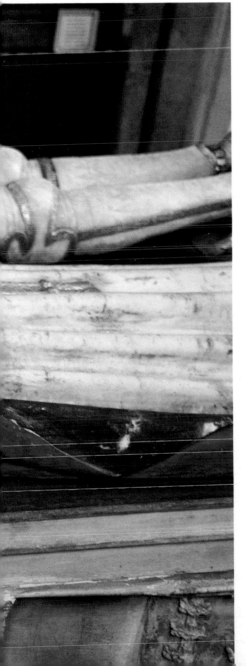

One of the most fascinating churches in Suffolk – Dennington. The tomb figures of Lord and Lady Bardolph are particularly fine. His title came from the lady so it is she who lies on his right.

eagle with wings spread, at hers a wyvern, the heraldic beast with a serpent's tail, a dragon's head, only two legs, and wings. There is red on these foot-rests, but the figures are plain alabaster with parts of the armour and their jewellery picked out in gold, even the rings gold on their fingers, all renewed recently, and very well done. I am not particularly fond of tombs, but this, despite the gilding, is remarkably unostentatious; I found it both exciting and unexpected, the man's figure looking as though he might have been laid there straight from battle, a challenge to all who did not fight on Crispin Crispian's Day.

But the bench-ends is what we have come to see, for there is something quite extraordinary here. Coming up from Ipswich there are some very good bench-ends at Ufford – fine poppy-heads above the carved end-panels and arm-rests, also scroll-like carving along the rear of the bench-backs – all much more interesting to my mind than the elaborately carved font cover that is 'telescopic' and surmounted by a pelican in her piety pecking at her breast, which is what most people go there to see. But the Dennington bench-ends are so much more numerous, so very outstanding. All of them culminate in poppy-heads, and not just poppy-heads, but leaves of fruit as well, finials carved with animals that often look like dogs, but are mainly birds, including an eagle with two heads, and strange animals, and on one arm-rest three little faces peering out of a hole.

Bench-end and arm-rest carvings of what look like animals are supposed to be mythological and to have had a significance for medieval parishioners that is quite lost on most of today's visitors. But if you study them, particularly if you can sketch them and compare them with the illustrations in ecclesiastical manuscripts of the period, a certain similarity will be apparent. But one still needs to be expert on the deep-rooted beliefs and superstitions of the time to understand the symbolic meaning of it all. And when it comes to the sciapod, then the mind boggles.

You will find this revolting caricature of a human being most beautifully carved on a bench-end side panel. He is long-haired and bearded, dressed in the fashion of the fifteenth century, and he lies on his back with knees bent and two of the largest webbed feet you ever saw stretched back over his whole body to the head, and three little faces peep from under his left arm. It is said that his feet are raised to shield him from the sun and that when he is hungry he'll start chewing on those three little captives of his.

The handbook to this church is a model, the rector having done a great deal of research. The sciapod, for instance – scia means shade, but you won't find sciapod very readily in dictionaries or encyclopaedias. Yet it seems St Augustine knew about them, for he wrote of their fleetness of foot and the way they shaded themselves from the sun. There are pictures of them, apparently, in the British Museum, the Chapter House at Westminster Abbey and in the Bodleian. They are supposed to have had only one foot (the Dennington sciapod has definitely two) and on that one foot they used to leap very nimbly after the poor little creatures on which they fed. That is why the carver has shown three little heads tucked under the sciapod's arm, and their occupation of caves in the desert explains the arm-rest, near where the box-pews begin, with three heads peeping out of carved circles that presumably represent either caves or holes in the ground.

It is worth going a long way just to see that sciapod carving, for the myth of the sciapod goes back two dozen centuries, to a Persian report of them, in India, and this is the only carving of one outside of a few French churches.

As a complete contrast to Dennington, and the other larger churches of this coastal belt, Bramfield is again something special, thatched and on the shoulder of a hill, the round tower standing apart, very squat and solid, for it is Norman and a good five metres in diameter at its base, its top little higher than the church's chancel ridge. Inside the church the gem, to my mind, is not the 1629 marble masterpiece of Renaissance sculpture by Nicholas Stone, but the fifteenth-century wooden screen with gesso decoration and early colours. It really is one of the most beautiful little screens to be found anywhere. Five of the eight dado panels are painted, but it is the rood-loft – so small but still no better way to describe it; it is swung out in the form of a coving both sides, on the west with a curved fan vaulting in imitation of a stone roof and on the chancel side curved again but with an even more elaborate roof-like pattern.

And at Cratfield, barely six miles away up the valley of the Blyth, there is what Cautley – the great authority on Suffolk churches – has described as the finest font in the kingdom. The church is hidden away behind the trees that surround the big rectory and as you go into it this beautiful piece of stonework literally hits you in the face, standing very tall on a few steps, the stone so pale it looks almost like marble, the bowl bearing the Seven Sacraments and the Crucifixion carried by eight angels and eight figures seated at the foot of its tall stem.

All through this north-eastern part of Suffolk the churches tend to be on a bit of a hill, often in the centre of the village, so that the setting makes almost any of them worth visiting, the squat, square towers visible from a distance, and the grey of flint offset by the tiled roofs of surrounding cottage buildings, only the graveyard striking a discordant note, too many of the tombstones having been uprooted and set in straight lines because the villagers are no longer willing to mow between them in their original grave-marking positions.

There is another group of outstanding churches that straggles away north-west of the Old Draperies, roughly on the line Needham Market, Stowmarket, Bury St Edmunds, out as far as Mildenhall on the Suffolk border, which is the last of the great beamed and angeled roofs before the Fens.

Spring in Suffolk is willow-green and popples almost the colour of olives as they burst into leaf, daffodils nodding by cottage and farm. Once I went to Landwade, just north of Newmarket, in the spring, because I had been told it would be awash with daffodils. It was. 'To the chapel', said a small, discreet sign by a kissing-gate to the right of a private house, but it is large for a chapel, more like a small church with its squat square tower all buttressed and rising in five stages. The present building is a 1459 reconstruction of one that was there in 987, the whole

Reed-thatched churches are not so plentiful as they were – Thornham Parva is one of the best.

neat little edifice enclosed in a brick wall and glimmering a warm grey through the bare branches of a large oak. The smell of new mown grass filled the air, several acres of it, and a stream, or perhaps the remains of a moat, made an L-turn close to the east of the chapel to flow under a three-arched brick bridge. I had arrived by the farm lane, but as nobody was about I went out by the drive, which I had seen from the Exning road, the whole length of it bordered with daffodils.

This surely is the time of year to go church-gazing, the days lengthening, but cold winds still blowing, so that a cool interior is preferable to lingering in the sun, the sense of discovery, as each example of those long-dead workers' labours is revealed, like spring fever. Needham Market – this really is the roof to end all roofs, quite astonishing in its complexity; and yet the church itself presenting such a hunched, misshapen appearance, crouched against the High Street behind its shallow porch with that ridiculous little clock-faced steeple plonked on the top of it.

But once inside, one looks up and stands agape at the profusion of timbering. There is everything here, a hammerbeam roof with angel-embellished hammerbeams jutting out more than six feet, the braces supporting this out-thrust timbering hidden behind a wooden coving that is really rather like the curved roof of an old Pullman car, for it stretches the length of the nave both sides and is carved with flying angels and fleurons or flowers. And as if this were not enough, there are great cambered tie-beams running transversely across the church and storey-posts that appear to stand on the ends of angeled hammers, but are in fact hung. Here I must quote from Pevsner: 'Finally, and this is the most astonishing feature, the upper third of the storey-posts are cross connected, i.e. from west to east, by a timber-built clerestory with windows.' He says it creates 'the impression of a whole church in mid-air', and that's exactly how I have always felt about it. Nothing else matters but that incredible roof. It *is* the church, all the rest being fortunately plain, and looking up at it, one has to accept that Cautley is right when he claims it as 'the culminating achievement of the English carpenter'.

Bury's St Mary, of course, has a superb roof and at Barking in the south-east of this galaxy of fabulous timbering is another of those churches that are far too big for the present village. It is set apart with the old rectory so that it looks almost as though it belongs to an estate and inside are treasures nearly as rewarding as at Dennington, particularly the finely carved and very dainty wood screens, all virtually complete – crested parclose screens north and south and an entire rood screen, the light divisions unusually separated into three parts – also doors with tracery, and a fine, chunky, very simple roof.

There is only one thing to do when looking at this group of churches – work across country following your nose. There is so much. Little churches, big churches, some plain and simple, some more elaborate, but all full of fine wood, which is I think what gives them that feeling of

Woolpit church: inside, a symphony of black and white plaster, outside, a symphony of flint topped by an odd little steeple.

warmth. My favourites, other than those I have already mentioned, are Great Bricett, which is older than most, being part of an Augustinian priory, and has some early stained glass figures that Destructor Dowsing seems to have missed; Hitcham and Rattlesden with their double hammerbeams; Rougham – again for its roof; Drinkstone for its screen and benches; and I think Cockfield – like a smaller version of Long Melford, its setting is what attracts with the timber-framed and brick-nogged Church Cottage acting as a foil to the stone and flint flushwork. Also, for curiosity, East Bergholt's bell house, which is a single-storey, largely wooden building, so that the bell frame is on the ground and the bells rung by hand levers, all visible from the outside through a criss-cross timber grille that runs right round the building.

But then there is Crowfield, if you can find it. Like Caistor St Edmund,

Sudbury's St Gregory viewed from close by the Stour.

Cavendish – a lovely little church on the edge of a village green surrounded by timber-frame cottages. An artist's dream of a place.

also just east of the Ipswich–Norwich road, it is up a little gravel track, standing like a barn in the middle of fields, a moated barn, for there is water here. It has the only timber-framed chancel in Suffolk, the beams exposed inside as well as outside, an east window all in oak that looks as though it were ornate stone and a glassed-in timber-roofed porch with two beautifully decorated tie-beams. Badley is another of these lost little churches that are difficult to find, a small gem of a church that nobody has tried to improve, so that it remains much as it was when it was built, largely in the thirteenth century, the oak unstained and silvery-grey. Alas, like most of these lonely churches, it is now kept locked, which I fear is also true of quite a number of the less remote, even some of those that are set in the midst of town and village.

Barking I like for its setting as much as for its screens and roof. But of all this group of churches the one that takes my breath away is Woolpit. So simple, such a symphony in near-black and white. Open the door and there it all is – double hammerbeams, angels all over the place, an   *211* almost perfect rood canopied screen, pinched it is thought from another church, and carved benches. No need to go any further, just stand there by the door and drink it in, the wood all dark, stark against the white of the walls, a wonderful, almost shocking simplicity, one of the most perfect interior compositions I have ever seen.

A tributary branch of these wool churches reaches westward through Sudbury to Cavendish and Clare, and north-west up the valley of the Glem to Denston's almost untouched fifteenth-century church. Sudbury's St Gregory is beautifully set and very fine, and so it should be for Sudbury was one of the richest of the wool towns, the chancel built, or more likely rebuilt, by Simon de Sudbury, Archbishop of Canterbury, in the fourteenth century. Cavendish, however, is my favourite of this group, partly for its flushworked clerestory and the tower with its comfortably furnished ringing chamber, but more particularly for its position at the head of a great triangle of a green edged with timbered and thatched cottages and the road so wide in the approach – this and Long Melford are why I always enjoy driving to Cambridge despite the architectural horrors of Haverhill.

Also in this group is Acton, just east of Long Melford, not nearly as impressive-looking as Assington, perhaps because it stands well back from the village instead of looming over one on a winter's night like something out of Domesday, but it has one great claim to fame, for it is the home of the Bures brass, which Pevsner regards as 'one of the oldest and one of the finest in England'. I have so far said little about brasses and Dowsing seems to have ignored them entirely, though he was a very thorough smasher for his 6s 8d fee, using bow and gun as well as hammer in his great work of destruction. There are probably more good brasses in Norfolk than in Suffolk, but the Bures brass, which is almost in the next village to us, is certainly the most outstanding in East Anglia – the chain-mailed figure of Sir Robert de Bures with shield, surcoat and sword, hands clasped in prayer, legs crossed at the knee, and at his feet a lion couchant with a funny face. Surprisingly, if this is intended to be life-size, the figure measures six feet six inches. The date is around 1320, early in England for such very fine engraving.

My problem with East Anglian village churches – and it will be yours if you make the pilgrimage – is that there is always another and another that I haven't seen, and should, and when I have, I am full of the excitement of discovery – often for its setting, nothing more. I made time quite recently, coming back from Colchester station, to look at Nayland's St James again, a church I have passed so many times. It was early morning, nobody about, the sky a cloudless blue, and in that hard, brittle light the oak-timbered and colour-washed cottages and houses clustered around it, the tumble of their roofs . . . I had the sense of walking round some fabulous Tudor stage set. This is just something I normally pass by going and coming from London, just one of so many village stage sets. But then that is Suffolk.

Upwell with Outwell is one long village street. Here in the churchyard the tombstones of the dead are lined up as though to parade their elaborate stonework.

9. The Clays

This is the heart of East Anglia. Here the weeds grow ten feet tall and in winter Flanders and the Falklands have nothing on the sugar beet lanes for mud. Outside of the heaths and sandlings, the chalklands, the fens and the swamplands of the estuaries, most of East Anglia is a good rich glutinous clay, which in rain turns to good rich glutinous mud, and in drought bakes hard – like clay! Here, until recently, those kings and queens of the forest, oak and ash, ruled supreme, mixing with elm and lime and alder to provide material for the boat people who used river and estuary the way we use lanes and highways. From these clayland forests came also the timber-framed dwellings that were so quickly erected – initially in 'raisings', like a barn – wherever man found or made himself a clearing. Flints, knapped to razor sharpness, provided axes that could fell and trim the trees.

Development was slow, the land heavy. In Long Melford there is an old black-beamed fifteenth-century inn where the clear-cut figure of a woodwose is carved into the head of a supporting upright. The woodwose were the little wild men of the woods, a legendary people as totally apart as those inhabitants of the Fens who walked on stilts and fought like Luddites against the draining of the marshes. If they ever existed, then the woodwose must have been gentler than the 'fen tigers', neither fighting nor adapting – just fading into oblivion.

In the great period of ecclesiastical building, when every pagan site, and every cluster of dwellings large enough to be called a hamlet, was provided with a place of Christian worship, the presence of those same forests ensured that the flint and rubble walls of the churches should be capped with timbered roofs, oak providing the material, not only of the heavy beams and rafters, but also of the marvellous carvings – of winged angels, of saints, of devils, too, and local characters, sometimes the carver himself, the timber and the carvings extending in the larger, richer churches to bench-ends, screens and font covers.

The heart and soul of this land is surely Bury St Edmunds, and here I must digress for a moment to give something of the strange story of the martyr king whose once incorrupt remains still cause ecclesiastical controversy and whose ruined abbey may well have left a legacy of incalculable worth walled up in some cellar. The abbey itself is a delight, set there in the middle of Bury town, between Angel Hill and the little

The green of the willows and the brown of the plough, a typical East Anglian scene – preparing the ground for spring sowing of the heavy lands near Higham, Suffolk.

river Linnet, a huge area of gardens and ruins totalling almost 140,000 square metres with little remaining but part of the walls and two massive gates of what had been before the Dissolution one of the wealthiest and most powerful Benedictine complexes in the whole of England.

Half the older houses in Bury must be built of the stone from these ruins, the extent of which is immediately apparent as you pass through the Great Gate into the Abbey Gardens, also the solidity and richness of its construction, for the gate itself, completed in 1353 and 18.9 metres high, is massively constructed, superbly decorated. The other remaining gateway is to the south and led directly to the Abbey Church, a vast building that was over 154 metres long with a front wider than any of our other medieval churches; this, the Norman Gate, is more than two centuries earlier than the Great Gate and 7.32 metres higher.

To drive past these gates late at night when Crown Street and Angel Hill are deserted always gives me a feeling of the clocks turned back and myself in an age before the Dissolution, the wonderful façade of grey-brown stone starting at Honey Hill with the fourteenth-century church of St Mary, its tower beside it to the north, then the Norman Gate close south of the early sixteenth-century parish church of St James, since 1914 the cathedral. Crown Street then broadens into the big open space of Angel Hill with the old creeper-covered hostelry, where Pickwick learned he was to be sued for breach of promise, directly facing the Great Gate, and behind it to the west, the grid-patterned narrow streets first laid out for well over three hundred houses by the monastery's Abbot Baldwin a few years after the Norman Conquest. Like Norwich, Bury still has many wonderful old houses, Moyse's Hall in particular, but the shrine and the body of St Edmund are gone now and pilgrims no longer beat a path to the abbey, only tourists.

Back in Saxon days the kingdom of East Angles, comprising North Folk and South Folk, preserved its independence from the larger kingdoms of England because it was geographically out on a limb, the undrained fens and marshlands below the Wash protecting it from Mercia and the Stour river from Wessex. The Stour doesn't look much of a barrier today, except when it floods, but in the ninth century it was all fen and marsh in its lower reaches and thick forest higher up, the main crossing point Bures. Edmund himself came from across the sea, from old Saxony, but he was a descendant of the House of Uffa that had ruled East Anglia from the middle of the sixth century until 794 when Ethelbert was murdered by Offa of Mercia.

Half a century of chaos followed as Mercia gradually extended its dominion over Norfolk, Wessex over Suffolk, and another Offa, vassal king in Norfolk, passed through Saxony on his way to the Crusades, and having no heir named Edmund his successor.

Charlemagne had conquered Saxony back in 775, so that England was something of an island buffer state between a Christian continental power and the Scandinavians who were still pagan, still maritime marauders;

The Abbey ruins of Bury St Edmunds contrast very sharply with the well-maintained fabric of St Mary's church to show the destructive effect of the Reformation.

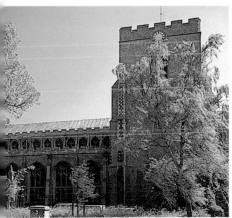

and the way into England was through the East Coast estuaries. Offa never returned. He died in the Dardanelles, sending back to Edmund the royal signet ring and also perhaps a fragment of what he believed to be the True Cross that he had picked up on his travels.

Edmund succeeded at a time when the Danes were pressing in upon the East Coast, which explains why he did not land at Dunwich or Lowestoft, but sailed right round Norfolk to Maidensbure, which was in the Wash near Hunstanton. He had to wait the better part of a year while his emissaries negotiated with their Wessex overlords. He spent the time learning the Psalter by heart. The Danish raids continued, the coastal areas becoming depopulated. Wessex needed a strong East Anglia as a buffer state, and so, finally, he was crowned at Bures in the very

south of Suffolk where Wessex influence was strongest. It was Christmas Day, 855.

He reigned for fourteen years. An excellently researched little book, written by a Roman Catholic parish priest in Bury and printed and published in Lavenham (it reads in part like a detective story and includes some fanciful passages), suggests that, though a very devout king, he did have some success in organising resistance to the Danish coastal raids. But then, in 865, the Danes made their first real bid for conquest, landing a great army in the east coast estuaries. The main objective was almost certainly Northumbria, but they needed horses for their cavalry and it was impracticable to bring horses across the North Sea, coming as they were from Denmark, some from Friesland, and the distance well over 300 miles.

They got their horses, trained their cavalry, plundered East Anglia's harvest and sailed the following October. York fell, Northumbria was theirs, the one-time cultural centre of Christian Europe finished. They went for Mercia then, but by 868 were back at York having been faced with an alliance of Mercia and Wessex, and with the King of Wessex was his young brother Alfred.

Meanwhile, Edmund was presumably hastily training up his fighting men, for he was at the relief of Nottingham and held the field against the Danes at Thetford where they had set up their winter camp. But part of the Danish forces were away in their ships sacking the islands in the Fens, including Ely. The best defence line was probably the Devil's Dyke or Ditch, a seven-mile, sixty-foot trench on Newmarket Heath; that's even deeper than Offa's Dyke that stretches from the Dee to my Cadora woodland on the Wye. But presumably it was already outflanked, the Danes having landed on the shore of the fen 'sea' near Soham, forcing Edmund to move back into the heart of Norfolk, maybe even heading for an old resistance area, the Broadland marshes just east of Norwich. There was no battle, it seems. King Edmund, always deeply religious, was now caught up in the frenzy of martyrdom. He would die, like Christ, for his people; and like Christ, his death would be the unifying force that would give his people the strength to resist.

It is this that makes the story of St Edmund something that moves all those who down the years have had the keeping of his relics. With the East Anglians resisting and causing heavy casualties, the Danes directed their energies to the destruction of the leader. Was there a broken treaty? The Bury priest, Bryan Houghton, thinks there was. It would explain why the messenger demanding Edmund's submission should have been described by Abbo as coming *unexpectedly*. Admittedly Abbo was writing his *Passion of St Edmund* some 115 years after the event, but he spent two years at Ramsey before being appointed abbot of the Cluniac house of Fleury and had recorded the story from Archbishop Dunstan, who as a youngster had been at Bury with Athelstan when that king was given a full account of what had happened by Edmund's aged armour-bearer.

According to this account Edmund was surrounded, captured, chained and beaten, then tied to a tree and lashed, still crying the Saviour's name. Arrows were shot and still he was not dead, still the name of Jesus on his lips, so the head was struck from the body. And then, because religion, any religion, exercised a great influence on people who were innately superstitious – and because perhaps a treaty had been broken and a cruel and cowardly act perpetrated on the foremost figure in East Anglia – the head was not paraded in public but discarded in a forest thicket.

Now the story moves out of history into legend, for Edmund, like Arthur, was a subject for propaganda, so that it is hard to tell fact from fiction, bearing in mind we are still in a period when virtually all information is verbal and memorised. This is not to say that it is inaccurate for, as has been proved by Homer, the minds of even simple peasants were automatically trained to a degree of verbal accuracy that

If you go through the archway of the magnificently solid Norman Tower you find early houses that are quite a rare example of the way town dwellings were built into the walls of ecclesiastical buildings.

often amounted to almost total recall. The body recovered, the head was searched for and found, probably by a dog, but the Romulus and Remus story had already been good for many centuries, so it became a wolf. But one of the best of many portrayals of this episode is a bench-end woodcarving close to our home in Hadleigh church, and here the rather human-headed animal has an elaborate collar round its neck, suggesting it was, in fact, one of the King's dogs that found the head of its master.

Alfred on his accession in 871 was quick to use the martyr king as a unifying force. Coins were minted carrying his image; and in Denmark, too, after the Danish king's conversion to Christianity. Edmund was canonised, his body taken to Beodericsworth. Incorrupt, it grew a beard that had to be trimmed and nails that had to be pared. These became relics in themselves, eventually hung over the altar at his shrine. The severed head had miraculously become reattached to the body. When Sweyn Forkbeard, King of Denmark, mounted a new invasion, Ailwin, who had appointed himself guardian of the shrine, pushed the body on a wheeled litter all the way to London for greater safety.

There it remained for three years. The Archbishop of Canterbury tried to buy the fragment of the True Cross, which was still hung around the neck of the body, for a large sum of money. The Bishop of London tried to seize it. In the end Ailwin wheeled the body back to Beodericsworth, going by a route often used by people driving into East Anglia today, via Edmonton and Ongar, where the body rested in the little wooden church at Greensted, then up through Braintree along part of the old Roman road. Sweyn landed, plundered England, and Ailwin, who had been visited by his saint in a vision, journeyed north to the Danish king's headquarters at Gainsborough to make the extraordinary pronouncement that Edmund had told him he would protect his people. Sweyn died, it is said, the very next day.

Doubtless this explains in part Canute's consideration for the shrine when he became king, renaming Beodericsworth the Burgh of St Edmund in 1020 and founding what was to become one of the greatest Benedictine monasteries in the land with Ailwin as its bishop and some eighty monks drafted in from his old abbey of Hulme. By 1032 the great abbey church was complete and Canute was present when St Edmund's body was transferred to its new shrine. The ceremony called for another verification of the incorrupt remains by Ailwin.

This matter of verification is periodically repeated until 1198. King John came to Bury, so did his barons, the oaths they swore at their meeting there on November 20th, 1214, leading to the ratification of Magna Carta in the following year. Now, suddenly, all is confusion, the argument over the succession following the death of King John resulting in the Dauphin of France fighting and losing a battle for the succession on English soil, at Lincoln, and later sending cavalry to Bury – for gold or for relics? Did Melun, the cavalry commander, seize the remains?

No verifications occur after this; not after the demolition of the old

Ickworth, seat of the Hervey family; the massive Rotunda seen through the trees of the park.

The terrace entrance and a closer view of the Rotunda which was the brainchild of that much-travelled Earl-Bishop for whom all those Bristol hotels were named.

chapel, presumably in a search for the body; not even following the fire that destroyed so much of the abbey in 1465. There was, it seems, no body – certainly no incorrupt body. But, strangely, the great abbey of St Sernin at Toulouse, shortly after the Melun raid on Bury, suddenly displayed a marked enthusiasm for St Edmund. He became one of the city's saintly protectors – *S. Eadmundus Rex Angliae*, with Eadmundus spelt, not in the French manner, but as in England, as on the coffin. And this abbey could now boast among its relics a piece of the True Cross.

Meanwhile, back in Bury, the sanctity of the abbey was vested in the body's coverings, not in the body itself. Right up to the Dissolution, which followed the Act of Supremacy that made Henry VIII head of the Church of England, there was no verification. It was the 1539 Parliament that dissolved the larger monasteries, vesting their property in the King, and St Edmund's Abbey was high on the list. Thomas Cromwell was Vicar-General at the time and the Commissioners he sent were instructed to raze the shrine to the ground and remove all bones and ornaments. Abbot Reeve handed the Abbey over to them on November 5th, 1539, and their first report mentions finding such vanity and superstition, instancing nail parings and enough bits of the Holy Cross to make a whole cross, but nothing about a body, and the shrine itself described as rich and very 'comberous' to deface.

Forget the body and the shrine for a moment . . . what about the wealth of the Abbey? It was supposed to have been immensely rich. All that wealth was, of course, inventoried, but Abbot Reeve would have had plenty of warning, the smaller monasteries having been dissolved several years before. When Dorothy and I first came to East Anglia there was a charming, somewhat Dickensian character, who took a glass of sherry with us periodically while discussing our wine requirements. He also talked at length about the Abbey's treasure. He was convinced that it was hidden somewhere in the vicinity of Bury; Reeve, he thought, too clever a man not to have got the bulk of it away. He could have fudged the inventory and would have had at least one night's warning of the Commissioners' arrival. A November night, twelve hours of darkness – time to get a heavily loaded horsedrawn wagon a dozen miles away and into hiding. As our visitor represented one of the oldest wine merchants in East Anglia he was a regular caller at most of the great houses, halls and farms in the vicinity of Bury St Edmunds, where he lived. He had seen a lot of cellars, but no whisper of the treasure. Sometimes, with a shining Pickwickian smile, he would hint that searching for it would give him something to do in retirement.

I have often thought how strange it would be to buy a house in West Suffolk and in the course of alterations, or the installation of a heating plant in the cellars, stumble upon the abbey's hidden wealth. It would be like finding the Cocos Island treasure, all the wealth of Lima cathedral hidden there by a Bristol brig, the *Mary Deare*, after which I had named a book, and later a boat. It is worth remembering that Abbot Reeve, after handing over the Abbey, retired to a house in Crown Street, and though he was given a pension of 500 marks, he was dead within five months.

As far as St Edmund's body is concerned, it is now fairly evident that it was, in fact, carried off to Toulouse – at any rate, the story is no stranger than the manner in which the shrine statue of Our Lady of Ipswich landed up behind the High Altar of the Sanctuario di Nostra Signora delle Grazie at Nettuno between Naples and Rome shortly after the Dissolution. There was a verification of the martyr king's remains there in 1644 – not of an incorrupt body, but of a skeleton with certain parts missing, the skull with lower jaw detached and three loose teeth. At the beginning of this century Toulouse agreed to relinquish the body, but not the head, so that it could lie in splendour in the new Westminster Cathedral. It came to England via Rome, was housed temporarily at Arundel while the cathedral was being completed, and there presumably it still is, in the Duke of Norfolk's castle, its authenticity having been called into question. But it can still generate enough heat to prevent the granting of the parish priest's request for its return to Bury, though he did apparently get the three loose teeth direct from Toulouse.

One further point that I find fascinating is that as well as a support grant of an annual fourpence per carucate of land levied throughout East Anglia – a carucate was the area a team of eight oxen with one plough could till in a year – the Confessor's queen left virtually all her Suffolk estates to the Abbey. Unfortunately the fourpenny levy was appropriated in 1096 by Bishop de Losinga for the construction of Norwich cathedral, but Queen Emma's estates remained and these more or less coincide with what we know as West Suffolk today. So a great deal of the clay lands, and the seats of the Suffolk nobility, were centred on Bury, and in a way Bury still draws its levy from this part of the county, every beet lorry during the winter 'campaign' turning its muddy wheels towards the huge sugar beet factory.

Here, in these heavy lands, it was quite a long time before horses replaced oxen, the powerful Suffolk breed being developed to power the plough through the fertile clays. Then came steampower, traction engines working the fields, drawing plough and thresher on long steel hawsers. A whole new industry grew up based on the fertility of fen and clay. But it was the diesel tractor and combine harvester, the huge growth in mechanisation following the Second World War, that really changed the face of this part of East Anglia.

Also the introduction of hormone sprays. By the selective elimination of all growth but the corn crop, these hormone weedkillers boosted production. All was suddenly green, a universal drab productive green as wheat and barley ruled supreme.

Within a few years we saw East Anglia become like the prairie lands we knew in Canada and the States, hedges ripped out, ditches filled, and the sound of the chainsaw ever present as the hedgerow trees were

Farming in the corn belts of East Anglia is highly mechanised.
Combine-harvesting near Higham in Suffolk.

225

plundered to make room for larger and larger ploughs, bigger combines, the featureless vistas ever widening.

The wheatbelt farmer, now totally industrialised, has his plough virtually hitched to the rear of his combine, so that in late summer, early autumn hardly a month separates the gold of the corn and the brown of the plough, and in that short interval the skies are dark and the evenings red with the fire-hazardous, air-polluting disposal of the threshed stalks of wheat for which there is no profitable use, the yellow of stubble prairie turned in a moment to a burned black landscape.

This burning goes on sometimes till quite late in the autumn, dependent, of course, on the weather. If the harvest is early, a blazing August running into a fine September, then the harvest moon really is the harvest moon. But if it's a wet summer, the corn ripening late or too full of moisture, then the farmer who owns his own combine and is not dependent on contractors will wait. 'They're like a lot of sheep, soon as they see their neighbour harvesting they all rush to get their crops in.' That particular farmer friend worked on the principle that East Anglia's 'Indian summer' always comes to those who wait, and in all the years I have been here he has hardly ever been wrong. Though kiln drying of the corn is fairly universal now, the cost of drying is high and an important factor in the profit per hectare.

Sometimes, it seems, the burning of the stubble comes so late it runs on into Guy Fawkes' Day. Certainly it now seems to have taken over from the bonfire as the autumn spectacular. There was a time when every village had its own bonfire, many of the farmers too, and always it seemed between six thirty and seven, so that if we were going out on the evening of November 5th the drive through the dark lanes would be lit by the pinpoint glow of fire after fire, and as many of them were, like our own, close to the church, tower after tower would stand out, square and solid in the night, as though floodlit.

Now the bonfires – which go back much further than Guy Fawkes and the other conspirators of 1605, to pagan times – are largely confined to pubs, even the fireworks no longer a home display, but shared as a communal event. And not only pubs. Great houses like Melford Hall have followed the example of Lewes and opened their grounds to the public for an organised display. But however big that display it is but a candle to the free spectacular put on by farmers over a period that often extends for a full month.

Scorched hedgerows and clanging firebells were for a long time the inevitable accompaniments. Now the law has stepped in and, with the perimeter scarfed, the danger of a runaway blaze is lessened. There aren't many hedgerows left anyway. As a result the farmer is less inclined to

And after the harvest the burning. This is one of the unacceptable faces of farming
– fire and the black fallout that follows.

wait around for the still of a quiet evening and the crackle of fields blazing can be heard at any time of the day, vast palls of black smoke visible for miles across the flat East Anglian landscape.

The sound of one of these stubble blazes is quite frightening. Several times I have been in the Great Wood when one of the fields that border it has been fired and the machine-gun crackle of wheat stalks bursting has been so loud I could have sworn it was the trees themselves that were on fire. The first time this happened I ran back to the car and drove right round the wood, so sure was I that I was hearing the sound of trees burning and would have to call out the fire brigade. But by the time I got to the source of the noise the fire was almost out and not a tree had even been singed. That sound of burning straw is carried very distinctly on the wind, the noise of it rising rapidly to a holocaust crescendo, then dying out quite suddenly.

This hut in the Great Wood was once a place for the guns to rest. During World War II bombs were stored in the wood. Now the forestry is a splendid mixture of trees.

But to see it at night, that really is a spectacle. So often when the days are drawing in and we have been driving out to dinner, there in the dark of the moon, far away on the horizon, a burgeoning glow appears, hazed in mist or reflected red on the low bellies of clouds. Sometimes that is all we see of it. Other times the road we are on seems to lead right into the furnace, so that the glow of it rapidly turns to leaping flames, then a line of fire galloping like a horse of the Apocalypse across the dark back of the land. Hedges, trees, the outline of a building, all black and stark against the leaping fire, rolling clouds of flame-red smoke, the noise and the smell of burning. And men moving, dark silhouettes hurling rags of flame or beating at the edge of a field where a rogue fire has blossomed, the black outlines of a tractor looking like a gun, the whole scene a macabre reminder of early films and a long-ago war, Hill 60, Ypres, the Somme.

And you drive on into the dark of the night thinking of poppies and Armistice Day so near. But the traffic is no longer stilled at eleven, the silence no longer kept . . . Has something been lost? Has the world changed so much that we can no longer spare two minutes of our time?

It is on these still dark autumn nights, driving into the darkness or sitting before a roaring log fire, that the mind turns in upon itself, thinking of age-old things. Soon it will be time to go to the woods for a Norway spruce that will furnish the children's corner of the church. Soon it will be Christmas. That at least remains, deep-rooted in our being, a festival as old as man, the last of the autumn plenty before the cold and the scrimping of winter comes. What if the coal and the oil ran out? What if there was war? What if any of the thousand and one disasters man is heir to actually occurred and there was no more frozen food in the supermarket, no more electricity and only wood to heat our homes through the cold dark winter months? Then the towns would know what the country is all about and we would regret the loss of our forest and hedgerow trees, our lack of foresight in not replacing the seed corn of our woods gone long since for charcoal and men o' war, and more recently to that wretched little beetle that has carried Dutch elm disease to half the great trees of England.

Autumn is the season for reflection, both in nature and in man. But not, I would add, for pessimism. Hope, not despair, is autumn's message. Look at the trees, the buds of the chestnut, those sticky sweet buds already formed. To walk in the woods in late autumn, after the leaf fall, is to see the promise of renewal, nature's promise. On a golden day with the sun shining through mist, sparkling on the frozen white of the grass, lighting the bare branches overhead, the dark of the haws gleaming bronze, the red of the hips brighter than any lips, and occasionally, just occasionally, that subtle orange-red of the spindle berries – then look up and your heart will lift, for there, glistening damp and bright in the sun, are the buds of next year's leaves. On such a day even the poplars look ready to be dressed again in green and the daintiness of birch and aspen

229

carry their own thin brown spears with the certainty of a new beginning already begun, the beech, too.

That is why I like to be in England for the winter. It is a good time for writing, short days, long evenings, forming what will later blossom into a book. And in the Great Wood only the ash looks drab, no longer queenly with her black buds standing two by two, hard and unyielding against the cold to come.

I do much of my thinking in the Great Wood, so many scenes worked out, a whole story line refashioned, a piece of dialogue framed on the mind's tongue, so clear I might have spoken it aloud – the trees, the dog, the grasses and the birds, all unseen, my mind locked in on the problem of the day. A mile walked and nothing seen but what is in the mind. What a waste of a beautiful day, yet what satisfaction if just one line has fallen into place or a character found himself again, the story moving on.

Then summer comes and we go to the Wood to watch the sun go down and listen to the nightingales. There we have what we think must be the longest bar in England. There are half a dozen of them in fact, each about seventy yards long, concrete and brick loading ramps constructed for bombing-up the airstrikes that once left almost nightly for Berlin and the Ruhr from the airfield that bordered the wood. The hardcore of these solid ramps is marvellous for storing up heat, so that we have warmth in the cool of the evening whether we are leaning against the wall or sitting on it, and dog roses have climbed twenty feet above us.

The sun goes down as we drink our wine and eat our supper. There are big, beautifully marked grass snakes and slow worms that lie quiet and polished and look like vipers. We hardly ever see the nightingales that produce such incredible, throbbing, gurgling song, bird calling to bird from oak to oak and in the high ash trees. Strange – I hardly notice them in the mornings when they sing even harder, but then there are other birds, the robin almost as good a songster, and there are visual distractions. Once we heard a corncrake and once there were purple emperors, the Wood being one of the few in East Anglia where they had been reported seen in the topmost branches of oaks.

But birds and insects, the whole environment, are under constant and increasing pressure. Particularly in East Anglia. Henry Williamson's little classic about the hardness of life on a Norfolk farm, though published in 1941, covered the period when Britain's agriculture was swamped by the flood of cheap imported foods from the Empire. It could never be written now. Land was cheap then. One of the largest fruit growers of Suffolk, driving us round his orchards in the fifties, could still boast that he had never paid more than a fiver for any of the great rolling sweep of

The feather from an overflying swan a-glitter with the morning dew or 'dag'.

The Great Wood looking down to the main entrance. The corn land beyond was once a bomber airfield.

acres we were looking at, the trees so neat and regimented, all heavy with blossom, the grass beneath them newly cut, the scent of hay mingled with apple, pear and peach, the sound of bees whenever we stopped the car. Now the value of that land has increased 400 times. But agricultural riches bring attendant problems, and added to the land hungriness of farmers has been an additional and quite exceptional factor – the eastern counties of England have since the sixties been virtually the fastest growing area of the country. Not only has national policy encouraged industrial estates and a shift of population out of the once overcrowded East End of London, but the high cost of living in London, particularly the high cost of City rents, has resulted in a natural drift east and north, Chelmsford, Colchester, Ipswich and Norwich housing an increasing number of evacuated London offices.

The pressure on the countryside has thus been twofold. In addition to the farmers' search for ever-increasing yields to meet competition, the towns have been eating up productive acres at an alarming rate, improved roads, bypasses, housing and industrial estates, sewage works, all the infrastructure that accompanies growing and increasingly prosperous communities. It has been pretty much a bandit snatch, the private enterprise of the farming community on the one hand seizing every extra foot of tillable soil, trees, ditches, hedges and wild patches disappearing, ponds and swamps drained, and on the other, the community at large, particularly the growing numbers in the towns, absorbing hundreds upon hundreds of acres for road vehicles, factories, housing, for effluent and waste disposal.

The rape of the environment has, in fact, been as massive as that started by the King and Bedford in the Fens, or the even more widespread effect of the enclosure of rivers and estuaries within artificial banks. But at least that resulted in land reclamation, even though it destroyed a whole way of life that had continued virtually unchanged for centuries and caused great harm to fishing and maritime communities on the coast by silting. Unfortunately, as far as resettlement and industrialisation is concerned, what has been happening in these same counties recently is land destruction. Roads, factories and urban housing do not grow food.

Whether the purple emperor has disappeared as a result of crop-spraying I do not know, but chemicals are a deadly agricultural weapon and in summer the buzz of the low-flying crop-sprayer is to be heard almost everywhere, something that does not occur in the towns. And anybody who has carefully read the small print will realise that spraying from aircraft is only as safe as the man who pilots it and those who mix the contents of its tanks. Several chemicals that were once widely and indiscriminately used have been abandoned in the last two or three decades, some of them only just in time. An occasional owl can now be heard in the clay lands, the hawks are back and there are mice again to feed predators. But it is no accident that the kestrels hover over the fringes of motorways – these, like the MoD properties, are the new

undisturbed habitats. Towns were once regarded as unhealthy places. Now I am not so sure. Diesel and the sulphur fall-out from central heating are bad, but consider how taxation has encouraged farmers to seek any means in a good year to plough profits back into the land. And for 'improvements', including the ripping out of hedges, they get a grant. The removal of hedges and the filling in of ditches was the first great grant-aided improvement. More recently it has been drainage. There are even drains set alongside ditches so that the ditch need never be cleaned. The result is a very fast run-off from the land into streams and rivers. There is thus no reserve of water held in the soil as there was once. Soon more and more crops will have to be irrigated by watersprays. This will affect the water table as well as the reservoirs and underground supplies which are already depleted. And with the run-off from the land comes the residue of everything the farmer has fed into his crops, the fertilisers, the sprays, the lime, the effluent. Given a period of heavy rain the water in my stream has a milky, dull look to it, as though it had been contaminated by a factory. And that is just what has happened, the factory upstream of me not an industrial one, but farmland. It is a very long time since children playing in the stream caught eels and I cannot remember when I last saw any smallfry.

Industrialised farming has meant an industrial back-up largely centred on Ipswich – Fisons, of course, for sprays and fertilisers, and a host of farm machinery makers and suppliers. But though the gods of wheat and barley now rule supreme, courtesy of CAP and the Common Market, East Anglia continues in the mould of Turnip Townshend and Coke of Holkham, an area where specialist and innovative husbandry is practised. The work of Leonard Hills at the Henry Doubleday Foundation in Bocking near Braintree and of the Soil Association at Haughley near Stowmarket is not exactly commercial, but it has led to a 40,000 acre farming co-operative at nearby Needham Market specialising in organically grown crops, and this group has broken out of the health-food shops into supermarkets. Another agricultural innovation, and one that has become highly commercial, started in the same locality. In fact the last of the crumbling sheds that housed the original battery chicken concept was until recently still visible barely a mile from the Great Wood, a dilapidated monument to the ultimate in animal degradation. This unacceptable face of intensified farming has been refined and refined until pigs and calves as well as poultry have been squeezed into pens that restrict movement, the ultimate in the unacceptable being, of course, the animal laboratories where experiments that most people would rather not know about are carried out for the testing of commercial products.

But, like the Roman and early Saxon coins so persistently turned up

Rape in Spring. This bright yellow, strong-smelling crop is grown for its seed oil. Next year it may be lupin seed.

Bullocks fattening for market in the lush green of May-time at Stratford St. Mary.

by the plough or ferreted out by metal detector enthusiasts, there are two sides to the agricultural coin. The bright side is that the clear sunlight, the brilliant autumns and the proximity to the continent has ensured that this is where the bulk of our seed crops have traditionally been grown and ripened. To be 'in clover' could well apply to a farmer with a field of seed ripening in a good autumn. Now you can get almost as much for a field of wheat to swell the mountain and it's not often you see the creamy sheen of Kersey White stretching away to the far hedgerow. Even rarer is the blue of flax that was once so common over towards the coast. But acres of seed, from onion to bean, from brassica to rootcrop, can be seen wherever the farmer decides to specialise, and there are others who turn flat strips of rich land over to rhubarb and like crops that you would hardly expect to see outside of a shed or an allotment. Colman's at Norwich is synonymous with English mustard – and incidentally with the fastest sail boat in the world, *Crossbow II*. Thompson and Morgan of Ipswich, supplying the world's gardens since the middle of last century, claimed the world's largest seed catalogue.

There was a time when half a dozen East Anglian maltsters supplied the Highlands and Islands of Scotland with almost all the malt for their self-whiskies. Not any more, for in 1963 a new strain of barley was produced suitable for growing by the farmers of north-east Scotland and now eighty per cent of the whisky malt comes from Scotland itself. There is a certain similarity in this sudden transfer of production to the collapse of the wool industry two or three centuries earlier. One of the East Anglian maltsters that continues to supply malt to Scottish distilleries is centred on Stowmarket less than a dozen miles away. They also supply Japan, have accounted for half of Britain's malt extract exports and whilst a friend of ours ran it were a good example of a local agricultural industry that follows the East Anglian tradition of endeavouring to keep in the forefront of innovative cultivation. They have branched out into hydroponics, recycling their waste heat into several acres of greenhouses where tomatoes and roses in particular are grown with their roots in gravel and water which is drip-fed a fertilised diet.

I suppose you could call it a spin-off of the battery chicken idea. The carp they farm, too. And I suppose their diversification into genetics is a development from work that originated at Cambridge and other scientific centres around the world. But what they were doing at Stowmarket, and the more sophisticated genetic experiments being carried out at the John Innes Research Centre at Norwich, is of particular interest to all of us since it could provide the beginnings of a solution to one of the world's greatest ecological problems – the gradual and apparently inexorable spread of the desert.

Deserts occur when the tree cover has been removed, usually by humans for warmth, for construction of homes, for charcoal to cook by, and particularly by the need for ground space on which to grow food. This process of denudation is completed by browsing animals, goats

235

chiefly, that destroy the seedling trees. It is difficult for us to visualise the Libyan desert as the granary of the Roman Empire or to realise that the last forest in the Sahara disappeared only a century ago. The first step in the reclamation of an area that has become desert is to recreate the forest. A start has been made by Sheik Zeyd in the Abu Dhabi area of the Gulf and near Dubai. But to extend environmental planting to the millions of square miles of African, Arabian, Asian and Australian desert would require a vast output of seedling trees, an output quite beyond the capacity of existing tree nurseries.

Considerable progress has already been made. Trees eight to ten years old for the production of palm oil have been developed *en masse* from a single plant stock, and all are running true to the original stock. At Stowmarket, in a very small unit with a capacity of some 650,000 plants in a nine-month period, they began micropropagating against firm orders from nurseries for clematis, roses, chrysanthemums, all the more expensive plants, either for quick propagation of new varieties or for the development of a particularly robust strain. Micropropagation involves taking tissue from new growth – meristematic tissue – then getting it to take in a special solution so that it produces vegetative shoots that can be grown on in a rooting medium until finally the plant can be weaned. The closely guarded secrets are, of course, the special requirements of each genus, for heat, light intensity and day length, for nutrients and hormones, and finally the weaning techniques – there is a weak ring between the root growth and the plant cells that has to be strengthened before it can be put to grow on in a natural environment.

The tissue culturalist, using the 'laboratory' techniques, is in the main commercially orientated, but it doesn't require much of a sci-fi imagination to extrapolate the 'green revolution' concept of feeding the human multitude out of the laboratory to the broader prospects of making the deserts bloom again . . . or, of course, to genetically engineering a world of mutants so terrifying, or of such perfection, that the whole course and direction of life on earth is altered.

This, as I have said before, is a book of enthusiasm, and not one in which I would have wished to introduce such very disturbing thoughts. But East Anglia is rich in its food resources, both on the land and in the sea, and nobody with any imagination can live in such an area without being at least vaguely conscious of a whole host of very worrying problems that most people would prefer to keep well out of sight. And to preserve the balance I now propose to do just that by shying away from the subject and talking about roses instead.

Most of the specialisation to which I have referred has arisen as a result of the climatic uniqueness of East Anglia in an island very much influenced by an oceanic weather pattern. Sun and soil, those hard-

An October landscape near Higham Hill.

The gold of ripening barley, and feverfew flowers in Autumn fields near Dalham.

baking clays mixed with gravel, it is this that makes the southern half of the area as good for the rose as the Bordelais is for the grape. Cants of Colchester – most of our roses have come from them, and not those potted things with their cramped roots, but stock that has been lifted straight from the rosefield – are on our route down from London.

July through to September those rosefields out at Mile End on the Sudbury road are a riot of colour. We see them perhaps in unusual circumstances. Certainly nobody else is ever there because when we are leaving London we get up at five and leave at six to beat the rush hour and ensure that I have a full writing day when I get back to Suffolk. This means we are at Colchester at seven thirty and if it is one of those wonderful bright summer mornings with the sun burning up the last of the early morning haze and the promise of heat to come, then at Mile End I turn off down the potholed gravel track and after half a mile, there

237

in the flat land beyond the sheds is a great rectangle of colour. The paths that intersect it are baked hard and brown. The warmth shimmers over the brilliance of millions of blooms and the air is heavy with the scent of them.

To walk row after row after row, so many names and blooms of all sorts in all stages from bud to overblown, white through palest pink to red so velvet dark it is the black of dried blood, and all the time the scent, the overwhelming heady scent – and nobody else there so that for a moment you are in Wonderland, the temporary owner of the largest, the finest, the most lovely cornucopial garden of roses in the world.

A vehicle appears, three men, one of them the manager. It is eight o'clock and work is about to begin, but for a few minutes, after he has got over his surprise at finding anybody in his rosefields at that hour, there is time to talk, about the rose show he has just attended and what he plans to exhibit at the next, and always a few words of advice, about black spot or mildew, which varieties are really disease-resistant, or what happened after that terrible 1982 December when so much was caught with the sap not yet down and feared lost, yet still most good stock ultimately managed to spring anew from the base.

And after that, as you drive into the heavy heartland of East Anglia, you will be very conscious during those few hot summer months of the wealth of roses blooming in every roadside garden. In fact, there are moments when the whole land seems to be one immense garden. And there are nurseries and specialist horticulturalists everywhere. I often regret that Barcock's nurseries or Beth Chatto's very specialised gardens at Elmstead are not also on our way home from London. Fred Barcock, in particular, for he started up at Drinkstone about the time we came to East Anglia and has been like a father to our Suffolk garden, his green-fingered knowledge, given so generously to us and to many others, apparently regarded by him as something to be shared with anybody whose enjoyment of growing things makes them fellow enthusiasts.

Elder in the Fens in June, bluebells and marsh marigolds in the woods and fields.

The glorious blood red of the poppies; a glimpse of what the countryside was like before sprays killed out the wild flowers.

10. Heaths and Sandlings

There was a time when I didn't know a tsuga from a thuya and thought *pinus contorta* must be an anatomical aberration. But then I went to Canada, wrote a book called *Campbell's Kingdom* and ever since then I have been hooked on trees. You can have all the other plants in the world, but a tree, with its marvellous built-in mechanism for pumping water and cleansing the atmosphere, is as sacred to me as it is to a number of primitive tribes around the world. The late Lord Bradford, who described himself as a dendrophile, once told me he had enquired of a well-known healer what he did to renew himself when drained of all the energy he had poured out for others. The answer was a very simple one – 'I lean my back against a tree for a while and absorb a little of its strength.' Since then I have tried to do just that, with what success I am never quite sure. All I can say is that in the process of finding a comfortable rest for my back and trying to think what the living cells and fibres of that tree are doing day in, day out, twenty-four hours a day, the mind becomes strangely empty and there is a wonderful sense of relaxation, almost of relief. I think if I were better at it, or perhaps made the effort to do it more often, I might get to a stage of mental weightlessness that would be very close to the disembodiment threshold.

Extensive travel in a country as vast as Canada has the inevitable effect of making the islands of one's birth seem quite diminutive, so that when I was offered 35,000 acres of the most spectacularly beautiful part of the Highlands at what now seems a quite ridiculous figure of seven shillings and sixpence per acre, it wasn't the distance I would have to travel that made me turn it down. It was high, bare mountain country, a lot of it, and I would have enjoyed it, the wildness appealing to my Highland blood. But in the ribbon of lowlands beside the loch there were a lot of crofts, and after reading the Crofters' Act, the thought of having to spend the rest of my life writing my guts out for a hundred crofters an' all an' all . . . so we bought the Great Wood a few miles from our Suffolk home. This was the first of our forests, a very overgrown neglected wood of oak underplanted with hazel, the coppice cover so high and thick it was no place to visit when the moon was high! And there was a single-track railway line running through a cutting and a bridge over it, but the trains were so few and the sound of them so muffled they were like ghost trains. In the end nothing ran and they tore up the rails, selling the track to the local council for a walkway, the woods either side gradually closing in to give it the appearance of a tunnel.

The King's Forest in May with the beech in fresh green leaf.

Since the land was heavy calcareous boulder clay, quite the opposite of the light sandy soil of Breckland, Aldewood, Lynn and Wensum, the Great Wood has no relevance to these sandling areas except to indicate that, through personal experience, and by serving on national and regional timber-growing committees, I do know something about the problems of planting and establishing woodlands in an area of England where the rainfall can be as little as eighteen inches a year.

The sandlings are not the original forested areas of East Anglia. They were heaths and open spaces and as attractive to the Neolithic men arriving by way of what is now the North Sea as the downland and other open hill areas of southern England were to those moving north across what is now the Channel. The old forest areas, which were predominantly oak with other hardwoods, flourished mainly on the heavier lands, and these, being unsuitable for primitive agricultural implements, remained largely intact. Indeed, throughout the Middle Ages, the impassability of the forest tracks was a major hindrance to the passage of goods by wagon. This must have been the case until well into the Victorian period, possibly later, for recent research has revealed more than seventy brick-making sites in West Suffolk alone, and since most of them are small, they were obviously developed to supply the immediate locality, clay being readily available and transportation, other than by water, still difficult. In addition to the forest, the North Norfolk people were hemmed in by the Fens on one side, the Broads on the other, so that the only way out was by Breckland and Newmarket Heath where the sterile sand gives way to chalk that is in places as clear and open as downland.

It requires some imagination now to visualise what a blasted Lear-mad heath the Brecklands must have been when those goosegirls were still driving their leathershod flocks from Norfolk to London, for it has changed out of all recognition. This is now Thetford Forest, the largest in England, larger even than Kielder or the New Forest. And marching with the Forestry Commission land is an almost equally large no-go Ministry of Defence area. Once, at a friend's house, when I asked a general, who was visiting Colchester Garrison, whether it wasn't about time the Army disgorged some of the land requisitioned in World War II, I was somewhat disarmed by his claim to be the greatest conservationist in the country. His point was that the problems of tourist-polluted areas like the New Forest, with its 800 tons of dumped rubbish a year, just did not arise on the MoD lands. The public was barred, and with military use spasmodic, animals, insects and plants flourished virtually undisturbed. That was some time ago. Now there is a small conservation section at the MoD known as Defence Lands 3 dedicated to the creation of areas of wilderness and the propagation of endangered wildlife, anything from the Dartford warbler to the natterjack toad or the re-introduction of the great bustard.

It was in 1922 that the Forestry Commission made its first land purchase of a small area near Swaffham. Now, with the MoD lands, the

This is the barren Breckland country as it is now, largely conifer, but relieved with fire-breaks of beech or birch and some very beautiful amenity plantings.

total conserved and forested area of Breckland nationally owned covers almost 150 square miles, a huge block lying between and to the north-east of Brandon and Thetford.

To drive through it is a joy, for the road running from West Stow to Brandon was forested in the days when the Forestry Commission could afford to edge its commercial plots with amenity planting. Deciduous trees – oak and beech and chestnut – border the road, lovely cathedral-like groves. Some fine stands of softwoods, too, with everywhere long ride-glimpses deep into the forest with the verges of logging tracks providing a habitat for all sorts of creatures and plants that could never have existed when it was open heathland. And at the south-western end of it, near an old Saxon site at West Stow where post-holes have indicated a village of some eighty huts and halls, five replicas with split-log daub-filled walls and sedge thatching have been constructed, also a small clay oven, to show just what it was like for a tribal family living in a forest clearing fifteen hundred or so years ago.

There is considerable discussion in Britain now about the effect on the environment of the dark of conifer plantations, the need for more deciduous planting. This has grown with the grubbing out of the hedgerows for prairie farming in the corn belt and the destruction of so many millions of elms by Dutch elm disease. Compounding the complaint is the stage we have now reached in the growth of plantations started in the fifties and sixties. There was a big surge in those two decades due to a greater realisation of the enormous cost of our timber imports, also the ever-increasing rate of taxation. It is difficult for most people to comprehend a time scale to maturity of 100 years and more, but that is the time it takes an oak to grow. Other hardwoods are not much faster, beech perhaps slower. It depends on the soil. Softwoods, on the other hand, grow much faster, even on poor lands like the sandlings, and it is on the poorer lands that the Forestry Commission has concentrated its efforts. But two decades sees the softwood plantation still at the thicket stage, dark and dense, totally unwalkable and waiting for its first thinning.

Thetford, however, is relatively old with many compartments close to maturity. It is a place for walking, particularly in spring when the sky is clear and bright and a bitter wind is blowing, for the forest gives shelter and the rough boles of the trees shine red in shafts of sunlight. And, when the days are long, to get up with the dawn . . . I can be there as soon as the sun is up, walking half a dozen miles before breakfast at the old Bell at Thetford. This is where the timber-growers of East Anglia meet in committee, so that for me the forest has been a regular run, and in autumn, when the road is a swathe of leaf-gold, there are fungi, even by the roadside, so that sometimes I arrive at the Bell with the boot of the car loaded with parasol mushrooms or inky caps that have taken me only a moment's pause to cull.

In the early days of this man-made forest a good mixture of species was planted – Douglas fir and European larch as well as a variety of broadleaved trees. But in the main it was Scots pine, the only conifer, apart from the yew, that is native to Britain – until about 8,000 years ago forests of it covered much of the country. It had to be Scots pine, for the soil is poor, the rainfall a low twenty-three inches, and hardly a month goes by without the danger of ground frost, the spring planting time being particularly cold with searing east winds. Corsican was used to some extent, but this pine is difficult to establish as I know to my cost. However, it yields almost double the volume of timber and in later

Rendlesham, one of the finest stands of Corsican pine in Britain.

plantings has been used much more extensively.

There are deer in the forest, red, roe and fallow. In fact, there are deer in all the forested areas of East Anglia, often in small itinerant family groups that move from shelter to shelter. These and the hares have added to the difficulties of establishing plantations of oak and beech, not only in Breckland, but on the clays as well. I was reduced at one stage to fencing in areas as small as eight acres before planting, and even then we found it advisable to plant our oak in small groups scattered through softwood plantings, the idea being that two complete growths of pine could be achieved while the oaks were making their ponderous 100-year way to maturity.

I have dwelt a moment on the problems of growing timber in the eastern counties because Breckland and the really poor sandlings of the coastal belt are best suited for this. You have to remember that these forestry areas are being farmed just as intensively as the fields you see green with corn or yellow with rape, or brown under the winter plough. But it is tree farming on lands that are of little use for anything else. Walk through the forest and you will see all manner of animals, birds, plants, insects and fungi. You will also see here and there, at the ride-side or deep in the timber, the forest industry at work – felling, logging up, replanting, brashing, and at Brandon the final process in a timber conversion depot that covers some forty acres, the largest in the country.

I must admit these places always strike me as something similar to an abattoir, for I never look upon them without thinking of all we owe to trees – homes, furniture, warmth, the very air we breathe. I never hear the buzz of a chainsaw without feeling for the death of a friend, for it was the photosynthesis of the leaves and needles of trees that in the long ago cleansed the atmosphere of carbon dioxide so that life on earth became possible. And when it is a mature hardwood being felled, the thought uppermost in the mind must be that it takes but a moment to fell what has been a century and more in the growing. Each day a big mature oak pumps forty gallons of water into the air through its leaves, and it is this process that is so beneficial to the atmosphere we breathe. That is why I grow trees, not corn. Wood is such a wonderful, living material, and I have never met a forester who didn't reflect in some part of his personality the kindliness of his working environment.

The forests of Rendlesham, Tunstall, Dunwich and Waveney, totalling some fourteen square miles, are much nearer the North Sea than Thetford, on even sandier soil and with even less rainfall. Rendlesham and Tunstall in particular. Here in the sandlings are great stands of Corsican pine. Nothing to compare, of course, with the red-gold cathedral forests that mantle the mist-shrouded heights of Corsica itself, but still impressive, and the soil so poor. Perhaps I am prejudiced, having watched them develop from quite small trees, but I prefer these coastal forests to Breckland, the plantations more broken, patches of farmland, and always the flickering yellow of kissing-time gorse merging in summer with the

brighter brilliance of broom. A great place for fungi in the gold of autumn, a world removed that puts one in the mood on the way to Snape and the Aldeburgh Festival, and with the sea so near a greater variety of birds.

And just as the boulder clay area of the Old Draperies is Constable and Gainsborough country, so the coastal heaths are associated with the names FitzGerald and Crabbe, the one born near Woodbridge, the other at Aldeburgh. A customs officer's son, George Crabbe became a surgeon-apothecary, but then left Suffolk in 1780 for London where Dr Johnson helped to make his name with *The Village*. He then went into the Church and returned to Suffolk for a few years. This, for instance –

> When tides were neap, and in the sultry day,
>   Through the tall bounding mud-banks made their way,
>   Which on each side rose swelling, and below
>   The dark warm flood ran silently and slow;

is from his *Peter Grimes*, which was later to be the basis of what is probably Britten's greatest opera.

Edward FitzGerald was a man in a different mould, a linguist who started his free translating in Spanish – the *Six Dramas of Calderón*, then switched to Persian and produced, in 1859, his *Rubaiyat* of Omar Khayyam. Educated at King Edward VI Grammar School, Bury St Edmunds, and Trinity College, Cambridge, a friend of Thackeray and Tennyson, he was known as Old Fitz and was one of the 'Woodbridge Wits'. Also, and this is what I find so endearing in such a clever and poetic man, he loved what he called a good Splash of sailing – i.e. a good thrash to windward. He had a little sixteen-footer on the Deben in 1861, then two years later, filled with the same urgent desire I was to experience almost a century later, he got himself a 14-tonner, the *Scandal*, so that he could order his skipper to sail him across the Deben bar and out into the North Sea.

This was in the days, of course, when Harwich was a great naval port – from the house where he was born the topmasts of men-o'-war lying in Hollesley Bay during the Napoleonic wars were plainly visible. It was also a great yacht racing centre. His father owned a 50-ton cutter, the *Ruby* (referred to later, punning in the worst of tastes, as The Ruby Yacht). The Royal Harwich had already been in existence for some time, one of the earlier yacht clubs, and the year after Fitz got out of the Deben in his *Scandal* (with or without the top hat his fishing lugger partner, Posh, swore in his cups he wore at sea) the first of the 'Ocean Matches', forerunner of the world-wide ocean racing of today, was organised by the Royal Thames, which brought to the line 11 schooners, 3 yawls and 13 of those fast cutters that were based on the older revenue cutters that endeavoured to cope with the smuggling trade.

But Old Fitz was essentially an East Coaster, and his heart was in the Deben. Here is a quote from a book few people even know he wrote,

Tunstall in June, a Corsican pine forest that is even nearer the coast than Rendlesham.

Suffolk Sea Phrases, 'Why the old girl shuffles along like a Hedge-Sparrow!' said of a 'round bowed vessel – a "bruise-water" – spuffling thro' the water'. His grave at Boulge is marked with a Naishapur rose.

This is also the area of Britten and Pears . . . Pears singing *The Foggy Foggy Dew* – the weavers' trade, remember? – or that most East Anglian of all Britten's operas, *Curlew River*.

Here, too, but a little to the north, between Aldeburgh and Dunwich, is one of the country's most outstanding bird sanctuaries – Minsmere. It is right on the coast and even if you are not a member of the RSPB you can get sight of most of the birds by walking along the top of the sea defences. But best of all you need to go into the Reserve where there are 247 wooden hides big as stables with slits through which to watch such rarities as avocets, the piratical skua and all manner of geese, ducks, swans and waders.

The sandlings of the extreme north include only two small Forestry Commission areas, the Wensum and Lynn Forests, but the afforestation of this light sandy-soiled ridge spills over into the great estates. At Sandringham the plantations are all round the house and there is a ridge that looks down across the Wash. This sand-soil ridge extends intermittently all along the north of Norfolk, pines, and in places rhododendrons, growing where little else will grow so well, and glimpses of the sea.

This is summer tourist country and one of the major worries is FIRE. But though we think of fire as a high summer risk, the product of picnics or of cigarettes carelessly discarded in vegetation burned brown by the sun's heat, the risk is, in fact, greatest in the spring, when broadleaved trees are still bare, the sap not yet risen, the east wind blowing and the fabric of the forest all brittle with frost. That is when the forester prays and the farmer watches his soil blow, everybody's blood thinned by wind-chill and still no let-up, the winter endless, spring seemingly as far away as ever.

Walking the sandy ridges of these forests, or what remains of the original heathland, I am very conscious that this is where man began his occupation of the country. It goes back a long way, the Clactonian flint industry covering the great inter-glacial period of 400–200 thousand years ago. For those who know what to look for there is a real chance of finding worked flints brought to the surface by soil erosion. Having been with the Leakeys in both the Lake Turkhana and Olduvai regions of East Africa my head drops automatically, my eyes hungrily searching the ground.

At that distance of time the Clactonian artefacts are relatively crude, but in Neolithic times the heathland had the same attraction for Stone Age man as it had for the Neanderthals – it was clear of forest and swamp, with flint, the raw material of the hand tools on which their lives were becoming more and more dependent, everywhere available. Grime's Graves, cut into a clearing in Thetford Forest just north of Santon Downham, west of Peddars Way, is maintained as monument and prime example of the shallow diggings where man down the ages has mined flint for his hand tools, and his weapons. The whole area is a mass of small shafts and mines, nearly 400 of them, some connected by galleries that are now sealed off. Antler picks were used as digging tools in the low galleries where the flints were mined over 4,000 years ago. Until quite recently flint-knapping was still carried on intermittently by the local people, largely to meet an African demand, old flintlock guns still being in use among some of the tribesmen. The peak of the Brandon industry appears to have been the time of Wellington's Peninsular War when the call was for a million and a quarter gunflints a month.

Grime's Graves is the outstanding and preserved site, but there will have been local flint industries all over those heathlands, flint workings that only began to decline as the Beaker People moved in from the continent and the Bronze and Iron Ages got into their stride. As tools developed and hunting gave place to husbandry, it was these light lands, where there was little in the way of trees to hamper them, that attracted primitive farmers. The soil, of course, was quickly exhausted. This, and an increase in population, helped by the movement of settlers along age-old tracks like the Icknield and Peddars Way, caused a gradual disappearance of the woodlands immediately surrounding the heaths. Thus, Breckland and other open sandy areas were continually being expanded.

It is all old country, old in man's occupation of it, and it is one's knowledge of this that gives it such a feeling of antiquity, that sense of the Ice Age just receded and Neanderthal Man migrating northwards along the banks of the Rhine, across those plains that are now the North Sea.

The geological structure of East Anglia is basically Jurassic rock in the fenland area of the north-west, chalk in the centre as far south as the Ipswich-Haverhill line with London clay spilling over the border from Essex into Suffolk, and to the east the crags, which are mainly sand and shell from old seabeds. But these are the underlying formations, not what we see on the surface. What we see owes much to the effects of intense glaciation, the drifts producing surface deposits of till or boulder clay, such as we have in the Great Wood – bluish in colour and about as glutinous as molasses. In the post-glacial period there was a build-up of wind-blown sand and of course there was a steady accumulation of peat in all the low-lying marshlands. The watershed runs roughly from Sandringham in the north, past Diss and Bury to Saffron Walden, the rivers to the west of this line flowing north to the Wash, and all those to the east running direct into the North Sea.

'The pleasure of West Suffolk,' Defoe wrote, 'is much of it supported by the wealth of High Suffolk . . . for the richness of the land, and the application of the people to all kinds of improvement is scarce credible.' The richness of the land continues, as does the *application* of the people, and so also, when we first came to Suffolk, the distinction between East and West. But it remained a class distinction and nothing to do with topography, so that I am left wondering at the meaning of High-Suffolk, for in general the west of the county is the higher part.

The 'pleasure' of West Suffolk spills across the border into Cambridge-shire at Newmarket Heath, all classes rubbing shoulders in the presence of the English Thoroughbred. The Heath, which is basically chalk with

The end-product; conifer logs felled in the Breckland forests near Santon Downham.

a thin layer of gravel, was on the road from Norwich to London, ideal country for hunting and hawking, for the inevitable wagering of horse against horse – and it was also a nice lonely place for highwaymen to ply their trade. It was the Tudor kings who started the import of Arab stock and so began the development of the English breed of racehorse which we have since exported all over the world. The first Stuart, James I, took his pleasure on the Heath and attended some races there. There was also racing at Linton and Thetford. But it was Charles II who really put Newmarket on the map, riding his own horses there in 1671 to the nickname of Old Rowley.

In those days horse racing was very much confined to the locality. Travel wasn't easy and the horses competing had to get to the meeting on their own four hoofs – the first horsebox was a primitive affair drawn by a team of dray horses that took Lord Bentinck's colt Elis from Goodwood to Doncaster in 1836 to win the St Leger. By then there were over seventy meetings around Britain, ten of them at Newmarket, all rather like point-to-point meetings organised by local hunts in almost every county today.

We are back, of course, in the early stage-coach days when horse power was the sole means of travel for those who had the money to take the weight off their own two feet, so that there was a whole breed of humans living off the horse, drovers, copers, ostlers, gypsies, too, and all of them hangers-on at their local race meetings and, like the pickpockets and the Fagins, hoping a little of the gentry's silver would rub off on their itching palms. So, high and low met in uncontrolled proximity and the dozens of meetings were without any proper regulation till 1750, when the Jockey Club was formed to control racing on the Heath.

Eventually, the Jockey Club, with the monarch as President, became responsible for the regulation of horse racing throughout the country. Newmarket's position at the heart of British racing was further strengthened when Edward VII had the Royal Stud established at Sandringham. This, in brief, is the story of the Heath and now at last there is a museum at Newmarket so that the background of it is readily available to visitors and not something that has to be dug out of the staff at the Rutland Arms. I am not a racing man, so that though it is less than an hour away, I am an infrequent visitor, preferring the local hill farming atmosphere of Welsh pony shows, but whenever I am passing through Newmarket early in the morning I get great pleasure from the sight of strings of sleek, beautiful horses being ridden out to exercise on the gallops beside the Bury and Thetford roads. In the cold of winter, the breath of horse and rider smoking in the dawn, or Maytime, around five or six in the morning, the sun just rising and the mist still hanging, the shapes of horses moving with such a lovely gait on the edge of visibility. That is a sight for which

The dark of the forest near Santon Warren.

it is worth getting up before the sun, though you can still see strings of horses being ridden out much later in the mornings. Despite the chalk and the sand and the open grassland of the Heath, there is a Thames valley sense of richness about the secluded stables and houses, a great air of wealth. And watching the horses and their riders, the way the whole thing is organised, there is no doubt of it – this is a very thriving industry.

But back into Suffolk and that class distinction beteen West and East. It has become blurred now, and in any case, the West no longer lives off the East of the county. In the period of Empire and cheap imported foodstuffs many of the farms changed hands, and the dry sandling areas, which were never rich agriculturally, were particularly hard hit. This remained the position until quite recently. Then suddenly their cropping potential was revolutionised – by new seed strains, by the aerial spraying of pesticides and by hormone weedkillers, above all, by irrigation. There are farmers now who think largely in terms of water content, how much weight of water they can palm off on the public in the form of vegetables or fruit. You can see their farms in summertime, the sprayers like giant spiders rotating slowly, lifting and falling, a phantom dance that wavers ghostlike through fields of vegetable crops, some even moving on rails. In the Fens, too, but it is in these arid sand soil areas that the effect has been most marked.

Take a look at the private forestry on the Cromer Ridge, the growth so slow in the dry and the cold. Now it could all be profitably cultivated. But at Weasenham, close by the Townshend estate, I have seen a mixed stand of trees that makes nonsense of any such switch, the sort of trees I hadn't seen since walking through Stanley Park, Vancouver, before going to the Yukon. And this in what is almost a frost hollow, on soil light as silver sand with a two-inch layer of iron pan below that holds the water. Not the best land for growing trees, you would think, and yet they are fully a hundred feet high, the 'children' as it were of one of the Coke family, deciduous and conifer mixed, the species ranging from oak and sycamore to Douglas, western red cedar and some of the rarer firs.

Here was a plantation managed with loving care by the third generation, Richard Coke's grandfather having started it, and despite the fellings of two world wars it is a remarkable demonstration of the advantages of mixed planting, the soil improved and the rate of growth increased. A perfect tree, he pointed out, does not necessarily produce the best seedlings. These often come from rubbishy-looking, twisted trees that have had to fight hard to survive, like those wind-tortured, corkscrew Scots still to be seen on Breckland road verges.

This is a man who really understands his trees, and as I listened to him, I thought of Bradford and thanked God for the heaths and sandlings. It is these forested areas that provide relief from East Anglia's agrarian cultivation, a breathing space that enables us to relax, to put our backs against a tree and think about something other than the value of wheat.

Newmarket's business is horses and racing; a view of the town from the heath, once notorious for highwaymen, with horses going out to the gallops for their morning exercise.

11. The Arctic shore

It is virtually an expedition to visit the northernmost shore of the East Anglian bulge. It is not so much the distance, but the strangeness of it, and the need for suitable clothing. As all travellers discover, you need as many clothes for a weekend as you do for a fortnight, and to get the full flavour of this northern shore, where duck and geese flighting in on arctic winds have nothing but the sea between them and the polar icepack, you should go there in autumn.

October is migration month, spreading on into November. But all through the winter months there are birds to watch in their thousands, shingle beaches, dunes and saltings to walk in bleak isolation, the tide making in the narrow channels, curling round mudbanks and sweeping in from a sea that is far removed from the shore, until you reach the eastern end of it. And at that time of the year conditions really can be arctic. Nevertheless, those addicted to this coast will claim it as the most fascinating area in all England, ornithologists in particular. But then migration-watchers are a breed apart and the area has for them very much the same attraction as the Camargue in southern France.

For others I think the attraction is that it gives us all the feel of being on the edge of something vast, conscious all the time that the wind is a wind off water and ice – and only the birds to tell us of the miles and miles of it and what it is like. The atmosphere, even in summer, can be winter-bleak. So far as it can be said to have been tamed this has clearly been the work of tough farming and fishing communities, of sailors and wildfowlers. It is there, immediately recognisable, in the flint farms with their flint walls and flint barns, the doors built to give the wind free rein through the winnowing yard; in the small flint cottages that huddle shoulder-to-shoulder against any ribbon of water reaching in to terra firma and the chance of shelter; in old grass-grown staithes and silted creeks; in what is left of the wharfs, jetties, boats, lights and markers that existed in the old sailing days.

Now, of course, the retired and the second-homers have almost taken over, buying up poor flint cottages at low prices to adapt them for weekend use, while the children of those whose business was once rooted in the sea move out to the towns or to places like Wells where there are modern council houses. But as in my own timber-framed cottage village, the fortunate side effect of this influx of 'foreigners' is that the fabric of the little fishing and fowling communities is preserved, the flint and brick

Behind us is Blakeney, beyond the horizon lies the northernmost point of East Anglia – no sign of the sea, but that is typical of this arctic shore.

buildings maintained and improved.

My first experience of this coast was in wartime, firing guns at aerial targets trailed across bleak marshes. The range was just outside the village of Stiffkey, my memories of that visit mainly of flint buildings, the dreariness of those marshes with no sight of the sea, and the cold. Also the church, of course, for it was the Rector at Stiffkey that had got himself clawed to death in a lion's cage at Blackpool where he had insisted on having himself placed on display. Part of the camp where we were housed is still there, converted to leisure use, the semi-circular gun park above the arrow-straight low-tide 'road' of High Sand Creek is now a car park, and the church's flint-walled graveyard has goats grazing in it. The Hall, which is right next to the church, has round towers of flint and brick, and in the village there are several single storeyed cottages, attractive to look at, less so perhaps to live in so close to the road. Most of the village is very compressed, for the river is just to the south, virtually jamming cottages and coast road hard up against the low wooded hill that blocks it off from the marshes.

By the time I saw that coast again Dorothy and I were in the process of trying to become part of the East Anglian scene. It is, of course, at the furthest reach from our home, so that it usually involves at least one night away. On that first visit of exploration we decided to spend Christmas up there, at the village of Ingoldisthorpe near Hunstanton, attracted I think by the name, which is shortened, of course, to Ing'lsthorp, just as Hunstanton is to Hunst'on. There was a garden with the square tower of the church just beyond, and Christmas Eve was still and cold, a light dusting of snow riming the flintwork, everything bright in moonlight as we walked to the nightwatch service. And next day, in a church that looks out over the Wash, we found ourselves gazing up at the face of a Red Indian princess.

The memory of that face has haunted me ever since, partly for the incongruity of finding her there in a snow-rimed Norfolk church, partly because we knew the name from a visit to the States when we had driven down the dune coast of Virginia and North Carolina to Cape Hatteras. There are towns there called Suffolk and Norfolk, another named Raleigh, for it was Raleigh who laid claim to Virginia in 1584 and a year later landed the first English settlers.

That first settlement on Roanoke Island was abandoned, but in 1587 a new expedition sailed and it was in the reconstituted palisade of what became known as the 'Lost Colony' that we heard of Pocahontas, the Indian princess who crossed the Atlantic to be received at the court of the first Stuart king of England.

Her father, Powhatan, was the chieftain of the Indian tribes who

Cley with its fine windmill and the remains of a staithe where tall ships long ago sailed up on the Glaven tide to carry Norfolk's wool to Europe's weavers.

banded together in opposition to a new private venture expedition that had sailed into Chesapeake Bay in 1606 under the captaincy of John Smith, a Lincolnshire adventurer and explorer. They successfully established themselves at a place they called Jamestown, but the following year Smith was captured by Powhatan's Indians. Pocahontas, who was only eleven at the time, was either charmed by the personality of the man or else fascinated by the power and nature of the English; whatever it was, she stood between him and execution, 'his head in her arms'. She was still only sixteen when she was herself captured and taken to Jamestown as security for the lives of prisoners held by her father. There she became a Christian, and within a year she had fallen in love and had married a young Norfolk squire.

In 1616 John Rolfe took her back with him to England. She was in London, at Court, received everywhere as a princess, and it was the old, largely wooden London before the Fire. What must she have thought of it? And then to journey down into Norfolk, to the Wash coast where her pale-faced husband had been born, where he had family and friends. And everything packed into so short a time, for in less than a year he was on his way back to his 'farm' in Virginia. She was to follow him, but waiting for the ship at an inn at Gravesend she contracted smallpox and died. Her bones lie in a Greenwich churchyard, her sculptured features on a memorial tablet in John Rolfe's Norfolk church.

I won't tell you where to find her, but when you do I have no doubt you will be struck, as we were, by the extraordinary courage of this young woman from a race the Europeans were to destroy and very nearly exterminate. There she is in a little Stuart hat and high ruff with what looks like feathers in her right hand. The plaque, placed just to the right of the entrance to the Rolfe chapel in 1933, is by a pupil of Rodin. It describes her as 'Princess Matoaka Rebecka Pocahontas, daughter of Powhatan, hereditary overking of the Algonquin Indians of Virginia, born 1595, baptised 1613, died 1617.' And it adds, 'Her romantic marriage in 1614 to John Rolfe brought peace to the Settlement.' To look on that dark, incongruous alabaster face, there at the limit of her travels, knowing she was only just over twenty-one when she died an ocean away from her home, and in a land that must have seemed a whole world away from that of her Indian father – what an extraordinary story!

Near where we first had a home in London, in Red Lion Square, there was until recently a statue of her reclining in the nude with feathers in her hair, but I never knew it was Pocahontas until on a recent pilgrimage to that church by the Wash we saw two photographs of the statue just below the memorial plaque. She deserves to be commemorated, not just for her courage, but also for the fact that she is a piece of history personified, her arrival in England almost the first harbinger of the great empire that was to come; alas, she also stands witness to the deep religious strains and the Puritan streak that has been the cause of so much sorrow in East Anglia. Only four years after her death the *Mayflower* sailed for North America; another twenty-two years and there was civil war in England, some of the toughest of Cromwell's Ironsides raised in East Anglia, and some of the staunchest Catholics resident there.

How cold it must have seemed to her. The nearby resort of Hunstanton can be as bleak and windswept as Cromer or Sheringham forty miles away on the other side of the county, but on a fine summer day wind and sun can burn the skin off your back and nobody returns from a holiday on the north shore of East Anglia looking other than as bronzed as an Alpine skier. The editor of this book has a cottage on the Great Ouse just south of Lynn, sensibly tucked under the river's high banks, and once when I was discussing the book with him seated on a chair on top of the bank, I asked him how many days of the year he and his family could bask in the sun like this. He just looked at me and smiled. No word was necessary.

Holme-next-the-Sea, close by Hunstanton, is the north-western extremity of Norfolk. It is here that the converging paths of the Peddars and Icknield Ways finally meet, and end, something that makes me wonder whether the story of a king losing his jewels to the incoming tide as he crossed the Wash is not really a case of his baggage being brought down the Icknield Way to be loaded on a vessel at Holme and then lost at sea in a gale. Looking out now across the golf course and the Holme Dunes Nature Reserve, vistas of sand and coarse grass, the only building the remains of old coastal defences, one wonders why two such important tracks of the pre-Roman period should end at this desolate point. The land may be tilting downwards, but surely not at a rate that could make a crossing of the Wash possible when man first laid down those two ancient tracks, and then by the time of the Roman occupation the water so deep that a ferry service could have been run from the fortress at Holme – one of the Forts of the Saxon Shore – to the Lincolnshire coast.

Reclamation of the Wash remains a never-never prospect, much like the Channel Tunnel, but recently the Sandringham Estate has nibbled at the saltings to the west of Wolferton railway station. The level crossing is gone now, the grass high where the track once lay that brought Edward VII, Queen Alexandra, George V and his Queen Mary to Sandringham, but still the crowns that ring the tops of the platform lamps are kept gilded, the carrstone buildings in good repair. Now a new concrete road leads through the flats of reclaimed marsh to the pumping station and the new seabank which shuts off 710 acres from the saltings where people came to gather edible samphire. And Boatyard Creek, that once brought bargeloads of coal to the staithe by the main road, to the very point below the ridge of high land where the great surge of January '53 finally stopped, is gone now, the new seabank an extra barrier against the next big surge.

The beet was coming in when I was there, piled tractors moving over the brown, table-flat earth, and the wind blowing thirty knots and more off the Wash. But what chiefly struck me was how puny it all looked

Hunstanton seafront in July. It looks out over the Wash from a point on the coast very close to the end of the Peddars and Icknield droving ways.

against the vastness of the seascape beyond the remaining strip of saltmarsh. I have all the details of construction materials and cost – the carrstone roads and standings, the cross dykes, the mole ploughing, the infilling of creeks, the tile drains, all this in addition to the great bank and the pumping station just for seven hundred acres. And out there to the north-west is Peter Black Sand and Seal Sand, almost twenty miles of tidal shallows to be reclaimed. Perhaps that is what we should have done with our North Sea oil bonanza, for Sandringham's 700 acres are

producing good crops, and though nothing moves on the land when it's wet for fear of breaking down the soil structure, this restriction is of little moment to an estate of more than 20,000 acres, including some 1,500 acres of forestry.

Birdwatchers do not seem to have taken over the Wash the way they have the saltings of the north. Along that stretch of mudcreeks and marsh there must be at least twenty trusts, reservations and sanctuaries, as well as wildfowling areas and grazing land. But the Wash is more of a playground with miles of caravans and mobile homes fringing the coast from Heacham's south beach north towards Hunstanton. And beyond Hunstanton is Holme, the dunes swinging in a great arc, for Holme is truly next-the-sea; it marks the end of the Wash and the beginning of Brancaster Bay, and in Brancaster Bay there is something that has always fascinated me – the salt-cured remains of old woodlands half-buried in the wind-drifted sand and mostly covered by the tide.

Unfortunately, the times I have been there the tide has been fairly high, so that I have only once seen the actual stumps of the trees. However, lumps of the peat in which they were once growing are always visible, for these are scattered around the high tide mark. I have a piece of one in front of me now. It is brown and softish, like lignite, and easily mistaken for the coagulated tar remains of an oil slick, except that it is fibrous with no smell other than the salt in which it has been pickling; also, under the microscope, pale segments of crinkled weed are visible.

My recollection of what the stumps look like is rather hazy, but they have been described to me by the man who looks after the Great Wood for us. A keen ornithologist, he knows the area well. The 'forest', he says, is well down the beach and covered at high water, the stumps fairly clear when you see them and surprisingly soft. This confirms my own memory of them, and as he says, you would expect something that has survived the North Sea storms for so many years to be hard and rock-like.

But however interesting the remains of this old forest, it is not the point of going to Holme. Holme marks the division between the bleak dreariness of the Wash marshlands and the quite unbelievable, totally unique north-western coast, a world of improbable havens, with muddy and complicated approach channels winding through salt flats of marsh and sea-covered shallows, the whole area veined with innumerable creeks. Sand dunes and a high shingle bank are the ramparts that lie between the saltings and the sea, saltmarsh and creek the resort of fishermen, dinghy sailors, mussel and cockle gatherers, seals and seabirds. It has a wild, wild beauty, especially at dawn or dusk, and the wind bites shrewder than any place in Britain.

But wind or no, it is the wildness of it that attracts; people go there for something of the same reason they go to places like the Yukon. With your teeth chattering, the skeleton of your bones rattling to the iciest of cold air, and the geese flighting in, you can't worry about the rest of the world; or with a gale out of the north and a spring tide – what price the

The Wash at Hunstanton where board sailors have taken full advantage of the shallow, mudbank-protected waters. The Victorian pier disappeared at about this spot in the gale of 1976.

media and the news then, a surge on and the North Sea battering at your door?

From Holme through Thornham, Titchwell, Brancaster (the Roman Branodunum), Brancaster Staithe, the Burnhams, Overy Staithe, Holkham, Wells, Stiffkey, all the way to the Glaven estuary that runs inside Blakeney Point to Blakeney itself, and at one time beyond to Cley and on to Salthouse, more than twenty miles, it is a saltmarsh world, every village a harbour (of sorts) that required brave experienced men to pilot vessels in under sail. But from Salthouse on through Sheringham and Cromer, and along the crumbling, gravelly, cliff-lined coast, the saltmarsh is gone, the land in direct contact with the sea. Here the 'harbours' are really no more than shallow indents where ships could anchor with some protection from a headland and local fishermen launch clinker-built boats from open beaches.

The Sheringham or Cromer crabber was designed for working the offshore banks, which are of clean sand and rock and an ideal habitat for crustacea. These shingle boats are double-ended, lightly framed and planked, beamy as baskets, and all brightly painted. It is worth going up there in rough weather just to see them launch from the open beach or return after they have hauled their long lines, or shanks, of pots, rebaited and shot them again. And they go out in all weathers, for the pots must still be checked. Now they use outboard engines, but under oar-power, coming in with a north-easterly force 5 or 6, it must have been a great sight to see them broach-to at the beach edge, tipping the boats so that the waves broke against the keel.

These light crabbers are very different boats to the beach yawls that operated a little further down the coast in the days of sail, acting as pilot, life and salvage boats, and also as cargo carriers ferrying loads to off-lying vessels. The yawls were much heavier, oak-framed and operated by 'companies' who kept lookout like coastguards from tall watch-towers, grabbing any inshore business going. The boats were fast and they were open, at some seventy feet the largest open sailboats in European waters.

In those days the curved bulge of East Anglia's north-eastern shore was the sailor's nightmare, the tides strong, the prevailing wind onshore in winter. No shortage of pickings for the 'companies' and local fishermen, the beach itself yielding a fine harvest. Later the lifeboat crews performed truly heroic deeds. All of which was in my mind when I first saw this coast from seaward. I was bringing *Triune of Troy* down from Blyth in Northumberland to the Deben just after I had purchased her, skippering and navigating a boat of my own for the first time in my life. Looking back on it now, the boat tender and completely new to me, a scratch crew I barely knew, it was perhaps a little foolhardy, but by the grace of God the weather was good, the sea oily calm, seals coming out to meet us and the higher cliffs by Cromer emerging out of the haze as a pale, yellowish blur – a Turner seascape.

The border between the fifteenth-century cloth-weaving atmosphere of Suffolk and the grimmer Norman-Saxon feel of Norfolk always seems to me very clearly defined, particularly to the west of the region, where all roads seem to lead through the border town of Thetford. Here the Thet joins the Little Ouse and from time immemorial it has been the crossing point for travellers taking the open heath route across what we know as Newmarket Heath and on into what was once the empty, sand-blown land of the brecks. The castle mound was at one time all of thirty metres high with a clunch or chalk parapet and ramparts of wood, one of the very few ancient castles in East Anglia that was not built to defend a waterway.

When exactly all that earth was mounded up is obscure, but it must have been very early, because the Little Ouse was not made properly navigable until the middle of the seventeenth century and it was the Icknield Way crossing that the castle defended. The town's origins are also obscure, but the Danes are chronicled as having failed in an attack

The sea, the sun and the sand –
the light on this north-east corner of
the Wash can be dazzling.

on the place in 838, their dead perhaps occupying the eight burial mounds to the east of the town, and twenty-eight years later we know they wintered at Thetford because it was from there that they launched their attack on King Edmund's forces, just across the Little Ouse at Euston. It was this bitterly fought battle that was the prelude to his martyrdom in 870.

In those days, and for long afterwards, he who held Thetford held the key to Norfolk. The Danes knew it. Both Sweyne and Canute made it their capital. The Bigods knew it, too. Henry I held court there, for the Bigods, the first earls of Norfolk, were strong enough to challenge the king until Henry II built his great castle at Orford. Briefly, from 1070 to 1094, the Norman church made it a bishopric. Roger Bigod built a priory there, John o'Gaunt another, and it was Henry VIII who granted the town its charter shortly after dissolving those same priories. Most of the earlier Norfolks are buried there, not at Framlingham – the Bigods, the Moybrays and the early Howards who came from Stoke-by-Nayland and the Suffolk-Essex border. Thetford was never one of the weavers' towns. When the sheep disappeared, Breckland was left a grassless desert, the people mostly gone, for the town only began to industrialise itself very recently.

In the last two decades it has grown rapidly, spawning industrial estates and busily absorbing a large London overspill, so that the web of converging main roads now bypass the centre, making it difficult to see anything much of a very interesting and historic place, except of course if you walk. Provided I am not in a hurry, I now prefer to cross the Suffolk-Norfolk border a little to the east, either at South Lopham, or Garboldisham (Garb'lsham) where there are cottages that are an integral part of the heavy lands on which they stand, being built of large blocks of the stuff known as clay lump. At South Lopham the impact of the border crossing is much more direct, the Norman tower of the church, visible before you are even across the border, so massive it looks like a castle keep. The church itself, set in a big churchyard with yews and conifers, is very impressive, the tower almost a cube stuck in the middle of it, between a high nave and a high chancel, so that the whole effect of this strong, solid, largely flint building is as forbidding as a fortress.

Old Buckenham next, a thatched church with a Norman door, a village green the size of an airfield, and the remains of a castle and a priory. And then on into the land of Norfolk turkey, cider and duck, Attleborough's great turkey fair full of noisy free-ranging birds gone now, to be largely replaced by industrially farmed birds and their silent despatch to pre-ordained markets, sheds everywhere visible in this rather uninteresting countryside. A few miles more and the twin towers of Wymondham (Wy'ndham) are visible.

I suggest this as an alternative route north because Norfolk, at least as far as its archaeological remains are concerned, is predominantly Norman, and this way one gets the full impact of the period, particularly if the next stop after Wymondham is Norwich and its splendid cathedral tower. There is hardly anything in church architecture of the period so outstanding as this.

But great houses now – that is a different matter. The two that particularly fascinate me are Blickling and Oxburgh. Neither of them is Norman; Blickling was built in the years 1616–27, Oxburgh in 1482, and both are predominantly brick. That I should pick on just these two may seem strange in view of the county's rich agricultural base and historical background, but though there are big houses in Norfolk to match the many big estates, most are of comparatively recent vintage and few are the equal of the houses I know in other parts of East Anglia – Melford

The cliffs just north of Hunstanton are strangely banded with chalk and carrstone.

Hall and Gifford's Hall, or that marvellous little knight's castle of a tower at Little Wenham. These are all close to where we live in Suffolk, the last built as a fortified home in the late thirteenth century and still used periodically for shooting parties. Like the church at nearby Polstead, the bricks probably come from the first kiln operated in Britain since the Romans left. And Essex has even earlier houses, Beeleigh Abbey, St Osyth's and Leez priories, all dating from the twelfth to the fourteenth centuries.

Beeleigh Abbey, by the head of the Blackwater estuary near Maldon, we know particularly well because it was bought by Christina Foyle's father at the height of the wartime blitz and now she and her husband live there, their superb collection of books housed on the first floor in the thirteenth-century dorter or dormitory with its chestnut roof of collarbeamed and trussed rafters. The main body of the house is now timber-framed, but this was added much later, after the Dissolution. Almost immediately on entering you step down into the undercroft of the dormitory, also known very comfortably as the Warming House, with Purbeck marble columns and a superb fifteenth-century stone fireplace. Full of people, the great table laid and a fire blazing, this must surely be as fine a background for a winter party as any in East Anglia, and beyond it is the chapel and the chapter house, all built around 1225. At the entrance to the Blackwater, just across the Colne from Mersea Island, is another, equally important ecclesiastical building, St Osyth's Priory. This, because of its gateway, which Somerset de Chair restored and converted to his own use as a house, is unique, the flushwork panelling quite exceptional, so that it is certainly one of the finest monastic remains in the whole country.

The earliest occupied houses in Norfolk seem to be Caister Castle, which was built for Sir John Fastolf in less than four years beginning in 1432 – a very impressive place; the Middleton gateway of Lord Scales, which is brick and somewhat similar to Oxburgh; Elsing Hall perhaps, which is a few years later.

However, during the time when the timber-framed farmhouses of Suffolk were being built – from the thirteenth to the seventeenth centuries – there were a great number of land-owning families in Norfolk. In fact, as early as 1316, when the Nomina Villuram survey was carried out, there were some 440 lords of the manor, over six hundred at the time of the visitations of the Four Heralds two and a half centuries later. As for their property, when Sandringham was purchased for the Crown in 1862 there were still over two hundred large estates in Norfolk. Even now there are well over a hundred.

These fields of lavender just south of Hunstanton are close by the lands where an Indian princess from Raleigh's Virginia walked with her husband more than three and a half centuries ago. ▶

For confirmation take a look at Burke's and Savills *Guide to Country Houses in East Anglia*. No less than 130 pages are devoted to Norfolk, compared with sixty for Suffolk, forty-eight for Essex and only thirty-two for Cambridgeshire. The number of Norfolk houses actually described in detail is 462, most of the accompanying photographs supporting my somewhat jaundiced view of the architectural worth of most of them.

Take Sandringham, for instance. The house was redesigned nine years after the estate was purchased for Edward VII, then Prince of Wales and just coming of age. It was then partly rebuilt after a fire in 1891, a bad period for architecture so that, however comfortable inside, the exterior really does look rather more like a Frinton hotel than a stately home. One could almost wish they had bought Houghton Hall for the Prince since it was on offer at the time, but the Houghton lands are not nearly as extensive, or as attractive, and it was the land and the shooting that doubtless attracted him. The land, sandy-soiled along the ridge, attracts us all, for it is rhododendron country and to go there in late May, all the roads banked high with colour, is what Tony Stokes, that splendid eccentric of Hintlesham Hall, used to call a great 'arboreal experience'. Sandringham has its own carrstone quarry with the result that the superb garden walls with their rounded tops are faced in places with narrow brickettes of this dark, reddish-brown sandstone, as also are many of the estate houses, so that walls and buildings look as though they have been there since Roman days when those characteristically narrow bricks were kilned.

The most romantic building is surely York Cottage and it always surprises me that this has been converted to use as estate offices. It was originally the residence of bachelor guests, but was named for Prince George, Duke of York, when he married Princess Mary of Teck. They spent their honeymoon there, and when he came to the throne, rather than disturb his mother, who was occupying the 'Big House', they continued to stay at the cottage whenever they were visiting Sandringham until Queen Alexandra's death in 1925; in fact, all their children, except the eldest, were born there.

The effect of having one of the two 'recreational' Crown residences in Norfolk, plus the agricultural richness of the county, and the splendid shooting, is that most of the great houses have survived, only about fifty having been lost this century, despite all the problems of wars and taxation that have faced the owners. It has also encouraged others to move in, particularly men with an aggressive enthusiasm for knocking off driven birds and the money to invest in properties that run to several thousand acres.

With this sort of background, and the periodic presence of the Monarch, East Anglia was, I supppose, a natural nursery for that extraordinary organisation the Monarchist League. We were introduced to it by the Bristols, the late Marquis being the League's Chancellor and

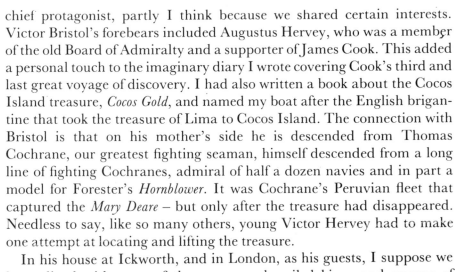

chief protagonist, partly I think because we shared certain interests. Victor Bristol's forebears included Augustus Hervey, who was a member of the old Board of Admiralty and a supporter of James Cook. This added a personal touch to the imaginary diary I wrote covering Cook's third and last great voyage of discovery. I had also written a book about the Cocos Island treasure, *Cocos Gold*, and named my boat after the English brigantine that took the treasure of Lima to Cocos Island. The connection with Bristol is that on his mother's side he is descended from Thomas Cochrane, our greatest fighting seaman, himself descended from a long line of fighting Cochranes, admiral of half a dozen navies and in part a model for Forester's *Hornblower*. It was Cochrane's Peruvian fleet that captured the *Mary Deare* – but only after the treasure had disappeared. Needless to say, like so many others, young Victor Hervey had to make one attempt at locating and lifting the treasure.

In his house at Ickworth, and in London, as his guests, I suppose we have dined with most of the uncrowned, exiled kings and queens of Europe, our attitude at first one of amazement that the trappings should still be there when there was no substance. And yet, as the years pass and presidents around the world take advantage of power to commit terrible crimes against their people, one begins to wonder . . .

The Herveys came into possession of Ickworth as far back as 1485, but it was the 4th Earl-Bishop, after whom all those Bristol hotels were named, who had the vast rotunda building erected. He planned the

Sandringham, the Monarch's personal property in Norfolk: the post office which is an estate cottage at West Newton, and a weather vane that belongs to the world of gun dogs.

wings as the repository for a large art collection, but this was seized by Napoleon and he died in Italy without ever seeing the building completed. It has been a white elephant ever since, a severe drain on successive generations until finally the family were able to hand all the eighteenth-century house over to the National Trust. Hengrave Hall, also near Bury, is even bigger, and earlier, having been built in the first half of the sixteenth century round a central courtyard. It is Gothic in style with elaborate turrets either side of the entrance and an equally elaborate bay window over, and the Oratory has its stained glass windows intact, probably the best of sixteenth-century glass still left in East Anglia. Where was Dowsing, one wonders – was he bought off?

In the far north of Norfolk, Holkham, pronounced Hoke'am, is like Ickworth, something of a monster – a huge grey block of Italian Palladian classical architecture, which according to the present Edward Coke, who has the problem of looking after it, was so well built that remarkably little maintenance has been necessary in more than two centuries. For the upkeep of it there is still an estate of some 25,000 acres (it was once nearer fifty thousand, and even just after the war it was 42,000), and what really makes the place so superb is the park with its

The remains of Binham Priory are some of the most impressive in Norfolk. This is the best view of them, across the fields.

beautifully landscaped lake and its deer, the great sweep and fold of the grass, and the way the main entrance gates face across the coastal road to an estate road running straight down to the sands of the North Sea.

All the northern part of East Anglia seems to have had a passion for Palladian houses, influenced by Italy and the Grand Tour. Houghton Hall, hidden behind its white gates, is another, the road to Sandringham flanked by wide grass verges set off by trees. South of Fakenham is the Townshend home, Raynham Hall, and further south still, just across the border at Thetford, the Grafton seat of Euston, Palladian again. Also Heveningham, further to the east and on the threshold of The Saints. Nothing flat about the country here in the upper reaches of the Blyth river, Capability Brown making good use of the sweep and roll of the park and the great grey pile looming over the lake against a forestry setting that glimmers with colour in the autumn. But for sheer ostentation I give you Elveden – a mammoth oriental-Irish palace sired by a Sikh maharajah, the final result out of Guinness family profits complete with work copied from the Taj Mahal. The bag, incidentally, for one big shoot was over 9,000 pheasants, a similar number of partridge, some 3,000 hares and 75,000 rabbits – this was in the days when poulterers and most butchers and fishmongers sold the produce of the big shoots at very reasonable prices.

The number of really big Norfolk houses is, I suppose, an indication of the attraction of an innovative and highly prosperous agricultural area for the really wealthy – as with those large yachts, anyone who enquired how much it cost to build and maintain a stately home in the style of the great Italian Renaissance architect, Andrea Palladio, obviously couldn't afford it. Men like Inigo Jones and Burlington were not exactly cheap and Capability Brown and the other landscape gardeners were just as uninhibited with other people's money in laying out the park surrounds.

But Blickling now; Blickling is a house that really appeals to me, the rooms so comfortable-looking, so liveable-in, the Long Gallery with its fabulous ceiling, the Russian tapestry with the Czar on a silly horse, an even sillier looking eagle above him delivering a laurel wreath crown, and in the background all hell let loose on the field of Poltawa; and is that really the original of Holbein's portrait of Henry VIII that one has known all one's life, there by the sombre oak of the grand staircase? No, alas, it is a copy.

But though the interior is much more enjoyable than most great houses, it is the first sight of it that always stops me in my tracks, the lawns, the gravel driveway, the red brick front reminding me of Melford Hall – except for that wretched wooden bell tower straddling it amidships – the way the warm, stone-trimmed façade is flanked by gabled and chimneyed outbuildings, and by the twin lines of Blickling's marvellous great yew hedges.

Yews! There are yews everywhere. Clipped once a year in early autumn

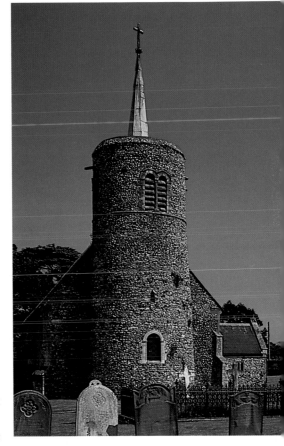

The church at Titchwell, between Hunstanton and the Burnhams, has a nice little Saxon tower.

271

they are used like walls, except in the sunken garden where they are clipped to ornamental shapes. Those are comparatively new yews, but the great yew hedges of the entrance, several yards thick and supported internally by staves, are somewhere close on 400 years old. Certainly they were there before the present house was built. Anne Boleyn would have known them as a child – long before she became Queen and bore the child that was to become the greatest of English queens. Seeing those old yew hedges, remembering the 1479 brass of Anna Boleyne headless by the chancel entrance of the church, I always have the feeling that the yews are there to remind us of this Tudor tragedy.

Something else that is unique to these gardens are the drooping, and in places layered, trees. The great turkey oak by the lake has spread the skirts of its branches over half an acre, the oriental planes are great swirls of light green, long-fingered leaves, and when you leave Lord Lothian's secret beech-hedged garden, following the ha-ha, there are several great limes that have drooped their branches to the ground in great arched curves so that they lie like fat grey boa constrictors along the grass.

The present house was built in the days when the Restoration monarchs were putting their stamp on Newmarket, but there was a Hall there in medieval times, and back in Saxon days King Harold had it as his manor. With the Conquest it passed into the hands of the Church as the home of de Losinga and other East Anglian bishops after the see was transferred from Thetford to Norwich. And only a few miles from Blickling is another moated hall – Mannington. Here it is the original house you are looking at, which is also true of Oxburgh, over to the west, but in that case the descendants of the original builders are still living there.

Oxburgh is about as perfect as an old house can be, a poem in brick and the equal of any of the smaller Loire chateaux; it even has a parterre, as Blickling once had. It is a battlemented manor house built of warm red brick round a central courtyard by Sir Edmund Bedingfeld. It has a moat and a great gatehouse that is very like the Deanery Tower at Hadleigh, which is probably why I remember it so clearly, being reminded of it every time I walk in the secluded peace of the graveyard square between Hadleigh's old timbered guildhall and its church.

The twin towers of the Oxburgh gatehouse stand with their feet in the water, a bridge over the moat running between them, through the great oak doors into the court where the English bonded brickwork towers eighty feet to the two corbelled turrets. Fortunately the major restoration, started soon after the Napoleonic wars, was carried out with loving care, so that the changes of the Victorian era are still in keeping with the original. To outward appearance it remains very much as it was conceived in Tudor times, the King's Room and the Queen's Room still brick-walled, the gatehouse unimpaired. Including the porters' lodges either side of the gateway there are a total of more than twenty-five separate rooms surrounding the courtyard.

Blickling Hall, one of the loveliest of the great houses of Norfolk. The main entrance gates lead to a great gravel sweep flanked by lawns and 400-year-old yew hedges.

A view of Blickling that shows the entrance over the moat with a glimpse of more yew hedges and the yellow brickwork of the almshouses that flank the front of the house.

I do not know of any other house in Norfolk, or indeed anywhere, that has been continuously in the ownership of one family through direct descent, father to son, for just over five centuries. The first time I saw Oxburgh we spent an afternoon there being shown over it by Henry Edgar Paston-Bedingfeld and his wife Mary, and it's not the priceless historic treasure of the Marian needlework I remember so much as Henry Bedingfeld's immense enthusiasm for the house.

It reminded us both of the hour or two we had spent in the company of the owners of a chateau north-east of Nantes. They, too, showed great warmth and affection for their ancestral home, but for them it had become something of a nightmare, the estate and their lives entirely devoted to providing money for the endless maintenance. This is the side of stately home management that is seldom revealed; there is a terrible poignancy in finding your family home become a millstone round your neck. Perhaps the most sensible and public spirited solution to this problem was undertaken by Suffolk friends of ours. Victor and Julia de Saumarez built a very beautiful, very modern house at the end of their superb Shrublands avenue – they called it The Vista – then converted the main house with its great entrance staircase into a health clinic. This required a great deal of faith for the Shrublands Clinic opened in the early sixties when a new Chancellor was making the financial pips of their likeliest customers squeak, and their dream wasn't just carrot juice for the over-flabby, but a proper health clinic. A really marvellous solution that proved successful because the de Saumarez virtually gave their lives to making it so.

But for the Bedingfelds it is different. There was a moment in World War II when the Hall was sold and – something I find quite incredible – the plan was to demolish it entirely. It was Henry Bedingfeld's grandmother who saved it, buying it back and handing it over to the National Trust. And since the family still live in part of it, this is a stately home without any tears. I think if I could look at the old brick walls of such a home and know that this had been the house of all my forebears, right back to the time of its building in 1482, I would be filled with the same pride and enthusiasm that Henry Bedingfeld displays. This is his home, still, after five centuries in which, through all the vicissitudes of history, the Bedingfelds have walked the difficult tight-rope of loyalty to Church and Crown, for they are a very Catholic family.

The Paston connection goes back to the marriage of the first baronet in Charles II's reign. This highly literate Norfolk family, whose home was in the small hamlet on the other side of the county that bears their name and who were such compulsive correspondents – particularly John Paston and his wife Margaret – have left us a picture of England at the time of the Wars of the Roses that is the earliest record to be preserved in such profusion of detail. More than a thousand letters, the greatest collection of their kind.

This is to me of far more note than the Marian hangings, though these

The house and the lake beyond.

275

are of great historic interest, having been worked by Mary Queen of Scots during the early and less rigid part of her long years of captivity.

North of Oxburgh, through Swaffham and Fakenham, it is 'Turnip' Townshend country, the great chalk expanse where six centuries ago vast numbers of sheep were pastured to provide wool for the Flemish weavers. Here, almost more than in south Suffolk, the Dutch connection was first established. And it was here, on his estates around Raynham Hall, another of those great Palladian houses, that the second earl, forced out of office by Walpole after a highly successful career in law and politics, devoted himself to the development of the four-course crop rotation that made full use of the newly introduced turnip. This was in 1730 and the Townshend order of batting was wheat, turnips, barley, then grass and clover. Up until that time the Roman three-course system of fallow, wheat, then beans had prevailed, this in turn having replaced the simpler corn, fallow, spring corn, fallow system of pre-Roman Britain. Only since the development of the fertiliser industry on a huge scale has monocropping been successful, and even then some periodic rotation with a root crop or beans is usually advisable. All the great estates, then the farmers, soon all England followed Townshend's example.

The Townshend estates must have marched, or possibly been intermingled, with those of Leicester, for the Cokes of Holkham once owned Castle Acre. Acquired in the course of extending their Norfolk land empire, they had the good sense to hand it over to the State and I always regard it as one of the prime reasons for visiting the north-western part of Norfolk. Unlike Oxburgh, which you come upon suddenly, hidden away behind trees and outbuildings, Castle Acre can only be surprised from the north. Approaching from the south the great earthworks, the Castle on its mound, the village with the Swaffham road running up between the houses and through the massively arched eleventh-century bailey gate, with the church beyond and just a glimpse of the priory away to the left, give an extraordinary feeling of history being flung at one out of the Norfolk countryside. The Norman castle was huge, the whole village of that time being within its bailey, but while the Normans undoubtedly raised the mound on which to build their keep, the original earthworks were erected much earlier, probably by the ancient Britons, for Castle Acre stands on Peddars Way.

The business of this village, like Walsingham just the other side of Fakenham, is ecclesiastical ruins and tourism. Just outside the bailey gate is a beautiful rectangular 'square' with limes down the centre, and to the west of it stands the church, midway between castle and priory, and it is the priory everyone comes to see. Not only is it the finest of all the ruined priories in East Anglia, but historically it is very much part of the trappings of Conquest, being of the Burgundian order of Cluny sponsored in England by the Conqueror's daughter, Gundreda. Gaunt stone and the green of grass, the slope of the land falling to the Nar, trees dripping and a bitter wind off the Wash . . . that is how I shall always see it, the ruins and that fantastic west front beautiful even in the rain.

Perhaps it deserves to be a ruin. For almost three centuries it was controlled by Cluny, a foreign establishment on English soil until the priors were naturalised. It was already in decline when the Reformation caught up with it and it passed to the Duke of Norfolk. But it is the castle's earthworks that I find really fascinating, such great quantities of earth to shift, the ditch and the huge mound and all the outer works man-made, and that same question again – when was it done, who did it, and for what particular reason?

From Castle Acre the Peddars Way runs straight as a die to Holme-next-the-Sea, Hunstanton lighthouse marking the turning point for east-bound ships coming out of King's Lynn and the beginning of those twenty odd miles of saltings, dune and shingle that end abruptly at Salthouse. No safe harbours after this. If a ship couldn't get into the Glaven by Blakeney Point then it had to make Great Yarmouth, hence

The gateway of Castle Rising keep: this great donjon dominates the surrounding earthworks which seem as extensive as those at Castle Acre some ten miles to the south-east.

the importance of this entrance to the Yare and the Broadland waterways in the days of sail, also no doubt the size of St Nicholas, the largest parish church in England. Over sixty miles of coastline, all shingle and sand, shallow cliffs and dunes, with off-lying banks where the North Sea tides rip over the shallows – 'a coast which is particularly famous for being one of the most dangerous and most fatal to the sailors in all England.'

That was Defoe's description of it. And to illustrate his point he wrote of a fleet of some 200 colliers caught by a north-easterly storm after passing Winterton Ness on the East Coast above Yarmouth – '140 sail were all driven onshore, and dashed to pieces, and very few of the people aboard were sav'd.' This was by Lynn deeps.

Lynn, incidentally, he describes as having more navigable rivers emptying themselves into the sea than at 'any one mouth of waters' in England, except the Thames and the Humber.

> By these navigable rivers the merchants of Lynn supply about six counties wholly, and three counties in part, with their goods, especially wine and coals. By the Little Ouse they send goods to Brandon and Thetford, by the Lake to Mildenhall, Barton Mills, and St Edmundsbury; by the river Grant to Cambridge, by the Great Ouse itself to Ely, to St Ives, to St Neots, to Barford Bridge, and to Bedford; by the river Nyne, to Peterboro'; by the dreynes and washes to Wysbich, to Spalding, Market Deeping, and Stamford; besides several counties in which their goods are carried by land carriage, from the places where the navigation of those rivers ends.

From which he deduced that Lynn brought in more coal than any port between London and Newcastle.

Lynn in the west, Great Yarmouth in the east, more than a hundred sea miles and only the salting ports between – Thornham, Brancaster, Burnham Overy Staithe, Wells, Blakeney, Cley, and Salthouse too before the eastern arm of the Glaven estuary was reclaimed for grazing – and all of them as tricky to enter as any in England. No wonder Defoe wrote of Great Yarmouth, 'the town facing to the west also, and open to the river, makes the finest key [quay or port] in England, if not in Europe, not inferior even to that of Marseilles itself. The ships ride here so close, and as it were, keeping up one another . . .'

It is much the same now. From the Haven swing bridge to the Yare mouth at Gorleston the river is lined with supply and container ships, more than ninety per cent of all the dock activity concerned with supplying and maintaining the offshore rigs and platforms, oil as well as gas. This is what Yarmouth is all about since the North Sea began to yield a different harvest, the great days of the herring fleet so remote that the appearance of even a small part of the Scottish fishing fleet causes an outcry – no room for fishermen in Yarmouth harbour now. South Quay gives a dockside view of the action. It also shows how the southward

Two views of Burnham Market that show the change of cottage building material in this part of Norfolk to flint with some brick. There are no less than six Burnhams, all huddled close to Nelson's birth place.

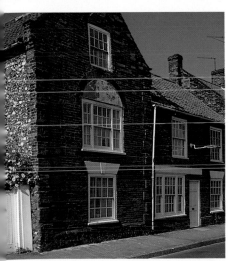

sweep of the tides down the Norfolk coast has built up the sand and shingle, pushing the Haven entrance further and further south. And the further down the Quay one goes, the smaller and older the buildings get, some of them shut, some half derelict. This is still a great place to start a small business.

It is something like twenty years ago that an ocean-racing friend of mine did just that when oil and gas were no more than a twinkle in North Sea Neptune's eye. He was a brigadier retiring early. Shipping members of the Royal Ocean Racing Club suggested he devote some of his sailing enthusiasm to supplying the rigs drilling for gas off the East Anglian coast. He bought a barge, earned £17 with it in the first month of operation. Then he bought a small coaster. In no time at all he was having his first special purpose vessel built. It was the start of Offshore Marine. Cunard bought it. By then, together with German partners, he was running over forty supply ships spread across the world, and when the great Cunard line went down and was bought up, his Offshore Marine was the only money-spinner. He got out of it after that and started up again, and again it was special purpose ships – 'I've finished with rigs, Ralph; I'm concentrating on production platforms only.' One of the two partners that started with him, in what was little more than a shack on Yarmouth's pebble and sand spit, has now switched to containers, for mud in particular, containers being essential for anything that goes out to the oil and gas fields.

South Quay, and all the spit area of Yarmouth bordering the river, has a frontier look about it. The seaside, on the other hand, though tawdry in places, has the more substantial appearance of continuity. Tourism and summer holidays are the main business of all the coast running northwards, and the coast itself has changed little in the near-three centuries since Defoe visited it, except, of course, the cliffs have been crumbling all the time. From Caister north to Sea Palling the Broadland sea defence is largely dune, called in some places Links as in Scotland, and the sands go on and on past Happisburgh with its red and white banded lighthouse and the length of the crumbling cliffs that stretch from Mundesley to Cromer. Even in the height of summer the sandline is so vast that you can walk for miles in a world that is half empty of any life but seabirds, and I never look on those sands but I think of friends who have hired coastline bungalows to give their families inexpensive holidays and found themselves in late evenings and early mornings lord of vast expanses of gleaming low tide flats. The emptiness of it all – just sea and sand – gives an extraordinary sense of space and a feeling of immense peace – London a million miles away instead of four hours by car.

Inland, this sense of having been removed into another world persists in the flintiness of the buildings. This becomes very marked when you reach the shingle coast beyond Cromer, but even on the Broadland coast there is flint, noticeably at Waxham just south of Sea Palling where, almost accidentally it seems, one stumbles on one of the first of those wonderful flint-walled farmsteads – Waxham Hall with its two gate-houses, the main north-eastern entrance fifteenth-century, the north-western Elizabethan, also one of the largest barns in the county.

Here, at the north-east limits of the Broadland flats in late September of a good summer, the smoke signals of inconsiderate farmers burning straw are visible for miles, a telltale of the extent to which the cattle-grazing marshland meadows have been drained and converted to wheat. Once, at that time of the year, I stayed the night in Cley, at the home of the Norfolk Naturalists Trust's warden, aptly-named Watchers Cottage and looking out across the marshes to the meres and hides of the bird sanctuary. There were cattle grazing where sailing ships had once gone up on the tide to Salthouse, greylags flighting in the dusk, Canada geese, too, and over the great bank of shingle that holds the sea

at bay long-rod fishermen were coming on to the beach for their evening's sport.

The NNT, founded in 1926, seems to have accepted the Bishop family as hierarchal guardians of their Cley sanctuary, the first of the family being followed by his grandson, then by his great-grandson who, until then, had been a reed-cutter. The sanctuary hides are neither as grand nor as numerous as those at Minsmere, but there is more water for the birds and the position is superb. There is also a splendid thatched information centre just back of the coast road that is manned daily by a roster of two volunteers, and being on the top of a steep rise, it has a view right across the marshes to the shingle bank, which is so high that there is no sign of the sea, only the distant shapes of coaster hulls moving like toys along the top of the bank itself. That September the birds, other than ducks and geese, recently sighted on the marshes were: avocets, black-tailed godwits, bar-tailed godwits, ruffs/reeves, redshank, spotted redshank, greenshank, curlew, curlew sandpipers, common sandpipers, green sandpipers, little stints, a bittern, bearded tits, and a snow bunting seen by coastguards.

The flatness, the marshness, the Camargue-like buffalo shapes of cattle, and the shingle bank, always the shingle bank, the sky so wide and a bird standing to its reflection on one leg in the nearest mere. And the village of Cley with its windmill, arms spread white against a grey sky, the whole place as full of pebbles as the great beach bank that guards it from the sea, and the long wall and extensive farm buildings of Cley Hall a mixture of flint and brickwork.

The church, when you have found it well beyond the seaport village, has the most enchanting setting of any of the coastal churches, looking down on the Glaven valley where Wiveton church stands on a mound above the river's bridge, the grey of the flint pale against the darker background of the marshes. So one gets two churches in one, for there is no way to have a better view of Wiveton's St Mary than to arrive at Cley church by the upper road, the light shining through the round windows of that fascinating, parapeted clerestory, and the shadow image of Wiveton beyond. Cinquefoiled and cusped circles is how Pevsner describes those clerestory windows – 'more vivacious' for being crowded together with small two-light windows. Certainly I have never seen anything like them. And if you go by the lower road, then the church is seen standing above a large cut-grass green, looking very impressive because of its south porch and transept ruins. You are at Newgate then and if you go on over the Glaven bridge you can stand on another, smaller green looking past the Wiveton church, back to Cley. It is fourteenth-century and if ever there was a church built on wool it surely

From Blakeney you can walk the dyke tops of the Glaven estuary lost to a world of boats, water and birds.

is St Margaret, which is why I regret so much that the staithe beside the windmill is now all grassland, for in the days before the Flemish weavers came to England it was from Cley that so much of Norfolk's wool was exported, the grass-grown staithe crowded with vessels, thousands of tonnes going foreign.

Thus Cley is for me the epitome of all the seaport villages bordering the north shore saltings. Having loved and married in the Sussex downland not far from where I was born, my mother's family Eastbourne people, I am at home with flint, so that villages like Cley and Stiffkey have the same chalk-based attraction for me as Friston and Jevington.

The range of birds seen at Cley is slightly different from those at Blakeney. With the branch of the estuary that ran up to Cley sealed off and the saltings reclaimed, the bird sanctuary pools are freshwater, whereas at Blakeney the tidal flow is right up to the staithe below the Blakeney Hotel, the estuary bordered by saltmarsh, the ebb and flow of the sea in a thousand muddy creeks providing a habitat and feeding ground that is all salt. To walk out past the dinghy park at dawn, along the top of the bank that stands between the anchored boats and the grazing cows, is to have a grandstand view of pools and creeks alive with the movement of birds, waders many of them, time flying because of the

Blakeney is one of the few places on the north Norfolk coast where boats can still sail right up to the town quay at high water.

variety seen through the binoculars. And the people you meet are often from as far afield as the migratory birds they have come to watch.

Admiralty charts are essential to any real appreciation of the saltmarshes, the large scale charts that show the mud creeks in detail. Only then is it possible to understand the extent of the tidal over-run, how it pours in through gaps like those at Blakeney Point and Scolt Head, flooding up all the muddy veins of this strange body of land, and to appreciate the dangers of low-tide exploration. Birds and their habitat are protected as far as possible, and the dunes are precious. From Salthouse to Blakeney Point, all is secure, the great shingle bank a barrier as solid as concrete. But west from the Point, all the way to Holme, the only barrier between saltmarsh and open sea is piled-up dunes of sand where the coarse grasses grow sparsely and every footstep spilling sand down the slope is a weakening of the coast's sea defences.

Everywhere, at every car park, village staithe or bathing beach, there are warning notices – warnings about the dangers of bathing, of getting cut off and overwhelmed by the incoming tide if you cross this creek or that marsh at low water, instructions about dune care, about keeping to the paths and avoiding disturbance to birds, and always, at the end of almost every track leading down to the saltmarsh, there is a statement 283 of what conservation group or trust has rights over it.

Only here and there is it possible to reach the sea proper by road – at Brancaster, at Holkham where there is even an estate boardwalk through the dunes for fear of a breach caused by tourist feet, and at Cley where a track runs down to the inner edge of the great shingle bank. There are one or two other places, but in general parking is close by the coast road and to reach the sea itself means venturing into the saltings either on foot or by boat, hence the warnings.

Just west of Holkham are the Burnhams. There are no less than six of them if you count Overy Staithe – Burnhams Deepdale, Norton, Overy, Market and Thorpe. Burnham Thorpe is the farthest inland and the place where Nelson was born, his father the rector there. 'What has poor Horatio done, who is so weak, that he above all the rest, should be sent to rough it out at sea,' wrote his uncle, Captain Suckling. Poor Horatio was twelve when he applied to join his uncle's ship, an indomitable spirit in a body weakened by that marshland menace, the ague. Cochrane and Cook, the only naval officers to achieve anything like his stature and fame, were never loved by their men the way Nelson was throughout the Fleet.

Why did he elect to go to sea? Why this route to power when he suffered from seasickness? The answer surely is the marshes that lay there just to the north of his home. This must have been his sea nursery, if not physically, then in fantasy, for all about him were men who lived by the sea, not only sailors bringing vessels into Burnham Overy Staithe, but fishermen and those who grubbed shellfish off the mudbanks. Exploring these creeks in a small boat, looking at the banks along the Wash and out beyond the dunes, it is easy to understand how the story got about that it was in those first twelve years of his life, spent there on the edge of those saltings, built out from the shore by the sweep of the tides bringing sand and shingle down from the Yorkshire coast, that he acquired the shallow water confidence to attack the French in Aboukir Bay on their landward side and so win the Battle of the Nile. But perhaps an even better training was the months he spent cutter piloting in the Thames estuary. Looking up at the figure of that one-armed man spotlighted on his column in Trafalgar Square, as I do every time I drive into London at night, I am always reminded of the cold north of East Anglia that helped to mould him into the fearless, very warm personality he became.

The seafarers of that coast, and all down along the eastern shore, are men of a similar stamp. There are not so many of them now, but when you meet them you know . . . They are an independent breed, obstinate as hell, cantankerous even, but to those they like they display a warmth and friendliness that is hard to match, and the quality of fearlessness is always there. They are, in fact, a breed apart with their own way of speaking, just as that northern shore is a world apart, totally different, almost foreign.

But I prefer Cley – it is wilder and flintier. And don't forget to call it Clye!

Author's note

The writing of this book has been a very personal experience, a looking back down the years that Dorothy and I have lived in East Anglia. They have been very full, very happy years and I do not believe any other part of Britain would have suited us so well as a working base.

It has been a place to which we have returned from many parts of the world, always with the same feeling of pleasure, and of relief, too, that there is such a world to return to, the beauty of it striking us afresh each time, unaffected by familiarity.

Reiteration can be tiresome, but all the things that contribute so much to the area – the beauty of the villages, those lovely churches, the strangeness of the Fens, the wildness of Breckland, the Broads and the mud-lined estuaries – all are such a relatively short distance from London, so that, though East Anglia has this very strange sense of being a world apart, it is still close enough to the centre of things for us not to feel cut off.

And something that is very important, an instinctive awareness of the arts to the extent that there is no surprise when a painter or a writer switches off, blocking everything out for a period in order to concentrate on the work in hand.

This is not, I think, due to Constable and Gainsborough, or Munnings, Seago, Benjamin Britten, Noland, Van der Post, Angus Wilson, Old Fitz, or any of the others that have produced fine work while living in East Anglia, but to the fact that there were so many priories here in the long ago, and when they were gone, there was always Cambridge to provide academic and artistic awareness. And, of course, all along the coast, among the seafaring and deep sea fishing communites, it was accepted that men would go off periodically, perhaps for months at a stretch. They were not forgotten just because they were away for a time.

It is a nice feeling, that – to know that you can drop out, disappear, block your mind off from everything but the work in hand, and still it will not seem strange or anything unusual. But that has not been the case with this book. Quite the reverse. Over the eighteen months to two years I have been writing it, instead of cutting myself off from my surroundings, I have become more deeply involved. This is because, even if I had lived in East Anglia all my life, there would still have been gaps in my knowledge of it that would have had to be filled. And memory can play dirty tricks.

Pocahontas, for instance. I was quite convinced her bust was on a carrstone pedestal looking out from a churchyard deep in snow, and that is how I would have described it if we had not gone there again to check. And the atmosphere of Fritton's little church so dependent upon the

The photographer, Neville Fox-Davies, who rented a cottage by the Stour for more than a year so that he could picture East Anglia in all seasons.

light, or the Broads so coloured by that first experience of sailing. Even Stiffkey needed to be seen again, the guns, the target planes, the black of the saltmarsh all mixed up with the flint village and so overlaid by war in the Mediterranean that it was more like a half-remembered dream.

In a novel the setting I have chosen has always been fairly recently explored. It is fresh in my mind, and being blessed with a near-photographic memory the impressions remain vivid for some considerable time. Place has always been tremendously important to me, travel as much a part of my life as writing. My belief that climate and terrain mould racial characteristics, that nobody can understand a people unless they have experienced the geography of their existence, this is what has impelled me to travel in areas of the world that are only now being opened up.

But to set a story in a particular area is vastly different to writing a whole book about the area itself. And in this case I have not been looking at it with the fresh eyes of the traveller, but as one returning to something grown familiar over the years. Thus I am no authority on East Anglia, so bear with me those of you who are. What I have attempted here is to show it as it has gradually revealed itself to me, displaying the mirror-image of it that has formed in my mind over the years.

Such personalised impressions can easily be distorted, both by mood and by circumstance. The mind is a kaleidoscope that is always coloured. Not so the camera, which records exactly what is there. Neville Fox-Davies has spent more than a year on the pictures for this book, which means that he has been able to capture the country at all seasons. Moreover, he left Norwich as a kid and had hardly been in East Anglia since, so he came to it with fresh eyes. I did not brief him, or do more than indicate the lines on which I was working, so that the visual image presented is entirely his own and gives the book I hope an extra dimension, the pictures not knowing the text, but complementing it.

For the writer the act of committing impressions to paper, not only points up the highlights, but concentration of mind produces a personal involvement. This is why I have always taken the opportunity to write a travel piece before starting on a novel, and why Dorothy has felt the urge to switch from plays to books. In East Anglia I have been on my home ground, but I have still found the same concentration of mind having the same effect. The act of writing about the area has given me a greater awareness of everything around me and a much greater understanding. In short, I have found it enormously satisfying and have become mentally far more personally involved than I would have been otherwise.

The author, Ralph Hammond Innes, with his wife Dorothy, looking out to the Deben bar which they crossed so often going foreign in their cruiser-racer Mary Deare.